THE
GREATNESS
OF FLAUBERT

Maurice Nadeau

THE GREATNESS OF FLAUBERT

TRANSLATED BY BARBARA BRAY

THE ALCOVE PRESS
LONDON
1972

INTERNATIONAL STANDARD BOOK NUMBER
0-85657-000-1

PRINTED IN THE UNITED STATES OF AMERICA

CONTENTS

PREFACE

FLAUBERT is just emerging from a long spell in limbo in France and becoming the subject of a wide range of different inquiries, and it seemed to me this might be a useful moment to set out my own critical thoughts gathered in my editorial work on the eighteen volumes of the Complete Works.*

I do not put forward any thesis. I am not a philosopher or a sociologist or an aesthetician or a psychoanalyst or an expert in linguistics—which is a pity, because both his works and his voluminous correspondence provide material for original approaches in a variety of disciplines. Without being far-fetched one could draw up an *Echec de Flaubert* as for Baudelaire;† or make a study of the very special way he found his voice; or show why the proprietor of Croisset also figures as a destroyer of those bourgeois values which sometimes governed his behavior, as for example in his choice of a business man as husband for his niece, and in his attitude towards the Paris Commune. Although it is no longer fashionable to reconstruct an author's psychology from his illnesses—in this case, epilepsy and syphilis—it is still considered permissible to dramatize his spiritual struggles and show how his work derives from an inadequately dealt-with Oedipus complex. In spite of the fact that Flaubert used to be taken for rather a simple fellow, not over-intelligent, the material is so abundant it gives scope for all kinds of brilliant applications. But I am not capable of such approaches.

*Gustave Flaubert, *Œuvres complètes* (Editions Rencontre, Lausanne).

†René Laforgue, *L'Echec de Baudelaire: Etude psychologique sur la neurose de Charles Baudelaire* (Denoël et Steele, Paris 1931).

I have no talent either for academic scholarship or for fictionalized biography. My only excuse for publishing this book is the admiration I have come to feel for Flaubert after a long relationship, during which I have read his works and letters so often I feel I really know him. I do not claim my picture of him is the only possible one, but at least it bears some resemblance to a subject not easy to catch. It was built up gradually from his books, his confidences, the statements he made and the attitudes he adopted, and from the testimony of his friends. I am naive enough to think he succeeded in his aim of becoming an artist. But I also believe that towards the end of his life he realized that this aim was not enough, and that *Bouvard and Pécuchet*, unfinished as it is and "impossible" as he thought it, may be regarded, as he wished, as his "testament."

The way he accomplished his aim of becoming an artist, through countless hazards, baffled rages, and long periods of despair, is so exemplary in itself that I simply recount it, without going into his reasons for embarking on it. Apart from his own statements on the subject, taken in their context, speculation on these reasons seems to me too conjectural to provide the basis of a true portrait.

It may be objected that this is to deprive oneself of the marvelous aids which the various new disciplines now put at the critic's disposal. Some critics have made excellent use of these new tools: Marie Bonaparte on Edgar Allen Poe, for example, Gaston Bachelard on Lautréamont, and, among others, Georges Poulet and Jean-Pierre Richard on Flaubert himself. But in addition to such studies, which really do throw light on a writer and his work, there are others—they need not be specified—which are mere illegitimate encroachments. It is not enough to see an author as an interesting "case," and then to use the "case," sometimes even unconsciously, as a pretext for what is really personal confession. Many commentators, in order to support their argument, treat the artist and the man as one and the same, and blame the one for the sins of the other. And yet all of them have read Proust's *Contre Sainte-Beuve*. But it is so tempting to see Flaubert as a bourgeois in revolt, timidly taking refuge in art. The next thing will be an explanation of Mallarmé in terms of a teacher who could not keep order in class, or of T. E. Lawrence's *Seven Pillars of Wisdom* as a penance imposed by a British agent on himself in order to acquit himself before history.

It is true Flaubert was neither a peasant nor a proletarian, and that he lived chiefly on his means. He did so, however, with increasing difficulty, and was ruined five years before his death. His father was a doctor; his mother's father was a doctor; his brother Achille became a doctor too. His background was thus professional; and in addition the family owned a certain amount of land. His father wanted Gustave too to choose a profession, and although he indulged in the luxury of a trip to the East, this was only after he had suffered several nervous attacks. His own personal extravagances did not go beyond a pied-à-terre in Paris, and he had to give up the lease of this when he was ruined. It should be added that the Flaubert family belonged to the liberal bourgeoisie of the Voltaire tradition, and that while Gustave was not altogether devoid of religious leanings he remained all his life a fierce anti-clerical. It was this which led him to take early socialism for a modern version of Christianity.

Of course the words "bourgeois," "artist," and "revolutionary" have such flexible connotations they can even be turned into entities and set to grapple with each other. Though Flaubert himself tends to lose out in such restricted debates, it is possible to derive some general conclusions from them about the fate of the artist in a capitalist society. But I have preferred to stick to Flaubert—for example to the young man who when his father required him to choose a profession pretended to choose the law, and then put an end to his studies by producing the symptoms of serious illness. It would make a fine subject for a "psychosomatician," this youth refusing in advance any establishment in the world of doctors, barristers, judges, sub-prefects, notaries and attorneys—all open or unconscious accomplices of tradesmen, manufacturers, and financiers, those *fellateurs de l'utile*, "fellators of the utilitarian" who govern society. Very early on he declared he would play none but a "stop-gap" role in this society. To those who object that he did in fact accept the role of a writer, the answer is that he did so on terms which avoided an "established position" which seemed to him as shabby as all the rest. He wanted to follow his deepest inclination, but without having anything to do with the compromises entailed when writing leads to a kind of commerce. *"Ce qui serait beau, ce serait de publier d'un coup ses Oeuvres complètes* (The great thing would be to bring out one's Complete Works all at once)." A utopian idea perhaps, but it seemed to him a fine one. At all events he vowed not to go in for literary purveying or noble raptures:

> *Si jamais je prends une part active au monde, ce sera comme penseur et comme démoralisateur. Je ne ferai que dire la verité, mais elle sera horrible, cruelle et nue.* (If ever I take an active part in the world it will be as a thinker and demoralizer. I shall only tell the truth, but it will be horrible, cruel and naked.)

A strange ambition for the son of a comfortable bourgeois family from Rouen. One might ascribe it to youth—Flaubert was only eighteen at the time—if there were not so many witnesses to the fact that the promise was kept: Napoleon III's judges, for example, and the now-forgotten critics who accused the author of *Madame Bovary* and *L'Education sentimentale* of "wallowing in the gutter" and painting his pictures with "filth," out of a perverted desire to "debase what is lofty" and "extinguish all that shines: science, talent, patriotism, independence, nobility, modesty, honorably acquired fortune, courtesy and elegance, and all the virtues great and small. . . ." True, he had defenders, admirers even, and, towards the end of his life, followers. But it is too easily forgotten that they were in the minority; and re-reading the articles on *Madame Bovary* and especially *Salammbô* by Sainte-Beuve, the major critic of the period, one can see how equivocal his praise was. As for the favor of the public, that can be measured by the smallness of the sales of *L'Education sentimentale* in 1869.

But why on earth did Flaubert want to be a "demoralizer"? Was it because of the example of de Sade? He read him when

he was quite young, passed him on to his friends, and drew
lessons from him in "wisdom" and "philosophy." But *le
divin marquis* was not admitted to his literary Pantheon. His
gods were "Homer for the ancients and Shakespeare for the
moderns." Apart from a few contemporaries, his favorite
authors were Montaigne and Rabelais. All those he admired
were writers who dealt honestly with the truth, and once over
the fever of romanticism Flaubert saw that what he himself had
to do if he wished to measure up to his models was tell the truth
about his own times. But the world he lived in was a developing
industrial society: a world in which sham was already
triumphant; in which everything was bought and sold, including the appearance of virtue; in which self-interest vied
with conformism, deceit, and stupidity. It was the world of M.
Homais, the savage Père Roque, and Dambreuse the financier
—a world of stooges and sharks.

What made it all the more repulsive to Flaubert was that
while it was made up of various strata all fighting against one
another, this society made common cause against a common
enemy—art and artists, the champions of all that is not useful.
For Flaubert there was nothing to choose between the proletarian and the factory-owner: both had the same scorn and
resentment for everything which suggested man was more than
his social condition, and might aspire "*à la beauté, à la paix, à
l'harmonie.*" The first adopted a hostile attitude through ignorance the other through guilt, but both worshipped the same
"bourgeois" values. While Flaubert loathed the class to which
he himself belonged, he also feared the blind and sheep-like
masses who voted overwhelmingly for the *Prince-Président* and
delivered themselves bound hand and foot into the hands of
the tyrant. When, by the coup d'état of 1851, Louis Napoleon
became Emperor, Flaubert could smile ironically: he expected
nothing better of the "people." He seceded from all who "think
meanly" to bury himself in an individualism which was "the
enemy of all authority." He shut himself up at Croisset, with
the illustrious dead for company, to devote himself to the
worship of art.

Not, as has so often been said, to worship the abstract goddess of "beauty." The expression, which has had such ridicule poured on it, was never used by Flaubert. The idea of creating what was exquisite but merely ornamental would never have occurred to one who was an admirer of Shakespeare and Rabelais, a learned annotator of Voltaire, a contemporary of Hugo and Balzac. His aim was to grapple with his age, to denounce its faults and attack its diseases with scalpel and lancet. His master was not Stendhal, whom he considered too much of a dilettante, but Balzac; like Balzac he intended to observe society and present scenes from provincial and Paris life. But he was to go beyond the study and cataloguing of manners to the analysis prescribed by his pessimistic philosophy of life, his revolt against the social order or disorder, and his desire for ruthless diagnosis. What he meant by "beauty" did not imply any nobility in the materials of which it was composed—the elements could only be commonplace in themselves. What he meant was the judicious ordering of the materials in accordance with an over-all conception which was necessary, harmonious, and just. What he had in mind above all was a new use of prose which would give the novel a new dimension.

The body of work which Flaubert built up was one of social, philosophical, and moral criticism. By the most masterly manipulation of every kind of irony, and an observation which stripped away appearances and mingled derision with pity, he undermined bourgeois values and destroyed their foundations. His effort to forge a prose with the suggestiveness and density of poetry made him also one of the greatest of artists. He has been called the father of "realism," which he detested, and a long line of novelists have professed to follow his "method." It is more correct to call him the founder of the modern novel, invoked by Kafka, Joyce, Faulkner, and even some of our "nouveaux romanciers."

WHAT MAY NEED EMPHASIZING for those who read him a hundred years after he wrote is that he was perhaps the first to do away with the distinction, which still existed, as stubborn and noxious as ever, between form and content, idea and expression. Though he had only read Hegel indirectly through Victor Cousin, Flaubert knew—and it was primarily thus that he revealed his artistic consciousness—that content and form cannot be dissociated, that one secretes the other or calls it forth as its manifestation, that neither exists without the other. His creed was "*Il n'y a pas d'idée sans forme, pas de forme sans idée* (There is no idea without form and no form without idea)." As for his "style," though he agonized over it it was the very opposite of fabrication. For Flaubert, to write was to allow himself to be invested by "the objective" until he merged into it, and then, by "atrocious labor" and "fanatical and devoted perseverance" to "operate" on the compound formed by the interiorized "thing" or the exteriorized self and make it yield up the word which gives it its existence. In this way, "*le style, c'est la vie, le sang même de la pensée* (style is the very life-blood of thought)" though the "*chimie merveilleuse* (marvelous chemistry)" by which words explode into another world, another nature, "remains completely incomprehensible."

An artist's dream, no doubt, but one which has little in common with the narrow idea of art people usually have in mind when they accuse Flaubert of wanting to be nothing more than an "artist". It is really more the dream of a creator, in the modern sense of the term, of a creator so committed to his work it is absurd to ask whether it is addressed to a particular social class. Flaubert wrote for all, whether bourgeois or proletarian, who were able to read.

> *Ce qui me semble, à moi, le plus haut dans l'Art (et le plus difficile), ce n'est ni de faire rire, ni de faire pleurer, ni de vous mettre en rut ou en fureur, mais d'agir à la façon de la nature, c'est-à-dire de faire rêver.* (It seems to me that the highest—and the most difficult—thing in Art is not to make people laugh or cry or lust or rage, but to act as nature does, and give food for dream.)

Surely this is the loftiest possible "commitment." Flaubert ascribed to literature and the novel their most necessary and effective purpose.

The work is there to bear witness, standing out firmly against time, stoutly timbered and hewn, a house with windows open on the world and yet with many shadowy corners. It is a monument against stupidity, but it does not merely sneer at or berate a weakness common to us all; rather, it isolates and reduces it, to leave more room for the free play of tenderness, love, pity, and the sense of beauty and life—all that rejects "received ideas" and fear and conformism, and makes us men in spite of everything. It is a monument one can move about in freely, living long, if one chooses, in a single chamber, or changing the point of view and varying the prospect. It is the reader not the author who decides: the author is present, but, as was his intention, he is present like God in nature—everywhere and nowhere, invisible, intangible, careful not to encroach on the "will to be" with which he has endowed his creation.

This gives rise to the natural but vain desire to know what Flaubert was really like, to try to make out his nature, temperament, and behavior so as to be able to define his "personality." Is he the "kindly giant" some people described him as, or the "hysterical old woman" with whom his doctors had to deal? The ironist who irritated Maxime Du Camp, or the respectful friend who esteemed George Sand while hating her books? A quiet bourgeois, or an impenitent non-conformist with a distinct tinge of anarchism? Towards his friends he was kind, affectionate, full of delicacy and feeling; and yet they were sometimes taken aback by his fits of apoplectic rage. He lived a self-regarding life on his income; and ruined himself for his niece. He anathematized the world, and shed tears over a sunset. When still an adolescent in revolt against his environment, he showed astonishing filial obedience. He admired his father, and adored his mother so much he yielded to her authority up to her death, and even restricted his emotional attachments so that she should have no rival. He despised Napoleon *le Petit*. Why, then, did he accept a decoration from him? And why, having accepted it, did he proceed to douse his red ribbon in his coffee? He wrote: "*Tout était faux sous l'Empire, des cocottes jusqu'à la littérature* (Everything was fake under the Empire, from light women to literature)." But this did not stop him from thinking the end of the world had come when the tyranny which he had always considered hateful and ridiculous ended. He denounced the Communards, but was disgusted by the Versaillais and their Monsieur Thiers. He said he was anti-socialist, but like Saint-Simon dreamed of government by the fittest, including philosophers and scientists. He detested the modern world, but proclaimed the arrival of "dazzling psychic suns." Did he even realize the revolution he had brought about in the novel? Zola suspected not, when to his amazement Flaubert declared that in comparison with a phrase by Chateaubriand or Victor Hugo, "Madame Bovary *n'est que de la m—(Madame Bovary* is nothing but a load of s—)." His disciples swarmed round urging him to found a school, but he flew into a rage and said he abhorred all "isms." His intelligence cannot have been flawless: no-one was more naive or easily taken in by appearances. Zola, who came from Aix, saw him as "a provincial."

BEHIND ALL THESE CONTRADICTIONS there must lie a fundamental conflict: he himself diagnosed it when as a youth he lamented to his friend Ernest Chevalier that he could not get hold of his own identity. His consciousness was avid, confused, Protean: we see him trying to introduce some order into it when he covered reams and reams of paper at full tilt—this was before *Madame Bovary*—in order to prove to himself that he existed. He was always putting on other people's personalities: Byron's, Chateaubriand's, Edgar Quinet's. He wanted *La Tentation de Saint Antoine* to be his *Faust*, to put into it not only his ethics, his philosophy, and his metaphysics, but his whole self. Du Camp and Bouilhet told him the *Tentation* was only fit for toilet-paper, and the howl that went up was not the cry of a wounded author, but of a rejected man who was to remain silent for two years. It was suggested he should tell the story of Eugène Delamare. Done! He set about the Norman tragedy as if it were an imposition, and began the dog's life it entailed

for him by insisting that the story revolted him and had nothing
to do with him. Yet when he had finished he said,"*Madame
Bovary, c'est moi.*" At the same time he also said, "She is living,
at this moment, in twenty villages of France." For him the
method he had built up, the style he had created, the example
he had set, counted for nothing. If it had not been for the
prosecution which followed publication and forced him to
defend his honor as an artist—and his bourgeois respectability—
he would have disowned his *Madame Bovary:* there was a
mistake, they had got the author all wrong. To show what he
was really like and to find it out himself, he changed course
completely with *Salammbô*, a "mirage of purple" which at least
would not get him accused of "realism," and which he based on
an unknown civilization and characters entirely foreign to him.

But when *Salammbô* was finished he took fright at what his
pen had produced. He did not recognize himself in it, and did
all he could to delay publication. Sainte-Beuve was not wrong
when he politely described the book as "sadistic," but Flaubert
was sure this face was not his own. He plunged into his memories, went over his own experiences, broke open the "royal
chamber" in which he had immured the great love of his life,
and, while appearing to apply his objective method once
again, launched into the heart-rending confession of the
Education sentimentale. But as well as being a confession, the
book is also a marvelous piece of observation which places its
author in his generation and that generation in its age. At the
time, however, people only saw it as a chaotic scrap of contemporary history; it aroused so little interest it scarcely sold
at all. Flaubert turned again to philosophy and the vast
metaphysical apparatus of the *Tentation*, "the work of his
whole life," a project he had kept going for twenty-five years.
People merely laughed at him for it. There was nothing left to
do but "spew out his spleen and spit on his contemporaries" in
the extravagant enterprise of *Bouvard et Pécuchet*. He decided to
"die himself of the stupidity of his two characters" and to put
on the mask of absurdity. It was like Jarry identifying himself
with Père Ubu.

There has never been a plainer or more striking example of the sufferings and grandeurs of writing, and of its ambiguous powers. With his faculty for "making himself feel things" to the point of hallucination, for identifying himself with his characters so closely that he suffered physically with them, for entering into a stone and growing with a plant, for vibrating in a sunbeam lighting up a room or a clump of undergrowth, and with his long and painfully cultivated gift of recreating life in its microscopic inner evolutions, Flaubert certainly succeeded in attaining his ambition: to create works of art that would "act" after the fashion of natural phenomena. But his main object escaped him: he was quite unable to use this creation to help himself to accede to being. Writing came between him and the world, constantly referring him, in the name of art, to a second nature which was not his own and in which he did not recognize himself. He stuck heroically to his project, but the effect was only to widen, from one book to another, the gulf which already at sixteen separated him from himself. It was no fault of his, and the greatest of those who came after him were to roll the same Sisyphean rock. Though it is a form of salvation, artistic creation is no more salvation itself than any other human activity. It only achieves less perishable objects, objects really worthy of mortal sacrifice and devotion. For his demonstration of this Flaubert remains, and deserves to remain, a model.

A PRECOCIOUS AUTHOR

THE DESIRE TO WRITE seized Gustave Flaubert very early. At nine years of age, when he could scarcely form his letters and was none too sure of his spelling, he told his friend Ernest Chevalier:

> *Si tu veux nous associer pour écrire, moi j'écrirai des comédies et toi tu écriras tes rêves, et comme il y a une dame qui vient chez papa et qui nous contes toujours de bêtises je les écrirait . . .* (If you like we could collaborate. I'll write comedies and you can write your dreams. And there's a lady who comes to see Papa who always talks nonsense, so I'll write it down . . .)

This was the first letter he wrote as an "author." Extraordinary as it is, however, it is scarcely proof of a vocation.

Together with his sister Caroline, Ernest Chevalier, and Alfred Le Poittevin, another friend five or six years their senior, Flaubert got up plays of all kinds in Dr. Flaubert's billiard-room. The billiard-table itself, pushed up against the wall, served as a stage. These children's games echoed the romantic theater, then in its heyday. Gustave and Ernest did not perform only their own plays. A letter from Flaubert to Chevalier refers to "dramatic proverbs," to Poursognac (*sic*),* and to Berquin, Scribe, and Carmontelle. Speaking later of his boyhood, Flaubert recalled his "frantic love for the stage." This passion was to remain with him all his life. In 1846 he wrote to Louise Colet: "I might have been a great actor if Heaven had had me born poorer."

By the time he was thirteen he had grown out of acting on

---

*A reference to Moliere's Monsieur de Pourceaugnac.

the billiard-table, but he went on writing plays. One was called *Frédégonde et Brunehaut,* another *Madame d'Ecouy.* There was a great prose drama in five acts entitled *Loys XI.* All these were written before his seventeenth year. His one idea of literary fame was success in the theater. His reveries were full of the sound of applause; he saw the auditorium "full of lights and gold" and calling for the author.

> *L'auteur, c'est bien moi, c'est mon nom—moi—moi, on me cherche dans les corridors, dans les loges; on se penche pour me voir, la toile se lève, je m'avance, quel enivrement!* (The author is me, it's my name they're calling—me—me. They search for me in the corridors, in the boxes. People crane forward to see me, the curtain goes up, I step forward. What ecstasy!)

When he was in the *cinquième classe* at school (*i.e.,* the second year of his secondary studies), he founded a journal called *Art et Progrès,* modelled on a Paris theater review, and copied into it notices of Alexandre Dumas's *Antony* and *Don Juan de Marana,* and other plays performed in Paris. He also included tales and short stories written by himself and his friends.

At the Collège Royal, Rouen

BUT IN OCTOBER 1832 he became a boarder at the Collège Royal, Rouen, and had to devote a certain amount of time to the compositions set by the French master, M. Gourgaud-Dugazon. He went to the trouble of copying them into an exercise-book under the collective title *Narrations et Discours* 1835-1836. They include *Matteo Falcone, ou Deux Cerceuils pour un Proscrit; Chevrin et le Roi de Prusse; Le Moine des Chartreux; La Dernière Scène de la Mort de Marguerite de Bourgogne; Portrait de Lord Byron;* and *San Pietro Ornano.* Except for the last, all these compositions follow the lead given by the teacher. The pupil endeavors to narrate, create atmosphere, and give his work unity of color. It is evident that he is gifted but unpractised, fond of effect, and inclined to take liberties with fact and probability. But already, and this is not unimportant, he deliberately indulges in aesthetic emotions.

Flaubert's preference at this stage for narrative, short story, and historical drama derived both from his reading—Hugo, Dumas, Walter Scott—and from the influence of his history master Adolphe Chéruel, a former pupil of Michelet who later became a professor at the Sorbonne. The young Flaubert produced works entitled *La Mort du Duc de Guise, Deux mains sur une Couronne; Chronique Normande du Xe Siècle; Le Secret de Philippe le Prudent, Roi d'Espagne; La Peste à Florence;* and his famous *Loys XI*. In all these, too, he bends truth to his own purpose and vouchsafes little of himself, except perhaps in *La Peste à Florence*, which tells of a rivalry between two brothers, the younger of whom murders the other. A psychologist might see in this some reflection of Gustave's coolness towards Achille, his elder brother, who was to succeed their father as chief surgeon at the Hôtel-Dieu.

It goes without saying that the young Flaubert was a "romantic," a furious romantic. Although he was a good pupil, his years at school bored him, and the only things he felt any nostalgia for in later years were a certain atmosphere of excitement and the extravagant imaginings of himself and some of his comrades.

The boys read what their elders produced in Paris, and were intoxicated with their daring. Their heads were turned by the French translation of *The Last of the Mohicans*, as by the bold, "satanic," and tumultuous career of Lord Byron. They all naturally looked forward to being rebels, adventurers, outlaws, and misunderstood artists when they grew up. In 1870, recalling his school friend and later close intimate Louis Bouilhet, Flaubert wrote:

> *On se crevait les yeux à lire, au dortoir, des romans, on portait un poignard dans sa poche comme Antony, on faisait plus : par dégoût de l'existence, Bar— se cassa la tête d'un coup de pistolet, And— se pendit avec sa cravate.* (We wore our eyes out reading novels in the dormitory. We carried knives around in our pockets like Antony. Some went even further. Bar—, out of disgust with life, put a bullet through his head. And— hung himself with his neck-tie.)

These "children of their age" refused in advance the insipid destiny offered by a bourgeois king in place of the epic of Napoleon.

The things Flaubert wrote for his own amusement reflect this atmosphere. After Dumas, Hugo, and Scott he adopted new models: Byron, whom he esteemed more and more; the Balzac of the *Contes Fantastiques;* the minor Romantics; the *"bousingots"*.* He invented narratives, all more or less fantastic, in which he tried to express an ethic, a philosophy of life, a metaphysic. He succeeded, though not without excesses, facile antitheses, and forced indignation, in *Un Parfum à sentir*, written in 1836, in which two women fight for the love of an acrobat. The wife is old, ugly, and neglected, and witnesses the triumph of the mistress, young, beautiful, sensual and cynical. When the story was finished its youthful author rhapsodized about the power bestowed by writing:

> *Vous ne savez peut-être pas quel plaisir c'est: composer! écrire! oh! écrire, c'est s'emparer du monde, de ses préjugés, de ses vertus et le résumer dans un livre: c'est sentir sa pensée naitre, grandir, vivre, se dresser debout sur son piédestal, et y rester toujours.* (You may not know the pleasure it is, to compose! to write! Oh, to write is to take possession of the world, with its prejudices and its virtues, and put it all in a book. It is to feel one's thought be born, grow, live, rise up on its pedestal, and remain there for ever.)

He is naively and touchingly astonished at what his pen has brought forth. "So I've just finished this strange, bizarre, incomprehensible book." He recounts the secrets of its gestation as if he were an established author. "I wrote the first chapter in one day. Then I didn't do any work on it for a month. Then I wrote five more chapters in a week, and in two days I finished it." Such aplomb, alas, forsook him later on.

He outdid the "black" Romantics, those who could only write with a grinning death's-head at their elbow. Such compositions as *Rage et Impuissance, La Danse des Morts, Ivre et Mort* and *Les*

---

*The *"bousingots"* were a group of young men who after the July revolution of 1830 affected unconventional dress and democratic opinions. The word is said to come from the English sailors' slang, "bowsing", a low tavern.

Funérailles du Docteur Mathurin are macabre affairs making it plain that life is only a brief transition leading to the void and composed of suffering and absurdity which neither ethics nor religion can disguise; if possible one should take it lightly, with a shrug of lofty recalcitrance. When Death comes on the scene, blind and triumphant, it is astonished that men, in their naivety, confidence and pride, have still not taken in this harsh lesson. Flaubert often imitates some medieval *danse macabre*, but he is not satisfied with mere spectacle, however harsh or even unbearable: he makes it express thoughts he has borrowed from Rabelais and Montaigne, his most recent discoveries, which he was to cherish all his life. His habitual state of mind at this time is skepticism and philosophic doubt, his fixed attitude one of mockery. Even at fifteen or sixteen he already took a dim view of life.

Writing as a Life-line

UNLIKE THE TWO SCHOOL-FELLOWS he refers to, Flaubert, though just as desperate and world-weary as they, did not kill himself. He put down on paper his disgust with existence and his horror of the world and of mankind. He took revenge through writing, which though he might not know it acted for him as a counter-irritant or safety-valve. It was his personal therapy for arresting the disease he shared with his whole generation. Taking himself as starting-point he constructed an image of life which accounted to himself for his own rebelliousness, set it against a general background, and made it into something more.

His favorite authors at once fostered this state of mind and gave it an outlet. The apprentice followed his masters in trying to clothe his thoughts and feelings, setting himself apart from his companions in a mode of being which at once gave just proportion to his own case and lent it added importance in his own eyes. For him, to write was to use the same instrument as, and thus to resemble, all those who shape the dreams and deeds of men; to lay claim to a place among the sacred host; to take one's stand amongst the things which have nothing to do with purely personal considerations. Having done this he could avoid any irregularity in ordinary life. The despairing rebel and nihilist had no difficulty in cherishing his mother, admiring his father, loving his sister, and always showing himself an obedient son, quite happy to live wrapped up in the family cocoon. School, after all, was of little importance to one who already looked on himself as an artist and put his trust in words.

He did not merely dream of being an artist. He proved it to himself, and, though he wrote only for himself, did all he could to prove it to others. He called the world to witness his tastes and feelings; even when he rough-handled the reader, he still tried to win him over, mixing general ideas and *pensées définitives* with naive confidences. He imitated those he had read, exaggerating even their most facile effects, but it was through imitation that he found and formed himself. Though influenced by the age in which he lived, and even more by his youth, he did more than merely follow the fashion. By an astonishingly sure instinct he turned to the greatest writers of all—Rabelais, Montaigne, Shakespeare. He read *Faust* on Easter Day when he was sixteen, and it was as if he had drunk strong wine. It was under the influence of Goethe that at eighteen he wrote *Smarh*, an ambitious work which also shows the influence of Byron and Edgar Quinet, and looks forward to the *Tentation*.

Full of himself and his ideas about life and the world, he poured forth heart and mind freely. The pen sped over the paper and scarcely ever looked back. He wrote in a fever, or at least in haste. He had so much to say!

He could also on occasion look around him at his contemporaries and pinpoint their absurdities and foibles, differentiating among what had long seemed to him an undifferentiated mass of social types and modes of life. *Une Leçon d'Histoire naturelle, Genre commis* (A Lesson in Natural History: the Genus "Clerk"), on the model of the "physiological studies" then in fashion, depicts a minor bureaucrat in concrete terms which are comically accurate but which excite as much pity as satire. It was published in *Le Colibri*, a fortnightly literary journal which appeared in Rouen, and through it can be glimpsed the twin countenances of Bouvard and Pécuchet, the odd heroes of the *"sacré bouquin"* on which Flaubert spent his last strength.

Le Garçon

THE DETESTATION which the young Flaubert felt for a life and a world supposed to have been organized by a superior will was not just intellectual and philosophical. It was also a matter of temperament. The child who had secretly watched his father dissecting corpses had very early taken the measure of men's pretensions, and of the wilful blindness which makes their hustle and bustle, their pleasure in life, and their ambitions all so comic. He found a bitter satisfaction in seeing his intuitions confirmed by the spectacle of universal stupidity. But neither now, nor later when he was a grown man and famous writer, did this make him put on airs of superiority. He was too well aware that he shared in the general stupidity, that it is a part of the human condition. But he would try, by describing it, to expose it and to limit its worst effects. At the age of sixteen, less patient, less subtle, and more ferocious, he vented his spleen on the character of the Garçon.

The Garçon, to whom he refers now and then in letters to his friends, is stupidity incarnate: at once a sort of Monsieur Prudhomme (a pompous bourgeois invented in 1852 by Henri Monnier) and a prefiguration of Père Ubu. Like Jarry's Ubu, Flaubert's Garçon was conceived in the class-room and perhaps partly based on one of the teachers; some of the other boys must have shared in his creation.

While he is the quintessence and caricature of the bourgeois in general, the Garçon also has his own personality. His acts and behavior are individualized. He moves about like a robot. He has a strident staccato laugh, all on one note, which expresses enormous self-satisfaction and annihilates all that is good, noble and generous. Flaubert and his friends used to produce this laugh in order to mock at others and at themselves, to pass a wordless judgment on all the absurdity of existence.

It was the only outlet for a kind of rebellion, and acted both as a password and as a reminder.

The Garçon has an excellent constitution, is a great eater and drinker, and is also much addicted to "it" (sex). He makes coarse and even scatological jokes. He professes liberal and progressive ideas in pompous language plentifully besprinkled with provincial phrases. His self-satisfaction and vanity are accompanied by less obviously bourgeois characteristics: he has a liking for outrageous practical jokes, makes a cynical practice of "all the vices," uses the greatest freedom in speech and behavior, and exhibits a streak of sadism. All these things, if they do not exactly make him sympathetic, do give body and variety to the character.

In fact Flaubert projects on to this grotesque and disagreeable parody both a deep hatred and a secret attraction. He denounces the bourgeois as a hypocrite, a gull in reality for all his false enthusiasms, a demagogue who is in fact only concerned with his own material interests, to which he clings tooth and nail. Yet at the same time Flaubert is drawn by this stupidity so stoutly rooted in life, by this self-assurance and good health, by this great rock against which dreams, magnanimous feelings, ideals and the productions of art all dash themselves to pieces. The Garçon does not ask himself questions— he lives, he has a clear conscience, he is happy. Is he not, in a way, to be envied by someone who cannot manage to establish his being around some nucleus which would give it solidity and permanence? At all events, the youth who was to take a more lasting revenge with Homais and Bournisien was for the moment somewhat impressed. Untroubled by doubt, untouched by anxiety, the bourgeois lived and did not dream. That was why the world was his.

A Foretaste of "Madame Bovary"

IN THE TWO STORIES, *Quidquid Volueris* and *Passion et Vertu*, in which he makes his début as an analyst, Flaubert applied the gifts he had used to discover his own "difference" to obtain a better knowledge of man in general. He still put much of himself into his characters, which sprang from an imagination fed on a black and sadistic romanticism, but he also tried to make them objective.

In *Quidquid Volueris* an ape-man who is the issue of a scientific union between man and monkey falls in love with his mistress, Adèle de Monville. What could be more natural, says the author. Why shouldn't he obey both sides of the dual nature he has been endowed with? He may look like an animal but he feels like a man. If he outrages Mme de Monville horribly before dashing his brains out and expiring on her corpse, the fault is in nature, and it is not a moral judgment which is called for but a condemnation of man's mad passion for experiment. The story is the psychological application of fantastic premises, though the scenes are strung together in accordance with a more bourgeois type of verisimilitude. It was probably with some pride that the author appended the sub-title, "Psychological Studies."

Passion et Vertu raises more disturbing questions. Mazza, though a married woman of thirty, is "still pure." "Thrusting aside all the desires which were born every day in her soul and which died the next," she did her "duty" in the arms of her husband, a banker. It was "a duty, nothing more—just like supervising the servants and dressing her children."

How, then, did the handsome Ernest, "a Don Juan rather than a Lovelace," manage to seduce her from the straight and narrow path? He did so by talking to her of love, by exciting her curiosity, by entering into her foolish, "half-mystical" feminine dreams. She succumbs, and with delight and amazement discovers pleasure. She falls madly in love, but her lover, frightened by the flames of the "volcano" he has brought to life, sends a letter breaking off the affair (a letter which might have been signed "Rodolphe," so clearly does it foreshadow his letter in *Madame Bovary*) and flees to America. But Mazza is not so easily got rid of. She cannot believe their love is dead, and poisons her husband and children so as to be free to follow Ernest. When another letter from him informs her he is going to marry and stay in America, she commits suicide.

Like Stendhal, Flaubert had found the subject in *La Gazette des Tribunaux*, which reported court cases, and it was not easy to divest the story of its original flavor of scandal and sensation. He shows he is a novelist by the way he tries to concentrate the interest on Mazza's mounting passion, though his knowledge of this subject is still derived from books—on the waves of despair which sweep through her at her lover's flight, and on the motives which make her murder husband and children. He endeavors to make the facts flow naturally from their psychological premises. He was unconsciously getting ready for *Madame Bovary*.

Thus we see him gradually interesting himself in consciousnesses other than his own, trying to understand them himself and make them comprehensible to others with the help of his imagination and his reading. Hie techniques are still those he was taught at school: description, narration, scenes with dialogue. But in spite of excesses, digressions, a tendency towards melodrama, and a habit of generalizing at every opportunity, he captures his reader's attention and carries him along without undue resistance. His talent is that of a gifted adolescent intoxicated with his own precocity.

I wish I was dead . . .

LIKE MANY YOUNG PEOPLE, he never ceased to be amazed at himself and his own singularity. Perhaps he may have been rather alarmed, too, at the ease with which he adopted these Wertherian and Byronic attitudes. Why did he feel this melancholy, this *ennui*, this attraction for death and the void? He realized they came to a certain extent from his environment and his reading. But, out of a desire for sincerity which is still as yet an imitation, he wanted to see how far he was infected with what he took to be an evil, and whether this evil was inevitably linked to the human condition.

Agonies, Pensées Sceptiques marks this attempt at self-survey. He says the work comes from the "heart and mind" of "a

wretched boy of sixteen," and dedicates it to his friend Alfred
Le Poittevin, who seemed to him to be better ordered, more
mature, more critical than himself, more radical in his refusals
and less easily taken in with words.

He does not avoid such naiveties as "Oh, thought! yet
another boundless sea . . . ," or such gestures of defiance as
"I am bored, I wish I were dead, or drunk, or God, so that I
could play some tricks. Oh, s—." He tries to say what he
means in the form of fables, three of which have for moral the
uselessness of hoping in the world or in men. He follows La
Rochefoucauld, Pascal, and Chamfort in cultivating aphorism
and maxim. Far from hampering it, this literary presentation
actually facilitates personal confession, and it would be a very
shortsighted reader who did not discern through all these
influences and imitations a personal suffering, a soul early
wounded and lucid too soon. Like the traveller in one of the
three fables, this soul is "hungry, cold, and thirsty." In the
indolent solitude where it perishes and looks on at its own
death, it literally does not know which God to turn to.
The young Flaubert, brought up in an agnostic milieu and
fond of describing himself as a "son of Voltaire," looked
for some divinity which might be a help and consolation.
Except during another crisis in 1840, he never came so near
believing in God as in these years of youthful despair. He might
be playing at being a writer, but he did so with a seriousness
which kept him from cheating with either his feelings or his
thoughts. He came successfully through the first test of his
budding career—that of expressing what was personal to
himself by means of a common instrument; that of making real
clothes out of cast-offs.

Meeting at Trouville

FLAUBERT'S DISCOVERY of Rousseau and the *Confessions* encouraged his youthful leaning towards personal confidences,
this time not in the form of "thoughts" but in sustained narra-

tive showing forth "a soul entire." The raw material was still to be himself, but presented in terms of a crisis complete with beginning, development, rebounds, ins and outs. This time he did not have to imagine it. All he had to do was re-live in recollection an adventure which appeared for the first time in *Mémoires d'un Fou* and was to echo through the rest of his life.

It happened in the school holidays of 1836, when he was fourteen-and-a-half. The Flaubert family had gone to Trouville, then a fishing village with a comparatively unfrequented beach. Flaubert's niece, Caroline Franklin-Grout, described Gustave, on hearsay evidence, as then being "like a young Greek . . . tall and slender, supple and graceful as an athlete," dressed in a "red flannel shirt," "coarse blue linen trousers," with "a scarf of the same color tied round his waist." One day he was walking along by the sea when he saw a lady's beach-cloak about to be covered by the waves. He moved it out of reach of the water and went on.

His good deed had been noticed, and when he entered the hotel dining-room for lunch a voice thanked him. When he turned round he saw a young woman sitting at a nearby table with her husband. "She looked at me. I blushed and lowered my eyes. What a look! How lovely she was! I can still see that blazing eye beneath its black brow gazing at me like a sun . . ."

He called her Maria. Her name was really Elisa Foucault. She was twenty-six, and living with Maurice Schlésinger, the music publisher. "Every morning" he went to see her bathing, gazed at "the contours of her limbs under her wet garments," and stared at her footprints. When she passed near him and "I heard the water dripping from her clothes and the rustle they made as she walked, my heart thudded; I lowered my eyes, the blood rushed to my head, I could scarcely breathe . . ." One day, seeing her suckle her little daughter, he experienced a "strange ecstasy": "How I devoured her with my eyes, how I longed only to touch that breast!" Then his romantic temperament took over: "It seemed to me that if I had placed my lips there my lips would have bitten with rage; and my heart melted with delight at the thought of the pleasure this kiss would bring."

But he was not to taste such joys. Even if by some strange chance they had been offered to him he would not have dared to accept. A moonlight excursion on the water with Maria's shoulder brushing his, and conversations about art and literature, were enough to fill his heart to overflowing. He imagined the young woman in the arms of her jovial and vulgar husband, and these visions drove him wild. But, to return to earth and to biography, he addressed Schlésinger as "*vénérable père Maurice*," and was jokingly addressed in return as "*mon fils*." He must have found it more painful to address Elisa as "mother." The holidays ended. They separated without an opportunity to say goodbye.

Mémoires d'un Fou (1838)

WHEN FLAUBERT WENT BACK to Trouville two years later, in 1838, Elisa was not there. Maurice Schlésinger had apparently been there with another woman, and then gone away again. The return to former scenes revived a ghost and unleashed a real and great love for the woman who was no longer there. Gustave made pilgrimages to the places where he had seen her, raked over his memories, had hallucinations. When he got back to Rouen, under the pressure of emotion and nostalgia and with a presentiment of possible happiness, he wrote the story of his love. He had started out, probably the previous winter, to give an account of his childhood, his "bored," "bothered," day-dreaming life at school, with its reading and its visions. As usual he had played about with generalizations. Now suddenly, he drew a line under all that, declared that "here the *Mémoires* really begin," and told the story of Trouville, solemnly, "with absolutely religious emotion." Maria was lost to him, and he was filled anew with a sense of the emptiness of existence. "Farewell! but I shall think of you for ever . . . "

Having sworn to tell all, he told of other loves: a charming intimacy with two English girls, sisters, of his own age, before he met Maria; a venal encounter he threw himself into after Maria was lost to him. Up till now all Flaubert's biographers took the two English girls to be Gertrude and Henriette, daughters of Admiral Collier, whom he met on the beach at Trouville and saw again in Paris. But M. Jean Bruneau says Flaubert could only have met the Collier sisters for the first time in 1842, four years after he wrote *Mémoires d'un Fou*.* As M. Bruneau at the same time accepts the *Mémoires* as "completely truthful," we find ourselves in a dilemma about the "English girls." But no-one doubts the authenticity of the lines: "A woman presented herself to me, and I took her; and I left her arms full of disgust and bitterness." It was his first experience, attempted out of adolescent "vanity" and because he was "ashamed" of his own "chastity." Nor is there any doubt that when he left this woman he thought of Elisa. "I was stricken with remorse, as if love of Maria was a religion, and I had profaned it."

Mémoires d'un Fou—Flaubert tried to make it illustrate the adage that madness is really wisdom—is not distinguished by originality of style or by sureness of composition; it was written in three different periods and in various manners. But it is the first story of Flaubert's in which the raw material is living and personal, where he delves into his own past and sees what happened over again in terms which are both emotional and artistic—experiences it in depth in all its consequences, and even more fully than he did at the time, than he did in "real life." This was to be one of the secret springs of his art. At the same time he threw over the narrative principles he had been taught at school. As he found, so he asserted himself.

Meeting in Marseilles

AT THE END of 1839 Flaubert left the Collège Royal and worked for his baccalauréat on his own. He passed on August 23, 1840, and as a reward was sent on a trip to Corsica in the charge

*Jean Bruneau, *Les Débuts littéraires de Gustave Flaubert, 1831-1845* (Armand Colin, Paris 1962).

of a friend of the family, Dr. Cloquet. In Marseilles (some say before he embarked for Corsica, others with more plausibility say on the way back) he had another amorous adventure which this time did not stop short midway.

The travellers put up at the Hôtel Richelieu in the rue de la Darse, run by Mme Foucaud and her daughter Eulalie, whose married name was de Langlade. Eulalie was the mother of a little girl, and was soon to rejoin her husband in Guiana. She was thirty-five years old, and reminded Flaubert physically of Elisa. He was attracted by her, and she was not insensible to the charm of this handsome youth. She gave herself to him, and he, though neither his heart nor his senses were entirely virgin, experienced for the first time physical love and sensual pleasure. It was heartrending for both of them when after two or three days they had to part. Later, much later, when he read the ardent letters she wrote him which he did not answer, he wondered, "with a strange sense of regret," if the "poor woman" had "really" loved him. He did not dare believe it. But he did not forget Eulalie any more than he forgot Elisa. In 1845, 1850, and again in 1858, he made pilgrimages to the Hôtel Richelieu, by then no longer a hotel and without a trace of its former inhabitants. The brief but intense episode of 1840 recurs in one form or another in *Novembre*, the first *Education sentimentale*, *Madame Bovary*, and even in *Salammbô* and the *Education sentimentale* of 1869. Every time Flaubert described the bitter delights of pleasure he drew from this same unfailing source.

A Private Journal

THE DIRECT EFFECTS of the Marseilles adventure can be seen in a journal which Flaubert kept at this time, before enrolling as a student in the Faculty of Law in Paris in November 1841.

Once again he went over his memories of school and found himself on the brink of despair. He even declared himself disillusioned with writing and the life he had imagined for himself as an author. He did not know where to turn. He was ready to believe "Christ existed," he invoked the "grace of God," and thought of "throwing himself at the foot of the Cross, and taking refuge on the wings of the dove."

Then suddenly the tone changes, and hope returns. He remembers a "certain day"—it was a Saturday—just like "today, in a room like mine, with a low ceiling and red tiles . . . " The confession stops short, but we have recognized the room in the Hôtel Richelieu and glimpsed what happened there and now lends him wings. There is no more talk of falling at the foot of the Cross, and if he had to choose between materialism and "spiritual" philosophy he thinks he would incline to the former. Writing is not a total disappointment when it has given one a critical eye capable of seeing faults which may be remedied; "a sense of rhythm, that's what I lack most, especially a long-winded style full of pretention." He was thinking of Chateaubriand, whom he read and re-read as a lesson in style. Then he set to work again.

In the Footsteps of René and Eulalie

IT WAS YET ANOTHER confession. He thought about it for a long time before he started, partly on the beach at Trouville, and he wrote it mainly in Paris, in 1841 and 1842, when he was supposed to be studying law. He called it *Novembre*—the sub-title was "Fragments Towards a Style," for one of his chief objects was to acquire the sense of rhythm he felt he lacked. His model is easily recognisable as Chateaubriand.

> *Dès le collège, j'etais triste: je m'y ennuyais, je m'y cuisais de désirs, j'avais d'ardentes aspirations vers une existence insensée et agitée, je rêvais les passions, j'aurais voulu toutes les avoir.* (Even at school I was sad: I was bored, I fabricated desires, I had ardent aspirations towards some wild and whirling existence, I dreamed of the passions and longed to experience them all . . .)

Drawing strength from his own phrases, he allows himself to go beyond the character he is supposed to be depicting and even beyond autobiography. He describes adolescence itself, with its appetites, terrors, despairs, its dreamy escapes into poetry and nature, its yearning towards the infinite. Women and love are the great secrets to be fathomed, and the great problem is how to give vent to the forces felt seething within. The adolescent, excluded from the world of adults, bewails his solitude; he rejects and despises the grown-up world, mainly because it rejects him. He can only enter it by bringing down the barriers which keep him out. If only he knew the pass-word! Then people would take him seriously, then he could believe in his own existence. Only women can give him the sense of existing; only women, by being interested in him, can prove to him that he is really alive.

Tired of waiting every day for "some great event," nourishing "a nameless rage against life, mankind, everything," hating even the sun and seeing death as "beautiful," he realizes that what is troubling him is "the demon of the flesh." "I can feel it living in every muscle, coursing through all my blood." His heart is bursting with love, he "can hardly breathe," he "agonises, full of desire." Then he flies, flees, to the woman who offers herself, to the brothel.

By a remarkable piece of luck, Marie is beautiful, gentle, discreet, loving, and, of course, does not stand on ceremony. The young man is "grave, somber rather than gay, serious, absorbed." He tries to dissimulate his "impatience, desire, and joy," but then collapses "overwhelmed with pleasure" and dying with delight. When he leaves Marie he "feels a different man": "I walked lightly, proudly, content, free, I had nothing more to learn, nothing more to feel or desire in life."

Is Flaubert recounting his first encounter with love that is bought and sold? He alluded to it before in *Mémoires d'un Fou*, that first experience which left him "full of bitterness and disgust." What he is now recollecting and describing is the Marseilles episode, and the intoxication he knew in the arms of Eulalie Foucaud. He tries to re-live what happened in every detail, tries to express all it imparted to him.

He goes back to see Marie the next day. Each is in ecstasies over the other's beauty. They communicate through a delirium of the heart and senses, stripping their souls bare. Like him,

Marie has encountered love for the first time. Before, she had sought for it desperately, giving free rein to a panic sexuality never assuaged. She had been a "*grande dame*," known luxury, men had killed themselves for her. But nothing had brought satisfaction. What she was looking for was a being "greater, nobler, stronger" than all the rest, whom she could love and who would love her. She had sought him even in the state to which she was now reduced, and at last the redeeming angel had come. She would never leave this "first lover," she would follow him to the ends of the earth. With "foolish vanity" he let her cut a lock of his hair; his heart too was overflowing, his senses sated, his mind intoxicated with pride. And yet he ran away, and with the strange question, "Did I already love her?" We seem to hear the echo, "Did she really love me?" To the young man who had early refused life and its gifts and was too sincere to pretend to be blasé, "real" love seemed impossible.

He had other reasons: first and foremost, his religious passion for Elisa Schlésinger, of which the prime necessity was that it should remain unfulfilled, and the next that no other passion should get in the way of it. As we shall have occasion to see, Flaubert lived in order to manufacture memories, and the more heartrending and frustrating these memories were, the more they excited in him the irony, at once bitter and wistful, which fed and justified his pessimism and nourished his work. He needed events to be irreversible and buried in the past in order to be able to exercise his strength and art in reviving them.

What is difficult to accept, on the plane of probability, is the prostitute's sudden "fated" love for a client, and the long account she is made to give to explain her fall and redemption. Here Flaubert is once more following fashion: Musset and Hugo, George Sand and Alexandre Dumas all brought tears to their readers' eyes with stories of fallen women redeemed by "*l'impossible amour.*"

But if Flaubert did not invent this theme, at least he added to it something entirely of his own. He takes such care with time, place, setting, nuance, detail, the countless feelings of the heart, the thousand vagaries of the mind, and is so skilful at conveying the sway of passion and the intoxication of the senses that anything he borrowed from others must have been a hindrance rather than a help. He is beginning not to take but to give: the confession has living blood in it, it exteriorizes itself with ease, assurance and felicity, the work exists in its own right. *Novembre* is one of the most remarkable Romantic autobiographies and at the same time Flaubert's first important work. Though he did not publish it he never disowned it; he let his friends read it, and, even after *Madame Bovary*, would have liked Baudelaire to know it. He possessed from the beginning the gift for writing naturally which he had to recover later with such labor.

Flaubert in the Flower of Youth

As THE AUTHOR HIMSELF says, *Novembre* is the last work of his youth. This ardent, desperate confession puts an end to autobiography and the outpourings of the self. Only a few months later, in February 1843, the law-student was to embark on his first novel, in which the writer effaced himself behind his characters and plot and the rules of the life he was trying to "represent." His writing then no longer resembled that of Byron, Hoffman, Balzac, Hugo or Chateaubriand, but bore his own stamp; meanwhile he was gradually working out an aesthetic from which he would not swerve. He would be ready then to write his major works.

The Flaubert we have just got to know, the young ante-Flaubert, is of course recognizable in the masterpieces, the seeds of which are to be found in the early work: *La Tentation* in *Smarh*, *Madame Bovary* in *Passion et Vertu*, *L'Education* in *Mémoires d'un Fou* and *Novembre*, *Bouvard et Pécuchet* in *Une Leçon d'Histoire naturelle, Genre commis*. He may have forgotten them, or even disowned them, but they came back to him.

But *we* cannot forget this Flaubert in the flower of his youth, so naive and serious, so solemn and spontaneous, so downright in his judgments, so disillusioned already about everything, so intimidating in the sureness of his vocation. He may have begun writing for fun, but then he was caught by it, and turned it into a outlet, a therapy, and soon a necessity, indistinguishable from life, and for him to be life itself. His cries and groans, his gloomy professions of faith and sweeping negations must not be taken too seriously. He breathed them in with the air of the age he lived in, so that they became his own, but he expresses them with an elation which suggests an underlying gusto. In a sense he is playing. When he recounts the melancholy episode at Trouville, or the shattering encounter in Marseilles, his writing bursts with life and warmth and sensuality. On the plane of sensation the work is rich and succulent: at the same time as he rejects the world he clasps it to his bosom.

Later he was ashamed of the not yet ripened fruits of this early spring. He was right, from the point of view of the writer he had become. But at the same time he was wrong: had he not been dazzled as he was, had he not known those despairs, had he not desired to salvage these experiences from time and found a bitter pleasure in re-living them, his masterpieces would have come to us as if from an unknown father. Nothing is more moving than to see him thus at the moment of choice, trying to carve out the course through which his genius will flow, groping his way like the narrator of *Novembre*:

> *Une création entière, immobile, irrévélée à elle-même, vivait sourdement sous ma vie; j'étais un chaos dormant de mille principes féconds qui ne savaient comment se manifester ni que faire d'eux-mêmes; ils cherchaient leur forme et attendaient leur moule. J'étais, dans la variété de mon être, comme une immense forêt de l'Inde.* (A whole creation, motionless, unrevealed to itself, was living secretly beneath my other life; I was a sleeping chaos of a thousand fertile principles which did not know how to manifest or what to do with themselves; they were seeking after their form, awaiting their mould. In the variety of my being I was like a vast Indian forest . . .)

"I SHALL ONLY
TELL THE TRUTH"

ALL HIS LIFE Flaubert was haunted by journeys, or rather by travel, as change of surroundings, escape, discovery. For him it meant uprooting himself from the milieu in which he lived and of which he soon came to see the pettiness. It was not long before he could no longer bear it, and began to fulminate against the citizens of Rouen, of Normandy and of France, with their utilitarian habits of living and thinking, their narrow morals and limited horizons. For the greater part of his life he shut himself away from all this, partly out of devotion to art, partly to escape from ordinary existence and dream himself into other and more magnificent climes.

When he was still a boy spending the holidays with his family at Trouville, the sight and sound of the sea already gave him a strange thrill. The great natural spectacles filled him with a longing for eternity and the infinite; his whole being melted into the elements. There was exaltation even in his melancholy broodings as a romantic adolescent, and every time he had to go back to Rouen and to school it was with greater regret.

The trip to Corsica after passing the baccalauréat promised to be something new altogether. He would be crossing the sea, the Mediterranean, steeped in classical memories. Often in his thoughts he had already sailed along its coasts, seen the countries of the South and a sun which had shone on Athens and Rome, been within reach of the East which had always been for him a vast reservoir of dreams. As he wrote to Ernest Chevalier, "I think I must have been transplanted by the winds into a land of mud, and that I was born elsewhere, because I've always had what seem like memories or intuitions of perfumed strands and blue seas. I was born to be Emperor of Cochin China, to smoke pipes 36 fathoms long, to have 6,000 wives and 1,400 minions, scimitars to cut off the heads of people whose faces I don't like, and marble fountains."

He would have liked to travel alone, without any tutor or companion, to go as the fancy took him, with no fixed plan. But this was out of the question in those days for a youth of eighteen-and-a-half. His first steps outside his own province were therefore to be chaperoned by Dr. Cloquet, the doctor's sister, and the Abbé Stéphany. The prospect was rather irksome. To have to admire things collectively, listen to everyone's comments, and go with them wherever they chose to go, would spoil all the joys of discovery. He left Rouen at the end of August 1840 with a mixture of eagerness and doubt.

They took the longest route to Marseilles, via Bordeaux, the Pyrenees, Toulouse, Languedoc, Carcassone, Narbonne, Nîmes and Arles. At each halt Flaubert made notes: on the landscapes, buildings and objects of interest, the people they met, and the incidents of the journey. These notes were largely written up on his return. For the career he meant to follow he needed to learn to see and describe *sur le motif*, "from the life," and for the first time he left the world of books behind. As he said several years later, "Travelling is serious work." It should leave traces behind in writing.

Nothing much happened as far as Bordeaux, except that for him the South seemed to begin at Poitiers. Nothing much happened at Bordeaux either; to him it looked just like Rouen. But he did not forget that Montaigne had been mayor of the city, and he went and looked at the manuscript of the *Essais* with "as much veneration as if it had been a sacred relic." The mummies in the Tour Saint-Michel did not impress him; he had seen plenty of corpses already. He was more interested by a visit to a porcelain factory, the memory of which he used in *L'Education sentimentale.*

He was delighted, though, with Bayonne and its hint of Spain. He said he "adored" the place and would like to live there. At Biarritz he made a vain attempt to save a couple of swimmers from drowning. The thrill of actually setting foot in Spain—in Fontarabbia and Irun—blinded him to Pau and even to the "superb mountains" of the Pyrenees, though he allowed that Gavarnie was unusual.

Narbonne, Nîmes, and Arles brought reminiscences of Roman history flooding back. He imagined the circuses, and the open-air performances of Plautus and Terence. But alas, "all splendor fades." Then, fortunately, there was the Mediterranean at last. "There is something tender and grave about it which makes one think of Greece, something immense and voluptuous which makes one think of the East. I went tunny-fishing in the baie des Oursins, and I might easily have been somewhere on the coast of Asia Minor." So one is not surprised that Marseilles makes him think of "the Persia of antiquity" or "Alexandria in the Middle Ages," and that he hears "a hundred strange tongues," and that by merely murmuring "Smyrna," "Constantinople," and "the banks of the Ganges" to himself, he conjures up endless visions: "All the perfumes of the East, pictures of life in the seraglio, caravans crossing the desert, great cities buried in sand, moonlight on the Bosphorus."

His spirits rose again on the boat going over to Ajaccio, though he was vexed at being sea-sick. Ashore he found a wild country in which nature was grandiose rather than appealing, and where the people were reserved but hospitable.

He applied himself to seeing, describing, narrating. Dr. Cloquet, who was finally left as his only companion, turned out to be pleasant, frank, intelligent and caustic. Flaubert could not have managed without him. They travelled on horseback or by mule through gorges, across the *maquis*, along the precipitous coast and through the depths of the forest. They stayed overnight with government officials or medical colleagues of Dr. Cloquet. They met the famous bandits, who looked very respectable. They lived the same primitive life as the Corsicans themselves, travelling all over the island along the two main river valleys and visiting the principal towns. Young Flaubert gathered and multiplied impressions. It was like living the adventure stories of his boyhood. What he made of it when he got back to Rouen was something more than a guide: it was a study in human geography and ethnography which does credit to his powers of observation. The narrative is lively, colorful, and full of personal sensation.

But above all it is unpretentious, good-natured, sometimes even detached: its author is just as much concerned with straight description as with sensation and expression. It is a romantic view of the world through a particular temperament, but instead of putting on airs like Chateaubriand or Lamartine it frankly reveals the naivety and astonishment of youth. The young Flaubert could not be disillusioned with the whole world without ever having seen any of it, and he was just as interested in discovery itself as in his own reaction to it. He composed a pleasant mixture of objective and subjective— there was a ready model in all the fashionable travel books which rarely rose above the mildly picturesque. He had Alexandre Dumas's *Voyage en Suisse* more in mind than Chateaubriand's *Atala*. The journey was over all too soon, but at least it supplied his lively and individual sensibility with material, and gave substance to dreams which up till then had often come only from textbooks. He was never to forget his first sight of the Mediterranean, Marseilles and its brief love-affair, or his first contact with a primitive way of life which conjured up the early days of man.

The Visit to Italy (April-May 1845)

BETWEEN THE TRIP to Corsica and the visit to Italy five years later many things happened. Flaubert finished with his youth in the course of a dramatic *crise de conscience* which thrust him back into the past as into another life altogether. He wrote the first *Education sentimentale*, which although it was put away in a drawer is the first of his works that really deserves to be called "Flaubertian." He dropped his law studies. Above all, he suffered the first attacks of the mysterious illness which helped to set him outside ordinary life and the world and turn him into "the hermit" of Croisset.

The first attack occurred in January 1844, when Flaubert was driving a gig back from Pont-l'Evêque to Rouen, accompanied by his brother Achille. They had been to Deauville about a house Dr. Flaubert was thinking of acquiring there, and at dusk on the way back, not far from an isolated inn and just as they were passing a cart, Gustave fainted and remained unconscious "for ten minutes." His brother bled him and brought him back to Rouen, where Dr. Flaubert prescribed a strict diet which forbade spirits, wine, tobacco and red meat, and a treatment of bleeding and large doses of sedatives. A few weeks later he had another attack. After that they occurred less frequently, sometimes with intervals of several years, but he was never entirely free of them. Maxime du Camp was the first to refer to Flaubert's illness as "epilepsy."

Was Flaubert really epileptic? Although his own descriptions of his attacks refer to sudden unexpected loss of consciousness, this does not seem to have been accompanied by the sort of convulsion characteristic of epilepsy. Commentators have spoken of nervous attacks, which means strictly nothing; of hysteria; of a nervous affliction caused by hyper-sensibility; even of specific diseases. Flaubert suffered even more morally than physically. His father's inappropriate treatment worsened an all-round loss of vitality. "I've suffered horribly, dear Ernest, since you last saw me," he wrote to his friend on February 9, 1844. For several months he was in a state near to despair.

At the beginning of 1845 his sister Caroline, his closest friend and confidante, got married. Although her husband was Emile Hamard, with whom he had been at school, Flaubert considered Caroline lost to him. But he agreed to make one of the family party that was to go with the couple on their honeymoon in Italy.

He wrote from Marseilles to Alfred Le Poittevin: "I wanted to see Aigues-Mortes, and I haven't seen Aigues-Mortes; I wanted to see Sainte-Baume and the cave where Madeleine wept, Marius's battle-field, and so on. I haven't seen any of them because I wasn't alone, I wasn't free. This makes twice I've seen the Mediterranean like a shop-keeper. Will the third time be any better?" He went to see the Hôtel Richelieu. "I walked past it, I saw the steps and the door. The shutters were closed, the hôtel is deserted. I could only just recognize it. Is that not a symbol? How long now the shutters of my heart have been closed, its step unused, once a bustling hostelry, now empty and echoing like a huge tomb without a corpse!" He was given news of Eulalie Foucaud, but said he lacked the "zest" to pursue inquiries.

They went along the coast road, through Fréjus, Nice, Toulon and Menton to Genoa. He noted down in telegraphese what was striking or unusual, usually without going into it and always without elation. The only comments were brief exclamations of melancholy or disillusion. Every so often he would come to life, then sink back into passiveness. His heart was not in it, at least until he got to Genoa, which really impressed him. "You walk on marble here," he wrote to Le Poittevin; "everything is marble—stairs, balconies, palaces. A really beautiful city." But he did not yield to enthusiasm. "There was a time when I would have had many more reflections to make than I have now." Now he was content just to look. "I turn my eyes on everything, naively and simply." He was storing up for later.

With characteristic seriousness he went systematically through the gallery at the Balbi Palace and gave a minute description of the pictures. He was greatly struck by Breughel's *Temptation of St. Anthony*, and returned a few days later to note down all the details: "It eclipsed all the rest of the gallery for me; I can't even remember the other pictures." A subtle mechanism had just started up: the seed of one of his most important works, one which was to preoccupy him all his life, had just been planted in his heart and mind.

Gustave was delighted when the rest of the family could not face going south as far as Naples. He expected wonders of Naples, and both his discovery of it and his memories would have been spoiled for ever if he did not go there alone or with Le Poittevin.

The homeward journey through Milan, the Simplon pass

and Switzerland evoked only literary emotions. At Chillon he mused over the name of Byron carved on one of the pillars of the famous prison. Byron had been the great love of his adolescence: "I laid my hand on my heart and felt it beat louder." At Clarens—misspelt by Flaubert as Clarence— Mme de Warren's house was no longer there. At Vevey he remembered Julie, heroine of *La Nouvelle Héloïse*, and *"le maître aux phrases ardentes"*. At Geneva, again, he thought of Rousseau: "What a man! What a soul! What an eruption, what a flow! How marvelous that there are people who think the *Confessions* an immoral book and Rousseau a scoundrel!" Ferney did not move him so much, though he tried to retrace Voltaire's footsteps. He met a man who had known him as a child: "I looked at him hungrily to see whether Voltaire hadn't left something there which I might gather up." At Besançon, all he was interested in was the house where Victor Hugo was born.

Then back to Rouen, "the port, the eternal port, and the cobbled courtyard. —And at last my room, the old surroundings, with the past behind me, and as always the dim semblance of a more scented breeze!" Also *"comme toujours,"* the pleasures of the journey did not really come home to Flaubert until the journey itself was over, and he could abandon himself to imagination, memory, and dream.

The Trip to Britanny (1847)

IN NOVEMBER 1845 Dr. Flaubert fell ill with an abscess in the thigh. He died on January 15, 1846. Two months later, on March 23, Flaubert's beloved sister Caroline also died, after giving birth to a daughter who was named after her. On July 6, Alfred Le Poittevin, Flaubert's intimate friend, awakener, and mentor, married. (His wife was Louise de Maupassant; Alfred's sister had married her brother and was to be the mother of Guy de Maupassant.) So 1846 was for Flaubert a year of bereavements and disappointments. He shut himself up at Croisset, inconsolable and sinking deeper and deeper into pessimism. "I don't see what other misfortune can happen to me," he wrote to Maxime Du Camp, "I'm resigned to every-thing, ready for anything. I've tightened sail and await squalls with my back to the wind and my head down." He had started having nervous attacks again.

He had met Du Camp in 1843 in Paris, when he was studying law. After an hour they were on familiar terms; they went to the theater together, and to other less public places. They and Louis de Cormenin and Alfred Le Poittevin had had marvelous parties at Dagneau's in the rue de l'Ancienne-Comédie, pouring out their philosophies and reconstructing the world. Once, in his room in the rue de l'Est, Flaubert took a manu-script out of a locked chest and made Du Camp read *Novembre*. "I had no difficulty in showing my enthusiasm," Du Camp wrote later in his *Souvenirs littéraires:* "I was spellbound and captivated. At last a great writer had been born to us, and I was receiving the good tidings." For these words much would be forgiven him whose sins against friendship were many.

In the spring of 1847 Maxime, taking pity on his friend's state, came to stay for a few weeks at Croisset. He tried to get Flaubert out of his depression by tempting him with the possibility of a walking tour, together, in Britanny. Mme Flaubert was against it, but good Dr. Cloquet said Gustave needed a change of air. The nervous illness the mother used as an argument to keep her son at home was used by the doctor as a reason for getting him away. It was arranged that the trip should take place the following spring; Mme Flaubert would travel by post-chaise and meet the two young men in the chief towns they visited.

The year's interval was necessary to prepare for the "serious business" of travelling. Gustave took charge of the historical preparations, and set to work systematically on the Rouen library. Du Camp was to take care of the rest, including the equipment they would need for the tour. During the months that followed they kept each other informed of their progress in the various fields of study they meant the trip to cover.

"On May 1 1847," wrote Du Camp, "as Paris was getting

ready to celebrate the King's name-day for the last time, we walked across the just awakened city, in our tourists' get-up, from the place de la Madeleine to the gare d'Orléans. We marched briskly along the quais, hitching our sacks up, smiting our sticks on the ground, gay, and as Flaubert said, '*seuls, indépendents, ensemble!*' . . . We were happy . . ." They were making for Touraine: their tour of Britanny was to begin with the châteaux of the Loire.

There is no need for us to follow them step by step. Flaubert himself has given an account of the journey. He is an eloquent, well-documented, ever-entertaining guide, and the reader will find in him at once a man who has deliberately shaken off his worries, a writer careful to give the freshest and most imme-diate expression to what he sees and feels, and a landscape which seems a thousand miles from Paris and is still untouched by modern civilization. There was only one cloud in the sky. In Tours, Flaubert had one of his attacks. But it was the only one.

Though the two travellers might look and behave like a couple of tramps, putting up at small inns and even sleeping in woods or in the open, and getting themselves questioned by gendarmes and customs officers, they did not forget their year of learned preparations now to be verified, nor the fact that they were writers. They took notes so enthusiastically they would have brought themselves to a standstill if they had not sensibly decided to leave the real writing-up until they got back. Each day they prepared for the town or district they were to visit next. They even foresaw and allowed for the unexpected. But this did not stop them from laughing and singing and larking about, or hatching far-fetched plans about Tiffauges, Quiberon, Saint-Malo and Mont-Saint-Michel. Above all it did not prevent Flaubert, who sometimes remembered the Garçon, from acting the goat. At the fair in Guérande he got drunk with the owner of a five-legged sheep on show there. The sheep was referred to as the "*jeune phénomène*," and this was what Flaubert kept calling Du Camp for some days after, to his annoyance. "When he got ideas like this into his head," wrote

Du Camp, "he was terrible, I might say unbearable, because there was no stopping him. You just had to let him play himself out, and sometimes that took longer than I could have wished."

Flaubert, who was later to declare his love for "all excesses," felt he had to declaim the episode of Velléda (the druidess in Chateaubriand's *Les Martyrs*) at the île de Sein in the baie des Trépassés, then comparatively unfrequented by tourists. In the middle of the night they spent in Combourg Du Camp was woken up by "a ringing voice." "The window was open, and you could see the house lit up by the moon and Flaubert standing there saying: 'Man, the time for you to migrate is not yet come. Wait for the wind of death to rise. Then you will spread your wings towards the unknown regions your heart yearns for!' 'Let's get some sleep,' I said. 'Let's talk!' said Flaubert. We were still talking about Chateaubriand when the sun rose over the trees."

The master's spell was over them as they climbed the winding stairs and went through the towers and chambers where his footsteps had echoed. He himself echoes in Flaubert's account of it all: "*J'ai pensé à cet homme qui a commencé là et qui a rempli un demi-siècle du tapage de sa douleur* . . . (I thought of the man who began there and who filled half a century with the clamor of his pain) . . . " The evocation is both grandiose and moving. The young writer was discharging his debts: "*N'est-ce pas ici que fut couvée notre douleur à nous autres, le golgotha même où le génie qui nous a nourris a sué son angoisse?* (Is it not here our own pain was born, is not this the Golgotha where the genius who nourished us lived out his anguish?)"

They went back through Vitré, Fougères, Vires, and Honfleur. The excursion had lasted three months. They decided to write it up together, after having re-read their notes and worked out a plan. Du Camp was to write the even chapters, Flaubert the odd. It was real literary work, a matter of deliberate composition and style which for the first time cost Flaubert a great deal of time and effort. He admitted to Louise Colet that, working together at the same table, he and Du Camp may sometimes have "mingled their pens." Flaubert himself polished and re-polished. Not that there was any question of publication. They had both decided against it because of certain remarks too challenging or too irreverent towards the establishment. For Flaubert, who was later to enunciate it in the form of a principle, it was a question of "pleasing himself"; an exercise which was to lead to a work of art. Flaubert's chapters of the big octavo volume, published by Caroline Franklin-Grout in 1885 under the title chosen by Flaubert, *Par les Champs et par les Grèves*, are sufficient unto themselves. They show that Flaubert had found the secret of ease through effort.

How Is One to Become a Writer?

THE YOUNG MAN we are about to leave, and who when we come back to him will be to a large extent an author already formed, is a figure at once attractive and disturbing. If we knew nothing about his future we should still guess he would become a writer. All his inclinations lead him to set down on paper the thoughts and feelings of a tumultuous personality, and to express a world whose mysteries he flatters himself, somewhat prematurely, he has penetrated. He tries to bring things together and give them form. He relates everything to his vocation.

But only on condition that the vocation does not lead to a situation or profession. His love of freedom, and in particular of his own liberty unrestricted by ties or obligations, makes him dread any kind of petrification. He rejects the possibilities of setting up as a writer, publishing, making a career. They are snares which would trap him in a world he spurns; they represent the threat of being sucked into a reality which means disintegration and death. He sees no essential difference between being a writer and being a grocer: both consist in trading and keeping shop, in converting being, the only reality, into having.

Writing, not only in its spontaneity but also in its hesitations and gropings, manifests being; it is liberty, a different form of life. The schoolboy cries, "*Vive les poètes!*" and in the sense in which he uses the word, poetry proposes its own ends, rejecting any utilitarian obligation. This does not mean it is a gratuitous activity: on the contrary, it leads to real knowledge, as distinct from mere learning: "There is more truth in a single scene of Shakespeare or an ode by Horace or Hugo than in all Michelet, all Montesquieu, and all Robertson . . ."

The opposition between poetry (*i.e.* writing) and the world, paralleling that between liberty and necessity, is one of the simple basic antitheses which Flaubert very early erected into principles of existence. At thirteen he was already talking of "the farcical joke called life"; a few years later he described life as "nauseating cooking," the mere smell of which was enough to make one vomit. It was even more revolting in its collective and social aspects. He ridiculed those who took life to be anything else than organized brigandage. He fumed against all the things men usually consume their lives trying to attain: happiness, security, power. The irresponsibility of youth made his ideas all the more radical: he could sport and dream without encumbrance in an ideal world.

When he had passed his baccalauréat and had to think seriously of making a choice in life, despair descended on him. What he would have liked was to prolong adolescence for ever and put off indefinitely the moment of choice: "It's a sad position to be in when all roads lie open before you, each as dusty, barren and crowded as the other, and you stand there perplexed, not knowing how to choose between them." The trouble was that they all led to the same goal—the establishment. His only weapon against such a prospect was irony: "For one must be a useful person and look after number one like the rest, doing good for humanity and guzzling up as much money as possible." But you cannot spend all your time jeering at necessity when it is bearing down on you and demanding a decision. Your first reaction may be to turn your back and sulk, to reject totally the world and the life it offers. But the second reaction may then be to surrender to necessity, bag and baggage. Both reactions are too absolute and too illusory to last long. There must be a compromise.

The young Flaubert exhibits the whole process. First reaction: "As for writing, I've completely renounced it, and I'm sure my name will never appear in print. I haven't the strength for it any more, I don't feel capable, and fortunately or unfortunately that's the truth." Second reaction: "So I'll be a stop-gap in society, I'll fill my place there, I'll be a steady, respectable man, anything you like; I'll be just like anyone else, like everyone, *comme il faut*—a lawyer, a doctor, a sub-prefect, a solicitor, an attorney, a judge of some sort, something stupid like all the rest, a man of the world or, stupider still, a member of one of the professions. For I'm going to have to be one of all these, and there's no middle course." And then the compromise: "Ah well! I've chosen, I've made up my mind: I'll do law . . ." Why law? Because "instead of leading to everything, law leads to nothing." By choosing to read law, Flaubert was in fact not choosing at all: he was leaving compromise every possible opportunity of splitting apart into antithesis—"*Il n'y a pas de milieu* (there is no middle course)." And since it was not a matter of cold reasoning, but of two extremes of feeling which met only in what was impossible or absurd, Flaubert no more actually gave up writing than he agreed to become a "stop-gap" in society. The apparent decision forced on him by necessity (and his family) was really only a putting off of the evil day. Flaubert, a timid rebel who dared not openly stand out against the commands of family and society, was getting ready to fail his exams as a means of turning back to his original plan. He failed his first-year exams at the first session in August 1842, but passed at the second attempt in December. But the following year he failed at both attempts. Even so he would normally be expected to get on with his studies. He reacted to this necessity by illness. The nervous affliction which came on him in 1844 was really a disguised, and ultimately successful, rebellion. The father, tyrannical out of a love which the son returned with the addition of admiration, fear and respect, gave up the struggle, and conceded the liberty, the freedom from obligation, and the sheltered existence the young man craved. The son, in order both to deserve his father's confidence and to assuage his own remorse for shirking what had been expected of him, made his work appear a huge and interminable labor. He would show the world that the work of the artist is harder and more heart-breaking than any other.

He did not set out t ocreate beauty. That was a creed he adopted later almost as if to justify his real raison d'être, which was to denounce the world, accuse and undermine it, so that the possibility of becoming established in it no longer existed for the writer.

> *Si jamais je prends une part active au monde, ce sera comme penseur et comme démoralisateur. Je ne ferai que dire la vérité, mais elle sera horrible, cruelle et nue.* (If ever I take an active part in the world, it will be as a thinker and demoralizer. I shall only tell the truth, but it will be horrible, cruel, and naked.)

The thinker constantly questions accepted ideas. The demoral-izer attacks the foundations of moral, religious, and social life. To tell the truth is to force men to face the nothingness of their condition. The nihilist thus finds reasons for interesting himself in the world he has rejected. He enters into it as a ferment of destruction.

The refusal of the world which the young Flaubert expresses with such conviction both in his early works and in his letters was the only positive force capable of welding together all the diffuse and contradictory tendencies of a nature which he himself later described as *brumeux*, "nebulous." His precocious activity as a writer would be less astonishing if it were not so constant and continuous. It was as if he were trying to fill a void which only grew deeper as, with an insatiability rarely parallel-ed, he piled up reading, observation, analysis, self-affirmations and professions of faith. This particular nihilist does not turn in on himself. He extravasates himself, spreads through the world, flows into the authors he admires, and imitates them, so that "manner" succeeds "manner" and one genre follows another. Not only is he at the age of imitation, but his "gift as an actor" enables him to apprehend vicariously feelings he is not yet old enough to have known, and to express ideas derived neither from long reflection nor from extensive experience. But borrowing is not living, and gesture and attitude did not deceive Flaubert, who used them simply to express himself. His habitual state of mind was anguish, anxiety, an *"ennui"* which turned into despair. His quest for a means of expression merged into the attempt to seize his own being, the oft-repeated endeavor to acquire *"une identité."* "Oh, what wouldn't I give to be either more stupid or more intelligent, more of an atheist or more of a mystic, but at any rate something complete and whole, an identity, in a word—something!" But he eluded his own grasp. He did not exist as an independent consciousness.

A Problem Solved on the Plane of Expression

REJECTION OF THE WORLD is the first affirmation of the self. The world is, to begin with, ordinary life, the utilitarian ways of the age one lives in, the age itself. It is also the laws of life, the metaphysical scandal of man's being born to die, the evident triumph of evil and suffering, the meaninglessness of a blind universe. Though Flaubert's nihilism was a fundamental part of himself, he borrowed his way of expressing it from Byron, from the Romantics, from the skeptics ancient and modern. In opposing a utilitarian society motivated by profit he was doing what every artist does: setting against a cramping and limited reality the creativeness of art, thought, and literature. In other words, he was basing his rejection on powerful forces which legitimized and even ennobled it. Though it was really only by solitary struggle that he could achieve his own "identity," he joined a great army whose aid he constantly and eclectically invoked: Byron, Goethe, Chateaubriand, Shakespeare, Montaigne, Spinoza, Sade, Hegel. But no sooner was he out of one wood than he entered another. The more he clarified the terms of his problem, the further away the solution receded. The affirmation of himself merged into a general affirmation of art and literature.

To write like Byron or Balzac or Chateaubriand was in a way to face the world and to exist. But at the same time it made use of a set of references which had nothing in common with the unique consciousness which was really seeking a place in the world. Flaubert was thus flung back on his own weakness and non-existence. The two crises, one in 1840, the other in 1842, which made him declare he was abandoning writing *"définitivement"* resulted not only from an inability to create his own personal mode of expression but also from an inability to be. He had rejected the ordinary world, and thought himself incapable of attaining to the world of literature whose representatives he regarded with "awe." He was thrown back on his own "nebulousness," that is, on an empty consciousness.

After the 1842 crisis, which he regarded as a break with his past, with his youth, as a cancelling-out of his former life, he returned to writing without elation or enthusiasm, gloomily looking at it as merely as good a way as another of "passing the time." It seemed just a means of getting out of studying law, of countering the demands of family and society. It was an evasion and escape as well as a sign of revolt.

It cannot be said Flaubert had found himself by the time this period of flight was over. But at least he had discovered an inner necessity which, instead of operating on the fringe of the other necessities imposed on him, actually set itself against them and successfully counter-balanced them: he was born to write—he knows it and proclaims it. He still admires all those he admired before, but they are no longer the cause of either undue excitement or discouragement. They form a horizon; it does not matter whether the horizon is near or far so long as he is going towards it. And going towards it at his own pace and in his own gait. After writing *Novembre* he bade farewell to Chateaubriand as he had already bade farewell to Byron and to Balzac. Henceforward he would concentrate on seeing the world through his own eyes, and on "representing" it by his own means. The "being" which he had exhausted himself trying to track down and which would probably remain elusive—at the end of his life he was still complaining of the void he had tried in vain to fill with masterpieces—was bestowed on him on the plane of words. The words the writer fashions and which are his alone. Being rises to the surface out of them like a phosphorescence; it is he who enables them to live and shine. What appeared to be a philosophical or metaphysical problem, was resolved by Flaubert on the plane of expression.

3
THE FIRST
"SENTIMENTAL EDUCATION"

FLAUBERT finished *Novembre* on October 25, 1842. In the
story itself he says goodbye to autobiography and confession. The narrator's friend observes:

> *Sans doute notre homme n'aura plus rien trouvé à dire; il se trouve au
> point ou l'on n'ecrit plus et ou l'on pense davantage; c'est à ce point qu'il
> s'arrêta, tant pis pour le lecteur!* (No doubt our hero found he had
> no more to say. There comes a point where one writes less and
> thinks more. And that's where he stopped. Too bad for the
> reader!)

Flaubert had reached the same point. He laid aside his pen
for several months in order to "think more."

This pause was of primary importance in his psychological
evolution and his development as a writer. He realized as much
a few years later, when he wrote to Louise Colet:

> *Celui qui vit maintenant et qui est moi ne fait que contempler l'autre, qui
> est mort. J'ai eu deux existences bien distinctes; des événements
> extérieurs ont été le symbole de la fin de la première et de la naissance de la
> seconde; tout cela est mathématique. Ma vie active, passionnée, émue,
> pleine de soubresauts opposés et de sensations multiples, a fini à vingt-
> deux ans. A cette époque, j'ai fait de grands progrès tout d'un coup; et
> autre chose est venu.* (He who lives now and is me only contem-
> plates the other, who is dead. I have had two quite distinct
> existences. External events symbolized the end of the first and
> the beginning of the second. All that is mathematics. My
> active life, full of passion and emotion, contradictory impulses
> and manifold sensations, ended when I was twenty-two. Then
> I suddenly made great progress; and something else emerged.)

Flaubert was twenty-two in 1843-1844. He had started on the
second year of his law studies in Paris. He knew Maxime Du

Camp and Louis de Cormenin, and one of his childhood friendships, that with Alfred Le Poittevin, had developed into close intimacy. He led a typical student's life, at once bored and bohemian, interspersed with lengthy discussions and visits to brothels. He often went to the studio of Pradier, the sculptor, and every Wednesday he dined with the Schlésingers. He saw a good deal of the Collier sisters, whom he had met at Trouville in 1842.

Was he still in love with Elisa? There can be no doubt of it. But the time of the "great love" and "religious" passion had perhaps ended after the nights in Marseilles with Eulalie, and it may be that Flaubert had thoughts of making his platonic relationship with Elisa more concrete, in spite of the discretion imposed on him as a friend of the family. But it is very unlikely that he succeeded. He went on hoping, however, for another six years. After that it was too late. The story of Elisa Schlésinger is reflected in that of Mme Arnoux.

Flaubert's relations with Gertrude and Henriette Collier remained more than friendly. Apparently he was fonder at first of the invalid younger sister, the "divine Henriette," so much so that the girl's mother began to think of a match. Then later he seems to have turned to Gertrude, who in an account written after her marriage says he kissed her ardently during a performance of *Faust* at the Opéra. The bonds slackened when the Colliers returned to London, but were taken up again later in terms of memory and nostalgia.

The freest of atmospheres reigned in Pradier's studio. Pradier gave the young man "advice," which his young wife Louise illustrated in a practical manner. She deceived her husband with zest, and Flaubert probably enjoyed her favors after 1845, when the couple separated. But for him it was only a passing affair.

The year 1843-1844, in which Flaubert failed his second law exam, seems to have been a period of voluntary chastity. According to what he told Louise Colet in 1846, this phase of impotence and disgust may have lasted even longer: "Two-and-a-half years—from the age of twenty-one to the age of twenty-

four—passed without my visiting Paphos." Another letter gives
the time as only two years, but says he thought of castrating
himself. In 1863 the Goncourts wrote: "Yesterday Flaubert
told me, 'I did not make love between the ages of twenty and
twenty-four, because I had promised myself not to. . .' " It is of
little importance whether it was one year, two years, two-and-a-
half years or four—what matters is that during a whole crucial
period Flaubert was concerned with other and more momen-
tous things than the youthful desires poured forth by the
narrator of *Novembre*. It was as if he disciplined his body in order
to attain a state in which he could assemble and concentrate his
forces.

This was before the nervous attack of January 1844, which
may have been the price he paid for his inner conflict. It marks a
watershed in his life, although, as he himself said, it was not so
much a cause as an effect. The change had already been made,
the skin cast; he saw, and we see, only its most spectacular
signs. His illness made him seek a sheltered and retired life of
study and literary creation, but he had already long been
hostile to the idea of taking any active part in the world. By
temperament, taste, and thought he had come to aim higher.
His goal was to express the life in which he refused to be an
object, to reflect it conscientiously, to "represent" it.

The First Flaubertian Novel

HE BEGAN the first *Education sentimentale* in February 1843
and finished it on January 7, 1845. Like *Novembre*, it was written
in several phases, three at least; the most productive was
the last (from May 1844 to January 1854), after the onset of his
illness. This puts paid to Du Camp's allegations about the
"sterility" resulting from Flaubert's "epilepsy."

The reason this work differs from the previous ones, and is the
first to deserve the adjective "Flaubertian," lies in the author's
attitude of mind, which arises as much from a change of
approach as from the acquisition of a technique. His main aim is
no longer to tell his own tale and express his own tastes, feelings,

and ideas, as in *Mémoires d'un Fou* and *Novembre*. Now he prefers to embody all these in characters.

He tries to show their behavior, the circles they move in, the events in their lives, the time and space in which they develop. Instead of making them declaim in strained and lofty terms, he attempts to make them speak as they naturally would according to situation, place, and circumstance. He stays as close as possible to the object, neither adding anything nor taking anything away. He abandons the romantic conception by which the self is always more important than the external world; he eschews a lyricism which he finds facile and insincere. He thinks less of Balzac and other contemporaries than of great models like Homer and Shakespeare.

All this represents an evolution, not a sudden conversion. It was prepared for by months of thought, reading, and discussion with Du Camp and especially Le Poittevin; by the difficult, crisis-ridden transition from adolescence to adulthood; by the shock of his mysterious illness; and by the sustained and systematic effort to find a style composed of something other than imitation and reminiscence. The process continued even while he was writing the book itself, as if Flaubert were completing his own "sentimental education" through the story of Henry and Jules. He is only a step ahead of his heroes; it is as if they helped him find himself. What makes this first *Education sentimentale* seem so modern is the way in which it helped to modify its author in the course of its writing.

There are two main plots and two main characters, not very closely connected. Henry Gosselin comes to Paris to continue his studies, leaving behind in his native town his friend Jules, a budding writer who has to take a job as an invoice clerk. They promise to meet again, probably in the university vacations, and meanwhile correspond about what they are thinking and feeling. Henry's story is told in the third person, Jules's in the first (as he is represented by letters).

Up till two-thirds of the way through, Henry predominates. He begins by getting to know Paris, then his mother installs him in M. Renaud's pension. A new world and a new life open before him, made up of lectures, private study, meals taken in common, and decorous receptions. There are vivid sketches of his fellow-students, who appear and disappear more in the interests of local color than because of the requirements of the plot.

"A Love like Ours"

THE PLOT CONSISTS of the love affair of which Henry is the hero. He has not failed to notice M. Renaud's young and pretty wife, nor to foster dreams about her. Her bearing, face and walk; the way her garments float about her as she strolls in the garden; her languid grace—all these speak vividly to the young man's imagination and to his just awakened senses. He timidly conveys how much it means to him to see and talk to her. The lady of the house, who must have had plenty of experience of this sort of thing, guesses what is the matter and responds to his advances. She even goes out of her way to provoke them, trying to disguise her coquetry as the effects of boredom. One Sunday afternoon she goes into the student's room, with far from innocent intentions. But we only guess this from imperceptible movements, almost invisible gestures, words that are bridges over chasms. The tumult in the heart of the young man, at once bold and terror-stricken; the young woman's provocations, sometimes premeditated and sometimes artless; the thunderbolt hanging over them which would throw them into one another's arms if Emilie Renaud were not so prudent; the things that are not said—Flaubert expresses them all with a power and truth and sensual force which makes this scene one of the summits of his art. Even in *Madame Bovary* or the second *Education sentimentale* there is nothing more perfect.

Emilie does not give herself to Henry straight away. On the contrary, she does her best to keep him in suspense by alternating encouragement and disappointment, so that he is torn all the time between exultation and despair. What happens during a meal, a reception given by M. Renaud, and a surprise visit by Emilie to his room, makes him think he is making progress; but he is severely punished for his presumption. One day she lets him clasp her to his heart, another she kisses him; she has everything under control. She will succumb in her own good time, when the fish is properly hooked. The author is already skilful at whetting the reader's impatience. He beguiles the time showing us the unsuspecting M. Renaud, a German student, two Portuguese brothers, and the petty life of the pension gradually being transformed by the growing complicity between the lovers. All this is a preparation for the consummation.

For the day of Henry's triumph eventually comes. He is beyond mere pride and the satisfaction of telling himself he has the respected wife of M. Renaud for a mistress. He has undergone a revelation—the revelation of physical love, sometimes tender, sometimes fierce, insatiable yet replete, cautious yet ready for any audacity. Emilie, who up to now was motivated perhaps by curiosity or boredom, yields herself utterly; she too has been swept away, lifted above herself. There are great outpourings of heart and soul. The two lovers can no longer bear everyday precaution, the presence of the husband, the atmosphere of the pension. In order to belong to one another in a way which accords with the truth of their feeling, they decide to run away to America.

But life together in a strange country with very little money is not all roses. They get to know each other better, they see each other put to the test, they begin to judge each other. The lover no longer experiences the same thrill, and is ashamed to see his passion waning. The mistress forces herself to endure hardship. They cannot bring themselves to admit that the feeling which was supposed to be eternal is dying by inches, while their homesickness for Europe grows, and they finally decide to go back. On the crossing Henry experiences something like relief. Emilie simply goes back to her husband. The end of the affair is shrouded in bitterness. One is hardly surprised that Henry becomes cynical and avid of "success," and fits himself out with the appropriate philosophy. All the author's interest, and all the reader's, now turns to Jules.

Jules's Disillusionments

WE HAVE ALREADY LEARNED from his letters to Henry that Jules was in love with a young actress on tour, who cheated him of some money and left him. The leáder of the company, whose mistress she was, had read a play of Jules's and said he would put it on, predicting a great success. He too went away without leaving any address. Disappointed in both ambition and love, visited by a strange vision of a mangy dog which reminds him of the spaniel he gave to the actress, Jules falls back on his vocation as an artist. It seems to him the only reality to which he can anchor his existence. He will write for himself alone, putting this solitary pleasure before everything else, before life itself.

This dual "sentimental education" has produced bitter fruit for both its heroes. Henry has trodden the path from grand passion to disillusionment, and though the lesson he learns may be of practical use to him in everyday life, it finishes him morally. He is ripe for a "position," marriage, or other loves. Good luck to him! He is of no further interest to the author.

Jules seems to him to be made of different stuff. Lucinde tricked him—but he was very young. Bernardi took him in also—but that does not mean he is without talent, or that that talent will not one day show results. But he was aiming too low: the artist's goal is not to get pleasure from life or to make his works satisfy earthly ambitions. Let us listen carefully: Jules's thoughts on these matters, the distance he sets between life and art, his notion of the end of artistic activity, are very likely to be the ideas of Flaubert in 1845.

"The Consciousness of the World"

JULES'S IDEAS come to him in the first place from his reading. He wants to be a writer, and having been through romanticism and found that its lyricism and fantasy only throw him back on his own wild imaginings, he methodically consults the authors of the past and "enters whole-heartedly into the great study of style." This leads him on to consider history and nature, both of which he embraces in all their complexity and variety, so that he is no longer astonished at anything. But he discovers a unity in nature and a constant in history—man—which are manifested in art.

> *Le monde étant devenu pour lui si large à contempler, il vit qu'il n'y avait, quant à l'art, rien en dehors de ses limites, ni réalité, ni possibilité d'être.* (The world having become for him so wide a subject of contemplation, he saw there was nothing beyond the limits of art, neither reality nor possibility of being.)

This on condition that the infinite is mirrored in art "as the sky is mirrored in the sea." The authors who give Jules this sense of the infinite are those who "have included mankind and nature within their circle": *i.e.* Homer and Shakespeare.

> *Tout l'homme ancien est dans le premier, l'homme moderne dans le second . . . Ils ont été si "vrais" qu'ils sont devenus "nécessaires"; ce qu'ils ont fait est leur œuvre en même temps que celle de Dieu; ils sont comme la conscience du monde puisque tous ses éléments s'y trouvent rassemblés et qu'on peut les saisir.* (All ancient man is in the first, all modern man in the second . . . They were so "true" they have become "necessary"; what they did is their work at the same time as God's; they are like the consciousness of the world in that all its elements are there and distinguishable in them.)

They were "simple" and "profound" geniuses, and sought not so much to show "the unfolding of a rich personality or the sway of strong feeling" as to efface themselves in a task which made absurd and irrelevant the accidents of their own existence and their own personal passions, so often the pride of lesser artists. They were less concerned with expressing themselves than with giving form and significance to a world which enthralled them with its vastness, majesty, and depth. What they achieved "is at once every individual's truth and truth in relation to the whole of creation, stamped by the hand of man without losing anything either of its reality or of its totality." Jules and Flaubert argue for the impersonality of the creative artist. In order to be able to understand and feel everything about men and things, past and present, he must forget himself and attain the objectivity of a God.

This aesthetic is based on a philosophy which presupposes that the world, for all its variety, is one, and governed by a principle from which all laws derive. It also presupposes that the laws of art correspond to those of life and are governed by a similar determinism. This means the artist does not have actually to experience all the feelings he describes, to live through all the adventures he relates, or to have known all the characters he presents. It is enough that he should enter into an artistic truth which will order the elements of living truth. Conversely, when he regards life in its particular aspects, his knowledge of constant and universal laws make it unnecessary for him to express his own personal thoughts and feelings. He thus inhabits both truth and "justice". Flaubert was to become so convinced that art is an exact parallel to life that he believed in the actual existence of what he had written. He would ask friends who were botanists or zoologists for specimens of strange plants or animals: they must exist because he had described them.

Life and art are subject to the same determinism, but whereas the ordinary person merely obeys its commands, the artist embraces them in their causes, effects, and consequences. The first is blind, the second clairvoyant. It follows that there is no need to live in order to represent life: to live might even blur the artist's vision. It is by setting himself apart from ordinary humanity and refusing to participate in its depravities and ambitions that the artist is able to perceive the relationships which define the ordinary man and which the ordinary man does not see. As he does not share in the common illusion, the artist is better able to exhibit it and can regard it with a higher degree of rigor.

Jules wonders whether there are as many possibilities for a 19th-century artist as there were for Homer and Shakespeare. By means of chosen examples he persuades himself that whatever the period and the apparent differences in man, he really has not changed: there are still liars, jealous lovers, and misers. The characters depicted by Molière and the passions animating the heroes of Shakespeare, everything that provided the material of comedy and tragedy and satire in the past, all still exists in profusion for the 19th-century artist. All he has to do to see clearly is to stand back, revealing permanent realities while describing appearances. It may even be that for him this is the only way to see how his own age differs from all the rest, and to show what are the particular problems that confront his contemporaries.

We watch Jules conducting his self-examination as an artist. He retraces his own line of development and formulates gradually acquired truths which he must now put to the test. It is this that constitutes his "sentimental education." He does not show the vanity of the inventor or the pride of the discoverer, but he has clearly seen his mission, and knows already how he will make himself worthy of it and by what means he will accomplish it. He means to fulfil his chosen task with his eyes open. He is ready to devote his time and strength and life to it because he has taken the measure of the vanity of life and of all other human tasks.

> *Il descendait si vite dans toutes les choses qu'il en voyait le néant du premier coup d'œil, comme ces sources à fleur de terre, dont on trouve le fond rien qu'en y plongeant les pieds.* (He fathomed all things so rapidly he saw their nothingness at first glance, like those shallow springs where one touches bottom as soon as one steps in.)

Only art defies the irony with which uncommon spirits judge all else, only art deserves to be one's sole preoccupation. When it is the art of Homer or Shakespeare, it would be a waste of time to try to "touch bottom."

Flaubert looking Over Jules's Shoulder

LIKE JULES, Flaubert had read a great deal: the ancients and the moderns, Montaigne and Rabelais, Montesquieu and Voltaire, La Bruyère and Chateaubriand. From all of them he derived lessons in style which were also revelations. He might not yet know what he wanted to express, but he knew how he would like to express it: by means of a style both supple and strong, colorful and vigorous, embracing the object in detail and in general, in shade and in flavor. He had learned that a writer is not great because of the loftiness of his ambition or the kind of subject he treats, or even necessarily because of his inner vision. He is great through expression—that is the strait gate through which one must struggle in order to reach all the rest. No style, no writer; form is content. Flaubert had read and profited by Hegel's *Aesthetics:* he knew better than Victor Cousin, the advocate of "art for art's sake" who gave a famous lecture on the subject, what "the true, the beautiful, and the good" meant for the artist.

Alfred Le Poittevin, his close friend and elder by five years, had also taught him a lot. The long philosophical discussions they had in 1845 were prepared for by the reading they did together, the confidences they exchanged, and the views about life they had aired to each other. Some people deny that Le Poittevin was really a Spinozan, but what is certain is that the monistic conception of the world expressed by Flaubert, in which every particle of matter is imbued with spirit, derives from Spinoza. As early as 1840-1841 Flaubert's private journal spurns Christian dualism: he says he "inclines towards materialism." He is a child of his age, and though he does not share its illusions about evolution in the arts, moral progress, and the virtue of numbers, he is a champion of determinism both in psychology and in the physical sciences. The impassivity of the artist is rather like that of the scientist contemplating his test-tubes. We shall have occasion to return to this.

At the same time as (through Jules) Flaubert formulates his aesthetic, he also tries to apply it in what is his first really organized work. It is not an unbroken narrative, but a real plot which twists and turns, thickens and is resolved in accordance with time, place, and circumstance. Instead of descriptions and confessions there are scenes embodying the action. The youthful novelist already knows the value of interval for giving an impression of real duration; he was to use it with great mastery in the second *Education sentimentale*. Though he puts himself first in Henry's situation, then in Jules's, he does not lose himself in either. He distances himself from them by means of irony. Although Emilie looks rather like Elisa and loves rather like Eulalie, she is also an original creation. To sum up, the author has made every effort to be objective, and scarcely intervenes personally at all in the story. He has done with effusions and noble or ignoble sentiments, with local color and the picturesque, with declarations of principle, with illustrating ethical and philosophical themes, with the literature of despair, or of satanism, or of humanitarianism—with all the things which were still common coin in the period reigned over by George Sand, Eugène Sue, and Alexandre Dumas.

An Imperfect Work, but Indispensable

BUT FLAUBERT PUT the book away in a drawer. He was not in a hurry to publish or even to show "his" truth. Perhaps, too, he realized that this *Education sentimentale* was not altogether what he could have wished. He may have aimed at an over-all conception, but the chief value of the book lies in episodes and isolated passages: the growth and slow disintegration of Henry's love; life in the pension; the love passages between Henry and Emilie; the episode of the dog that follows Jules. The two plots do not join together; they are not even parallel; they turn their backs on one another. The story is virtually over when Emilie returns to her husband. The author prolongs it artificially by making Jules expound his own aesthetic theories and bestowing on Henry a fate he has not deserved. He becomes explanatory and didactic.

"I'd need to rewrite or at least go over the whole thing, re-do two or three chapters, and put in one that's missing," he wrote to Louise Colet in 1852. But he could not bring himself to it. He preferred to work at *Madame Bovary*. Whereas in *L'Education sentimentale* "although causes are shown, and results, the connection between cause and effect is not shown at all," in *Madame Bovary* the inevitable unfolding of events was to appear implacably.

Although the first *Education* and that of 1869 both have the same title they are not at all alike. One is certainly not a sketch for the other; they are two distinct works. Nevertheless the story of Frédéric Moreau is also the story of an "*éducation*," an education through love and life, with the joys and sorrows attached to them, which preludes the emergence of the hero's fate. He too has an alter ego, Deslauriers, and the whole story is bathed in the same irony, ends in the same bitterness. Yes, it is the same and yet not the same. The great *Education* does not only depict an ill-starred love, an impossible passion; it is more than the tragic encounter of Mme Arnoux and Frédéric. It possesses dimensions which the story of Henry and Jules does not have: the dimensions given by the hopes and disillusions of a generation, of an age, of a life which began well and then fades away into apathy. When he wrote the first *Education* Flaubert had no more than an intuitive knowledge of what the world was like; his only experience was amorous. For all that does not relate to love his method is still that of Balzac. And he is still learning his job.

He does not need excuses and does not ask indulgence. Already he is sure in perception, elegant in invention, and skilful in the use of words. His mind is quite uncluttered by all the preoccupations which encumbered his contemporaries, Balzac, Victor Hugo and George Sand included. He makes straight for the facts, and that is what he presents to us: it is up to us to accommodate ourselves as best we can. We accommodate ourselves so well to the first *Education sentimentale* that we no longer see it overshadowed by the second and merely its harbinger. It exists in its own right, just as the love of Emilie and Henry is different from that of Emma for Rodolphe and from that of Frédéric for Marie Arnoux; just as Jules cuts the umbilical cord which still joined him to his youth and his illusions in a way that is unique. It is something that happens only once and that we could not have done without.

4
THE FIRST "TEMPTATION
OF SAINT ANTHONY"

I T WAS in 1845, during the visit to Italy with his family, that
Flaubert first conceived the idea of writing *La Tentation de
Saint Antoine*. In the Balbi Palace in Genoa he was struck by
a painting by Breughel which gave a crude representation of the
seductions that beset the hermit. He came back later to study
it at greater length. In a letter dated Milan, May 13, 1845,
he tells Alfred Le Poittevin how he would like to "arrange" the
saint's adventures for the theater, even though he does not
consider himself altogether up to it.

The subject would enable him to express in a dramatic poem
a long-cherished philosophical conception of life and the
world. He had already made some first attempts in such
ambitious but maladroit work as *Rêve d'Enfer*, *La Danse des
Morts*, and above all *Smarh*, in all of which Satan is somehow
introduced to hold forth about the infinity of the universe and
the mystery of creation, and to try to confound his adversaries.
In all man believes or imagines about the universe, nothing is
certain or based on tangible realities. Every logical system,
every faith, is doubtful. Nothing is true but the existence of evil
and the annihilation of death which is the end of all. The
youthful author's two main characteristics are a skepticism
derived from the reading of Montaigne and a pessimism derived from Byron and a certain type of Romanticism.

Flaubert had read and re-read Byron's *Cain*, and *Smarh* is very
much marked by its influence. It was from Byron that Flaubert
got the idea that "the world is perhaps one vast hell in which
everything is punished for being alive," and the notion that
whoever it was, God or devil, who invented life only to lead to
death, should be accursed: "He created only to destroy."

Flaubert also draws on other contemporary sources, especially Edgar Quinet's *Ahasvérus* (published in 1833), a prose epic brimming with a philosophic lyricism that must have appealed to the young Flaubert. It shows debates between Eternity and the Void, introduces fabulous creatures whose existence denies the wisdom of the Creator, and after discussing the philosophical basis of evil tries to find a better solution than Christianity, which is held to have sidestepped the problem.

All these influences are found again in *La Tentation*, of which the general conception and dramatic form nevertheless seem to owe most to Goethe. When he was only twelve or thirteen, Flaubert had been entranced by *Faust*, just translated by Gérard de Nerval. All his life he remembered the circumstances of this revelation: it was just before Easter, under the trees of the Cours-la-Reine, and all the bells in Rouen were ringing for the Resurrection. The discovery of the masterpiece kindled the boy's enthusiasm; it opened his eyes to the world and his mind to the comprehension of life; he probably vowed to follow Goethe and find a way of expressing in words what he felt within him. Saint Anthony, too, was a solitary hero exposed to all the temptations of the flesh, the heart, and the mind; and though the comparison with the actual character of Faust ends here, Flaubert did use the same form as Goethe to bring together in one vast philosophical symbol all the many and various ways in which humanity tries to give itself reasons for living, acting, and creating. The shattering laugh of the devil brings the whole vast house of cards tumbling down, but this does not stop the hermit from persisting in the strict task which makes him a saint. Like *Faust*, *La Tentation* contains an implicit moral about life. And it was so deep in the marrow of the author's bones that for twenty-five years, in the intervals between masterpieces, he kept coming back to it. As he himself said, his *Saint Antoine* was the "great affair" of his life.

Old Legrain's Puppet Show

ALTHOUGH BREUGHEL'S PICTURE was the immediate stimulus, one of the reasons it acted on Flaubert was that it aroused in

him a host of old memories. Every year in October, during the
Foire Saint-Romain, an old man called Legrain put on a puppet
show which Flaubert would go and see on his way home from
school. The subject was the temptations of Saint Anthony. The
hermit was seen in his solitude, first in prayer, then in the toils
of all the emissaries of the devil. For all his cries of *"Messieurs
les démons, lassez-moi donc* (Pray, master devils, let me alone)!"
they tried to take away his pig and destroy his house. The saint
was only left in peace when the Almighty himself appeared and
bade his tormentors go back to hell. Old Legrain, well-known
for his gift of the gab, played all the parts, improvising against a
background reminiscent of the old mystery plays in its naivety
and vividness. Alone or with friends, Flaubert would look on
enchanted at these performances, practically identical from day
to day and from year to year. When he wrote to Alfred Le
Poittevin about his new project in 1845, Flaubert referred to
"old Legrain's booth."

The idea was solidly rooted in him for all sorts of reasons.
Childhood memories; his earliest literary and philosophical
influences; the desire to give vent to a lyric impulse which
would voice everything—thought, imagination, confession, his
ideas on life and the world, his image of himself; all converged
in the plan to relate, through the legend of the saint, his own
inner adventures and those of the whole human race.

In August 1846 he put up on his "ramparts" the Callot
engraving on the same subject, a different treatment from that
of Breughel but equally fantastic. His philosophical debate with
Le Poittevin made him even adopt some Spinozan views. He
devoured books. "I read and write ten hours a day", he told
Ernest Chevalier. Any evidence about Saint Anthony was grist to
his mill, whether it was genuine or apocryphal, from the biography by Athanasius, Bishop of Alexandria, who had known
Anthony when he was young, through medieval incunabula
to great scholarly tomes like the German G.F. Creuzer's ten
volumes on religious symbolism. He wanted to steep himself in
the exact colors of period, place, and customs; at the same time
as he described the temptations of the saint he wanted to show

all the beliefs of the fourth century. His reason was not only artistic meticulousness but also the belief that the decline of Alexandria presented a parallel with the second half of the nineteenth century. In both periods faith, belief and ethics were decried. In both, man was face to face with his own nothingness in a disintegrating world.

The 1849 Version and Its Judges

HE WAS TEMPORARILY DISTRACTED from his project by his trip to Britanny with Du Camp, but returned to it after February 1848, which saw the fall of Louis-Philippe and the setting up of the Second Republic. He solemnly noted down the day and the hour when he began to write: "May 24, at a quarter past three." During the summer Du Camp pressed him to go with him to the East; he renewed the suggestion in the spring of 1849. But in spite of his desire to go, Flaubert was inflexible: he had to finish *La Tentation*. Before he spread his sails he wanted to prove he was a writer, and he wanted to prove it to his friends Bouilhet and Du Camp. He was going to read the masterpiece to them when it was finished.

On "September 12 1849, at twenty past three in the afternoon, a sunny, windy day", he wrote the last words of his manuscript with the same solemnity and confidence as he had written the first. He told Du Camp and Bouilhet, who had come to hear him read it, "If you don't shout with enthusiasm it will be because nothing is capable of moving you!" For the next four days, a total of thirty-two hours, Flaubert droned on, savoring every sentence. His audience were completely impassive. They only exchanged glances. It had been agreed that they would not give their opinion until the reading was over. Mme Flaubert tried to take them aside, but they eluded her questions. Like them she sensed catastrophe. Before the last reading, which ended at about midnight, the two augurs had consulted together and decided to tell Flaubert he was on completely the wrong track. When he asked them to say frankly what they thought, the more timid and yet the braver of the two, Bouilhet, pronounced the verdict: "We think you should throw it on the fire and never mention it again!" Du Camp, who describes the scene in his *Souvenirs Littéraires*, says "Flaubert leapt up with a cry of horror." First he protested and roared and tried to argue; then, because he trusted his friends' judgment, he resigned himself and did not "mention it again". He had suffered a blow from which it would take him years to recover.

Bouilhet and Du Camp were not bad judges. But they were just not prepared for what they had to hear. They thought Flaubert would have written a historical reconstruction, or tried to relive the saint's experiences on the psychological plane. Instead they were subjected to a lyrical deluge which swept away both the saint and his times, and submerged the listeners as well. They sat in stupefaction as Anthony himself was succeeded by the seven deadly sins, the three theological virtues, the founders of numerous heresies (including Simon the Magician and Apollonius of Thyana), other characters supposed to represent Science and Logic, allegorical figures like the Pastor and the Courtesan, fabulous animals and monsters, the Queen of Sheba, a Sphinx, a Chimera, the Devil, idols, the principal Hindu gods and those of Greek and Roman mythology, the nine Muses. All these characters, or personified abstractions, besiege Saint Anthony, trying to seduce and corrupt him, in a dizzying flood of arguments. There is no dramatic action. Heresies and philosophical or metaphysical ideas merely succeed one another and cancel each other out. Anthony does not even have to take part in the discussion; he merely looks on. And if it should happen that his senses are inflamed by the paradisiac delights offered by the Queen of Sheba, or that his mind is excited by the grandiose and coherent system expounded by the devil, he need only fall back on his good sense or his staunch faith. The vacillations of his thoughts and feelings do not prevent his remaining essentially on an even keel.

But *La Tentation* was no more a drama than it was a historical novel or a psychological confession. It was a sort of side-show which made use of several different genres, and in which the author was all the characters. The saint's temptations are in fact those of the solitary. Who, according to Flaubert, is more solitary than the artist? He, too, has rejected ordinary life. And so as to be able to see and represent it better, he must include in his purview the essence and history of the whole universe, and all humanity in its wretched condition and its senseless hopes. The monster for which Du Camp and Bouilhet could not find a name was Flaubert. It was he himself who lay behind the hundred characters, the thousand arguments for and against, the firework display of images and metaphors, and the three or four great incompatible temptations—is it better to believe or to understand, to live or represent life, to be happy or to be lucid? Where Bouilhet and Du Camp expected an answer, Flaubert put a question mark. When the hermit, delivered from temptation, turns to the rising sun and begins to pray again, the devil disappears with a significant laugh, promising to be back soon. The whole thing may begin again the next night.

The Meaning of Saint Anthony

IT IS IN THE POSSIBILITY of its all starting again that the significance of the drama lies. What gives an opening to temptation in Anthony is not the saint but the man. It is because he remains a man while wanting to be a saint that he expresses the anguish of the human condition. The devil asks him, "Do you know where hell really is?" And, pointing to Anthony's breast: "There, until you have torn it out from under your ribs, you carry it with you; sin is in your breast, desolation in your head, and malediction in your nature . . ." Anthony, Flaubert, and man in general are one. One wonders how Flaubert's two friends, particularly Bouilhet, could have been so insensible to his desperation at being merely a man. Du Camp accused him of "*verbalisme*" ("phrases—fine, skilfully constructed, harmonious, often diffuse, made up grandiose images and strange metaphors—but nothing but phrases"). Bouilhet blamed his "excessive lyricism." Both of them missed the actual content of the work.

It is true that Anthony is a very static hero. If he had yielded to one of the temptations the others would *ipso facto* have become superfluous, and Flaubert would have been unable to mount his panorama of all the ideas mankind has manufactured through the ages of its relations with God and with the world. And if Anthony had been dragged down towards life and the satisfaction of his instincts and desires, he would no longer have been a saint. He is exposed to contradictory and equal forces, and his oscillations are not enough to furnish material for drama. But at least he is rooted in the tragedy of existence.

The devil almost wins. Philosophically, one might almost say he does win. He expounds to Anthony the only philosophical system Flaubert himself might accept: a Spinozism in which all the elements which make up the universe, and God himself, are linked in a necessary relationship determined by the All to which they belong. Although Flaubert had arrived at this view through much reading and through long conversations with Alfred Le Poittevin, he was too cautious not to reflect that it might come up against equally satisfying ones among all the vestiges that were to be reviewed. If Anthony resists in the name of his religion it is because Flaubert is honest and scrupulous enough to admit that faith and intellect are two different spheres. He did not want to exclude anything which for better or worse bore the mark of humanity. He wanted to be able to understand everything, accept everything.

What might also have thrown the two listeners is that *La Tentation* does not move towards any climax. There is no truth gradually built up by means of situation, character, and argument. The long road between beginning and end leads to no summit. Not that one can say that nothing happens, with that long procession of characters, those masses of arguments, those dialectical excursions. But by some mysterious process all the assets become liabilities. The characters are as insubstantial as shadows—or ghosts—and their words vanish as they do. The most challenging arguments are cancelled out by others more persuasive, which in their turn sink back into the quick-sands of fancy and imagination. The most closely argued discussions only beat the air. What the author intends to convey by this all-round demolition is that one truth is as good as another; there is no truth. It is like trying to arrive at the centre of an onion.

That was Flaubert's intention—to leave the reader more bereft than he was before, to convince him that nothing which man thinks, believes or imagines is sure, and that living is as meaningless as trying to understand the mystery of life. He wanted to disturb the reader's profoundest convictions and plunge him into doubt. This lesson in skepticism derives from Montaigne and leads to the garden of *Candide:* everyone does and thinks what he was born to do and think; we only obey our own nature.

As with Montaigne and his work, one might say that *La Tentation* is "consubstantial with its author." He put his whole self into it—his dreams, desires, temptations, his bitter philosophy of life, his "abandonments of style." So to challenge it was to challenge Flaubert himself, both as a writer and as a man. "I admit the faults you point out to me," he told his two judges, "but they are inherent in my nature. How can they be remedied?" He could see no solution. It was then Bouilhet is supposed to have advised him, as a penance, to tell the very bourgeois story of Eugène Delamare.

An Obsession

DURING ALL THE Middle Eastern journey Flaubert brooded over his setback, had doubts about his vocation, cross-questioned himself about the future. He talked about his problems to Du Camp, and wrote about them to Bouilhet and to his mother. For him it was two years of uncertainty and anguish.

A few months after he got back to Croisset, in September 1851, he resigned himself to beginning *Madame Bovary*, a task that was to take him five years. We know from his letters to Louise Colet how much he had to force himself, and how he simultaneously modified his own nature and worked out an aesthetic which would justify that nature while dealing a mortal blow to its lyricism, its imaginative flights, and its excessive fondness for image and metaphor. He is probably less himself in his masterpiece than in his failure, the *Tentation*, and although the heights he reaches in *Madame Bovary* represent his greatest artistic triumph—the victory in which he discovered himself—his softest spot was still for *La Tentation;* he never forgot it, and was always secretly thinking of going back to it. He sent it to Louise Colet to read, and she was enthusiastic. So he then pointed out its faults, with more perspicacity than Bouilhet and Du Camp put together.

> *C'est une œuvre manquée. Tu parles de perles. Mais les perles ne font pas le collier; c'est le fil. J'ai été moi-même dans* Saint Antoine *le saint Antoine et je l'ai oublie. C'est un personnage à faire (difficulté qui n'est pas mince). S'il y avait pour moi une façon quelconque de corriger ce livre, je serais bien content, car j'ai mis là beaucoup, beaucoup de temps et beaucoup d'amour. Mais ça n'a pas été assez mûri. De ce que j'avais beaucoup travaillé les éléments matériels du livre, la partie historique je veux dire, je me suis imaginé que le scénario était fait et je m'y suis mis. "Tout depend du plan."* Saint Antoine *en manque; la déduction des idées sévèrement suivie n'a point son parallélisme dans l'enchainement des faits. Avec beaucoup d'échafaudages dramatiques, le dramatique manque.* (It is a failure. You talk of pearls. But it is the string that makes a necklace, not the pearls. In *Saint Antoine* I myself was the saint, but I forgot it. It's a great rôle, which doesn't make things easy. If there was any way I could make the book better I'd be delighted—I put a lot into it, a lot of time and a lot of love. But it wasn't sufficiently thought out. Because I'd worked hard at the material elements, by which I mean the historical parts, I imagined it was all there, and I started. But "Everything depends on the plan." And *Saint Antoine* hasn't got one; the rigorous unfolding of the ideas is not paralleled in the sequence of events. There is a lot of dramatic scaffolding, but no drama.)

The principle that "everything depends on the plan" came from Goethe. Flaubert put it to the test in *Madame Bovary*, where not one detail, sentence or phrase was the result of chance. For the whole machine to live and function, each stroke must contribute to the over-all effect, and this entailed endless re-writing and correction. The work exhausted and repelled him; he said it put him off "bourgeois subjects" for ever. But he had learned how to govern his own nature.

When *Madame Bovary* was finished at the beginning of 1856, he threw himself into *La Tentation* again, anxious to put into practice the skills he had acquired since the first version. "It is something that weighs on my conscience," he wrote to Bouilhet, "and I shan't have any rest until I'm rid of this obsession."

But he did not mean to rewrite it entirely. His conception of the work had not changed; it still corresponded perfectly to his philosophy. What he intended was to put some life and vigor into it, to add movement, to strengthen the structure so as to make the over-all design clearer. For a start he cut all the lyrical passages and all the digressions he had indulged in, did away with redundant characters, and tried to make his hero more solid. He wrote to Bouilhet: "I've pruned . . . everything that seems to me out of place—no small matter, because the first part, which used to be 160 pages, is now only 74 when copied out again." The Theological Virtues now appeared only in Part II, and the spokesmen of the minor heresies were eliminated. In Part II he cut various colorful figures like the Woman with the dagger, the Woman with eyes unbandaged (Fornication), the Woman with frizzy hair (Impurity), Science, the whole episode of the Poets and Players, and "filled out" the character of Anthony with "two of three monologues which will finally introduce the temptations." By pruning Part III in a similar way he gave more importance to the dialogue "in space" between Anthony and the Devil. In all the whole thing had been reduced by half. It had gained in force and dramatic interest. The scenes are more solidly linked. Anthony is more convincingly a charcoal-burner withstanding all the assaults of knowledge and all the extravagances, often excessively logical or rational, of the intellect. It emerges more clearly that the temptations are either the result of his unsatisfied flesh, or of his solitary spirit, or the voice of his scrupulous conscience which scents "vice in disguise" in his virtues. The piece has kept its shifting colors and barbaric strangeness while becoming more or less an inner drama.

Another Setback

FLAUBERT WOULD HAVE LIKED to publish this 1856 version, of which the 1849 version can be regarded as a first draft. But he was angered by the reactions to *Madame Bovary* and afraid *La Tentation* would be lumped together with it, whereas he wanted to reveal the lyrical side of himself. He was not sure his friends were right in having "amputated" that "second man . . . in love with tirades, lyricism, great eagle flights, all the resonances of words and all the summits of thought." The *Tentation* did not deal with a subject which, like that of *Madame Bovary*, often sickened him by its vulgarity: in it he had "sung in his own voice." As he wrote to Louise Colet, "Having taken a subject where I was entirely free as to lyricism, impulse and abandon, I felt myself naturally at home, I only had to press on. I shall never know again the abandonments of style I indulged in for those eighteen long months." Not that he regarded the *Tentation* of 1856 as perfect. So far was this from the case that in 1874 he produced a third version, the official and definitive one, completely reworked and very different from the two previous versions. How close *La Tentation* was to his heart is shown by the way he kept coming back to it right up to the end of his life.

The prosecution which followed the publication of *Madame Bovary* in the *Revue de Paris* made Flaubert keep *Saint Antoine* tucked away. Judging by the way they had misunderstood Emma, the lawyers of Napoleon III would only take the saint's struggles against temptation as fresh attacks on morality and religion. Flaubert, not only the unwilling protagonist of a public scandal but also suffering from a wound to his artistic pride, did no more than publish extracts of *Saint Antoine* through Théophile Gautier, his friend, in the periodical *L'Artiste*. But as he had foreseen, this was more than enough. Pinard, the public prosecutor, made use of the extracts, referring among others to the fine scene of Apollonius of Thyana. The public in general was also disappointed and put out by this new "manner." Though he was not so upset as he had been by the previous failure in 1849, Flaubert set to work on a novel about Carthage which would enable him to get his final revenge on "bourgeois subjeçts." This meant a return to his real loves and what he took to be his real nature. He did not realise then that the writing of *Madame Bovary* had been worthwhile for him in spite of everything.

The 1856 *Tentation* has been unfairly relegated by that of 1874 into the limbo of scholars and critics. It was not published until 1908, by Louis Bertrand, under the title of *La Première Tentation de Saint Antoine*, though it was in fact the second. But it reveals a Flaubert it is not always easy to find in the highly organized works of his maturity.

5

A STORMY LIAISON

ONE EVENING in June 1846 Pradier introduced Flaubert to Louise Colet, saying, "Here's a lad who wants to go in for literature. You ought to give him some advice." The lad was twenty-four, handsome and ardent. Louise Colet was a well-known writer. On July 29 Flaubert saw "La Muse" again, posing in the sculptor's studio. "The light fell obliquely on her," doing justice to her figure. The model and the visitor exchanged glances, and met again. They went for two drives in the Bois de Boulogne, accompanied by Louise's little girl, Henriette. They became lovers. But on August 4 Flaubert went back to his mother at Croisset, where at midnight he wrote his mistress his first letter: "Yesterday, at this time, I was holding you in my arms . . . " It was the beginning of a stormy love affair and an important correspondence.

Flaubert was emerging from a long period of chastity. He was in the middle of a kind of intellectual molting-season, and turning his back on his youth. At the beginning of 1844 he had had the first attacks of his mysterious illness.

Without being entirely extinguished, his passion for Elisa Schlésinger had turned into a nostalgia which he deliberately fostered and which was always to retain this character. The encounter with Eulalie Foucaud in Marseilles in 1840 was just a brief flare-up. The Collier sisters may have been in love with Flaubert, but for him the relationship, first with Henriette, then with Gertrude, was never more than a sentimental flirtation. The two English girls merged in his memories with the beloved "phantoms of Trouville."

Flaubert's illness had accentuated his desire to withdraw from the life he said he hated, and kept him out of range of anything to do with love. He never wanted to marry, and regarded the marriages of his two friends Alfred Le Poittevin and Ernest Chevalier as surrenders to conformism, exciting his sarcasm as well as his regret. To found a family was to become a pillar of the society he loathed, to enter into a sort of shopkeeper's existence. He preferred the seclusion of the artist, and after his father's and sister's death confined his affections to devotion towards his mother, to whom he pre- served an attitude of dependence, and towards his niece, whom he undertook to educate himself. The encounter with Louise Colet "*le derangeait*," put him out. Although he played quite fair with her, he could not resign himself to the prospect of an uninterrupted and all-absorbing liaison. After two or three nights of love, he went back to Croisset, and he had no inten- tion of receiving his mistress there. Every so often he went to see her in Paris, or else they met mid-way, at Mantes.

"It Can't Be Helped! We Shall See . . ."

IN HIS VERY FIRST LETTER he assumed responsibility for the strangeness of this set-up. He blamed his own nature: "I'm afraid I'm cold, dry and selfish." He blamed the irrevocability of the life he had chosen. He tried to make his mistress see the situation clearly and not cherish any illusions. For the time being they were carried away by passion, and it was probably best not to think about the future. "To think is the quickest way to suffer." But he does point out the "shoals" lying ahead, though he pretends not be bothered by them: "Oh well, it can't be helped! We shall see." He tells her of his love, which must have been pretty intense to have overcome all the barriers he himself had set up. But unlike most ardent lovers, unlike what might have been expected of most young men of twenty- four who had won a mistress like Louise Colet, he does not say this love is going to be his whole existence.

Flaubert's hasty departure in spite of her tears, and the reserves about the future in these early love-letters, vexed Louise Colet by showing her the limits of her power. Her

answer was "sad, pained, resigned." Flaubert tried to console
her, and told her again that he loved her as far as he was capable,
but that he could not force his nature. "I warned you, my
unhappiness is contagious. I've got scabies, and woe to anyone
who touches me." One might have thought the situation was
quite clear and that an intelligent woman, however passionate,
would either have found such a love unsatisfactory and broken
the whole thing off, or accepted her lover as he described
himself from the outset. But Louise Colet was not very intelligent, and such an attitude only whetted her feminine
pride. Her passion seemed to her to give her the right to try to
change Flaubert's life and habits and transform him into her
passionate adorer. Her head was stuffed with romantic platitudes about love. Her husband was so accommodating that
she was very free, and after all, love was a woman's vocation—
and one, to judge from her writings, that must have seemed
to her especially suitable to a *femme de lettres*. Flaubert and La
Muse did not set out together in step. Everything derives
from this false start—the future disagreements, the continual
complaints, the demands of the woman who thought herself
neglected, the ruptures for which neither was particularly
responsible, and the final break which left Louise vindictive
and Flaubert slightly more bitter than before. La Muse
ignored all the warning signals. She was too sure of herself,
and underestimated the young man she had raised to the rank
of lover.

La Muse

SHE WAS in the swim, and good-looking—and at thirty-six her
blonde charms were at their height. She was born in Aix-en-
Provence, where her father was post-master, and married
Hippolyte Colet, a teacher of music at the Paris Conservatoire.
When she and Flaubert met she was already well known, not
so much for her writings, which were no more than mediocre,
as for her train of distinguished lovers and protectors. She had
granted her favors to Victor Cousin, professor of philosophy

at the Sorbonne, a member of the Académie, and the secretary of the influential *Revue des Deux Mondes;* the connection between them went on for many years more. Alphonse Karr, who edited a satirical paper, is alleged to have said, punning on her protector's name (*"cousin"* in French can mean gnat), that her pregnancy was due to the sting of a gnat (*"une piqûre de cousin"*). She was to have other adventures, sometimes sustained affairs, with a number of successful writers—Musset, Villemain, and Victor Hugo. In both 1851 and 1855 she dispensed to Musset the pleasures Flaubert was in no particular hurry to enjoy—and Flaubert knew about it and took no offence. After the break with Flaubert, she took as acknowledged lover Jules Husson Montfleury, the somewhat over-simplifying theorist of the "realism" which Flaubert was supposed to have fathered. In short, she was talked about, and acquired various not very respectful nicknames.

At a time when Flaubert had not published anything, she was at the height of her fame. She had a salon in the rue de Sèvres, just opposite Mme Récamier's in the Abbaye-aux-Bois; she had made friends with her so as to share her empire. She carried weight both in the newspapers and in the Académie, and made sure whatever she wrote was surrounded by all the publicity she could muster. She had no objection to rewarding writers and critics discreetly in kind.

There is no doubt the young provincial was fascinated, and in fact hooked, by her beauty, charm, and poise. What is less understandable is that she should have fallen in love with him, who had neither name nor position, and that she should have gone on for years with a relationship that was scarcely likely to advance her "career."

Was it a merely physical attachment that she tried to magnify into a passion? Although her lover's prowess was so unstinting it made her utter "cries of admiration," she had to be satisfied with meeting only once every two or three months, and then only when "la Bovary" didn't get in the way. It is hard to imagine a woman as keen on love as she was being content with such "alms," as she came to call them. Louise

Colet's biographer J. F. Jackson calculated that in the two years 1846-1848 the two lovers saw each other only six times. She nagged and complained, and although one can see how irritating this continual drone must have sounded to Flaubert, she has a right to some pity. Flaubert's admirers have combined to condemn her as narrow, ambitious, vindictive, a crank and a bluestocking. They forget she saw Flaubert as a lover not a genius, and that although the ridicule in the works designed to get her revenge has now boomeranged on her own silly head, one cannot deny that there were extenuating circumstances: she did love him. After her own fashion, unfortunately—without understanding and without trying to understand him.

One is even grateful to her for having been an opening on life for the recluse solely preoccupied with his work—on a life he had fled from too soon, with its pettinesses, its immense and incurable stupidity, its storms, its drizzle, but also its splendid days of sun. A little of Louise Colet went into Emma Bovary, and into the portraits of Rosanette and la Vatclaz. And who can say whether Flaubert would have pursued his labors to the end, and performed them so thoroughly, without the "recreation" she afforded him? Even if she had been no more than the occasion of the monumental correspondence, she would not have lived in vain.

He confided to her in his letters as to no one else. He kept her informed both of his personal secrets and of his secrets as an artist, the latter sometimes amounting, fortunately for the rest of us, to a lecture in aesthetics. His woes and anxieties, his enthusiasms and disgusts, he set them all down for her, keeping her up to date with his life and his day's work, trying to bring her into it as he related the difficult gestation of a work he wanted to be new and important, even if he did not think of publishing it. Louise Colet had read *Novembre*, *La Tentation*, the *Voyage en Bretagne*, and the first *Education*. She was interested by them, sometimes enthusiastic. Narrow though she might have been, she knew Flaubert towered above her as far as literary creation was concerned. She meant to make use of his advice and correction; she even took him as a guide in tactics, though he was hardly qualified to act as such. As for Flaubert, he wrote as he was, without circumlocution or formality, spontaneous and natural, sometimes naive, and always frank regardless of the consequences. He was writing to a mistress. This appears more than once, in spite of the fact that his niece, Mme Franklin-Grout, saw fit to suppress expressions which shocked her and any memories or confidences she thought unseemly. At the same time he was writing to a friend, a literary colleague, but one who was weak and timid and confused. He wanted to remove the scales from her eyes, make her share his own enthusiasm for art; he could not understand how she could be preoccupied with anything other than the work waiting to be done. When she pretended to be in difficulties over the planning or execution of some composition or other, he was in seventh heaven and loved her a thousand times more. She was meeting him on his own ground; she was no longer the "dear child" whom, although he was getting on for twelve years younger than she, he dominated by his experience and suffering; she was no longer a woman who can be reduced to what is politely called the heart.

But such satisfactions were only short-lived: the woman soon got the upper hand again, the mistress nagged and recriminated.

A Definition of Love

IF THEIR TEMPERAMENTS and preoccupations were different, the ideas each had about love were more different still.

Flaubert had only known one passion in his life—that which he had devoted first as a child, then as a young man, to Elisa Schlésinger. It was an unhappy love; one might almost say he wanted it to be so, because that corresponded to his conception of life. He had felt for Eulalie Foucaud, and still thought of her with gratitude and tenderness. But he had not replied to her letters—a love that was happy and requited seemed to him out of the question. When he met Louise Colet he had already "walled up" in his heart *"une chambre royale"* where his love for Elisa reposed and was sacrosanct. He would have thought it sacrilege to let Louisa enter there. He loved her, no doubt, but he knew where and in what circumstances he had met her, he had heard the talk about her, and he judged her "unworthy." That being so, he meant their relationship to be an exchange of services, in the fullest sense, as far as feeling, tenderness, and devotion were concerned. No less. No more. Without being either common or vulgar, this sort of love was one of the ordinary manifestations of life. For Flaubert, it was even the best. But it was of the order of that which is perishable, it had nothing to do with either predestination or grace.

This is what he tried to make her understand from the outset, when she had just given herself to him and he was still overflowing with gratitude. The heart had played its part in the physical ecstasy they had experienced. Why ask for the impossible when love, understood and experienced like that, makes one "good, confident, serene, and joyful", expands the heart, and confers delirious happiness modulating into "exquisite sweetness"? Isn't it enough that it answers a need which "cries out from one's depths" and produces a "limitless devotion"? Desire demands the renewal of pleasure, and so produces the need to belong to one another.

Unfortunately neither of them wished to make a whole universe of their love. With Flaubert the refusal was conscious and deliberate; with Louise Colet, that was what is amounted to in fact. She had to watch out for her own reputation, and for that of her husband and daughter; Flaubert, after a painful mutation, had chosen to be an artist and devote his life to his work. They did not belong to the same circles. One lived in Paris, the other in Croisset. It could only be a matter of compromises.

How could they make the best of things and bend reality to their desire? Flaubert tried to organize the situation, but Louise Colet refused to face it. She was afraid society would take her for what she appeared—a married woman who takes a lover. She wanted to magnify and so disguise this fact, to believe and make believe it was a great passion in the romantic manner, with lofty sentiments, eternal vows, folly and delirium.

She also sought more bourgeois assurances. If the liaison got to her husband's ears and she was compromised, was Flaubert ready to take her husband's place? Would he at least promise to think about the possibility? And supposing she had a child by him? At first she only hinted at all this, to show the magnitude of her sacrifice. What did she expect from him in return? Just that he should promise to love her "always"; by this she meant a vow of ideal *amour-passion* which also included all the more mundane obligations of everyday life.

Flaubert was frank and matter-of-fact. He said he was grateful and that he really did love her. But he refused to take on a future which seemed to him either a pipe-dream or too surely bound for disaster. In spite of his youth he instinctively knew enough about life to know that loves do not last for ever, and that the day would come—as late as possible, he hoped—when he and his mistress would be strangers to each other, perhaps hate each other. It happened to everyone; they could not escape it any more than anyone else. Moreover, his own make-up was such that he could not see life through rose-colored spectacles. For him everything headed towards disintegration, people and love-affairs alike:

> *Je n'ai jamais vu un enfant sans penser qu'il deviendrait un vieillard, ni un berceau sans songer à une tombe. La contemplation d'une femme nue me fait rêver à son squelette.* (I have never seen a child without thinking he would become an old man, nor seen a cradle without thinking of a grave. To look at a naked woman makes me think of her skeleton.)

He apologizes to Louise for shattering her illusions; it would have been better if she had not loved him. He tries to persuade her to stop. She goes out of her way to experience the very disappointment and pain he would like to spare her because he loves her. Over and over, his letters steadily convey a clear "take it or leave it."

Louise's Grievances

BUT LOUISE COLET WAS NOT A woman to give up easily. On the

contrary, she determined to overcome what she took to be superficial objections. She thought he was only trying to preserve his "bourgeois" way of life, and that he was afraid to cut free of his mother's apron-strings. According to her he disguised this egoism and timidity by "theatrical" airs, a "pose," and a "fatalism" which were either the result of his own pride or vanities borrowed from others greater than himself.

Flaubert did not deny he was an egoist. Who is not, if egoism means being true to oneself, obeying one's own personality, following one's own nature. Saint Vincent de Paul was just as much an egoist in obeying his thirst for charity as Caligula was in obeying his thirst for cruelty. Flaubert did not ask Louise Colet whether she did not think she was an egoist herself; he merely said "everyone deludes himself" in this matter. Everyone is an egoist to his neighbor.

Did he want to protect his "bourgeois" life? Of course. He had chosen the existence which suited him best for what he wanted to do. He had never cared for life in Paris, literary circles, and all the intrigues and jealousies and ambitions. If Louise Colet thought to drag him into all this as the opposite of a "bourgeois" existence, she was doubly mistaken. It was the work of art that counted, and this required silence, a sheltered existence. It was his good fortune to have just such conditions, and he would not find them in any other mode of life. La Muse replied that this was a very "vulgar existence"; but he would not exchange it for anything more brilliant. Did Louise, who tended to judge by appearances, not suspect that beneath that "vulgar existence there is another, a secret one, all bright and radiant for me alone, and which I show to no-one because they would laugh at it"? Yes, she did suspect it, and it was this that upset her. Her lover kept this door closed even to her. She knew it was not for fear of being laughed at. And she accused him again of pride and striking attitudes.

She touched a sensitive spot when she said he couldn't bring himself to leave his mother's apron-strings. He was dependent on Mme Flaubert: she watched over his every move, looked after his health, and ran the house. He had to beg her permission for the visit to Brittany, and plot with Dr. Cloquet to get her to let him go to the East. He had kept his liaison with Louise from her, and in order for them to meet every two or three months he resorted to stratagems which his mistress found either humiliating or comic. Surely he must suffer under this subjection, and if so, why did he not have the courage to put an end to it?

Here again Louise Colet was going by appearances. Though it might seem abnormal for a grown man to go on living as an obedient son, Flaubert did not suffer under this subjection (except sometimes from the inconveniences it caused later as his mother grew old); in fact, he said, it was his mother who was dependent on him and not the other way round. After the death of Dr. Flaubert and Caroline, he had not expected her to survive. In coming to live with him rather than in the Hôtel-Dieu with Achille and his family, she had put herself under his protection. She took care of him—she still worried about his nervous attacks—and he took care of her. She was the last tie left to him, and he considered it his duty to spare her any disappointment which might increase the sorrow of her double bereavement. If he shrank from telling her about his irregular liaison—which in the end she came to suspect, anyway—it was not so much that he feared her disapproval as that he did not want to wound her love. He owed himself to her. The tears of Louise, angry and frustrated, drove him to despair. The tears of Mme Flaubert would be unbearable. He had to choose between two women, between two loves which could not be compared, and he had chosen—chosen his mother, through a sensitiveness, on which no doubt psychoanalysis could comment, which also prescribed secrecy about his love affairs, and even exacted it from his mistress, who was married and the mother of a child. He could not bear her to make her irregular situation public, nor that she should come to Croisset on clandestine visits and leave before daylight. It would be humiliating for her, for him, and for his mother, and he meant to protect himself from it.

"For Six years I Loved a Woman Who Never Knew"

FLAUBERT SEEMED TO BE quite happy with the meetings in Paris and Mantes. Because he did not see her more often, because he refused to change his way of life and plan for the future, she accused him of taking advantage of her and treating her like a prostitute. He defended himself, taking the opportunity incidentally to challenge her prejudice against prostitutes. He regretted to have to inform her that he did not belong to "the vulgar race of men" for whom pleasure is the whole point of love and who are blind enough to be content with that. He did not despise Louise's charms, but he would be depriving himself of a greater pleasure if he did not associate them with her whole person: "There is something I love even more than your beautiful body, and that is you yourself." But this did not appease her. Though she did not doubt his sincerity, she did accuse him of being incapable of love.

It was a foolish thing to do. She was only asking for home truths which would make painful listening. Without mentioning Elisa by name, Flaubert revealed that "for six years I loved a woman who never knew"—meaning that love can do without declarations and vows, and in fact saying more: that he had experienced the passion of love so fully that it had eclipsed in advance any later attachment. This was proved by the fact that after that unspoken and unfulfilled love he had not loved again, "had not wanted to love." Can one love just at will? If Louise believed they had been brought together by a *coup de foudre*, she was now disabused. Flaubert had succumbed to her charms with his eyes open, perhaps deliberately. He did not wish to confuse the passion one feels once in a lifetime—and which he had felt—with the relationship he and Louise had entered into for their mutual pleasure. Nevertheless he did offer her a sincere and devoted love comprehending all the emotion of which he felt himself capable. He wanted it to be a communion of tenderness and physical delight, proceeding pleasantly and peacefully, without storms. According to the experience of the world on which he prided himself, to ask for more would be to delude oneself. Love does not bring "happiness." It merely enables one to "avoid *ennui*."

This resigned matter-of-factness angered Louise Colet. She forgot this was not her first affair and that in her situation she could not begin a completely new life; she claimed an influence which could only have been justified by sacrifices on her part which Flaubert did not require. She invoked the absoluteness of passion, exaggerated, drew false analogies. Flaubert brought her back to earth. She misinterpreted his declarations and confidences, attributing intentions to him which he did not have and constructing out of his letters a character in which he could not recognize himself. In fact, she was guided not so much by a quest for the absolute as by a false appraisal of the facts of their situation; he reproached her for entertaining visions which had nothing to do with reality.

Each meeting at the Hôtel du Grand-Cerf in Mantes set her fabricating fantasies again. She did not understand that her lover refused to belong to her all the time, and escaped as soon as she no longer held him in her arms. She would not accept his rejection of more frequent meetings, of the advantages of living in the same circles in Paris, and of the possibility of her being admitted at Croisset if he remained there. The same old question, already answered in so many different ways, kept cropping up: "Do you love me?" The harassed Flaubert endeavored to dot the i's:

> *Tu veux savoir si je t'aime? Eh bien! autant que je peux aimer, oui;*
> *c'est-à-dire que pour moi l'amour n'est pas la première chose de la vie,*
> *mais la seconde. C'est un lit ou on met un cœur pour se détendre. Or, on*
> *ne reste pas couché toute la journée. Toi, tu en fais un tambour pour*
> *régler le pas de l'existence! Non, non, mille fois non!* (You want to
> know whether I love you? Well, as much as I can love, yes;
> that's to say that for me love is not the first thing in life but the
> second. It's a bed where one puts one's heart to take a rest. But
> one doesn't stay lying down all day. You would make love a
> drum to beat time for the whole of existence. No, no, a thousand
> times no!)

For Flaubert "the first thing in life" was not to love but to write. Love was not an end in itself; it was the writer's way of occasionally putting himself before his goal, of resuming his own personal life: it was a rest, a concession, a relaxation. He and Louise had a different conception of love, a different conception of life, a different conception of literature.

But Louise returned to the charge with suicidal obstinacy, like a beast to the slaughter, or a martyr of *"Amour"* (Flaubert spelled it with three h's in order to mock at it). Since love was something universally revered, magnified, and forgiven all its errors and crimes, she tried to put her lover in the wrong and brand him an outlaw from ordinary mankind: the least he could do was admit he was a monster. Flaubert, his back to the wall, countered with another blow:

> *Pour moi, l'amour n'est pas et ne doit pas être au premier plan de la vie; il doit rester dans l'arrière-boutique.* (For me, love is not and should not be in the foreground of life; it has to stay at the back of the shop.)

This was not the view of Emma Bovary or Frédéric Moreau, whose fates were ruled by love. But their creator could not allow himself the same license. In order to depict love one had to remain outside it, just as in order to depict life one had to lead an existence apart. Flaubert was not trying to be cruel to his mistress; he was trying to be faithful to his artistic philosophy, which did not permit the slightest personal concession.

Apparently, after this unambiguous statement, set out in a letter dated April 30, 1847, the eve of Flaubert's departure to Brittany with Du Camp, Louise Colet was enlightened as to the true state of affairs. The two lovers broke off relations, except for occasional letters in which they addressed each other by the formal *"vous"*, and then for several years took no notice of each other.

Reprise

THEY BEGAN SEEING each other once more in July 1851, after Flaubert's trip to the Middle East. They had met again, doubtless by chance, and realized they were still attracted. Unfortunately their previous experience together did not help them: they took up where they had left off, each merely fortifying previous positions. Flaubert counselled La Muse, "*Lisez et ne rêvez pas* . . . Don't dream, read. Bury yourself in long study; there is no resource so reliable as the habit of dogged work . . . " In other words, love was still to remain "at the back of the shop." Such was the condition laid down by the lover, slightly more disillusioned than before, to the mistress, slightly more determined to hold the reins, and hoping to recover lost ground.

One wonders why they resumed the relationship. Did Flaubert think La Muse had mended her ways, that three-and-a-half years of separation had enabled her to think the situation over and look at it more sensibly? It is difficult to imagine Flaubert being optimistic. Perhaps he yielded to the power of memory, perhaps to masculine vanity: he had returned from the East prematurely old, half bald, and getting stout, and it may be that Louise's continued interest set him up again in his own eyes. Why should this strong man not have his weaknesses? At any rate he had already had the weakness to embark on an affair which he knew would "put him out."

La Muse's motives are more mysterious. She did not lack admirers; she had learned to know her previous lover at least to a certain extent, and must have known she would never convert him to her way of thinking. Her physical attachment to him was not so great as to preclude a long interval and several consolations: in July 1851 she had just emerged from a six-months' liaison with the deputy Désiré Bancel. This had been a "mad passion" of the kind she liked, but a disappointment. In retrospect, Flaubert's solid love without illusions was not without its charms. He may still have held her by his very obstinacy. She may now have seen him more clearly as one of the rare individuals strong enough to become what he had set out to be—an artist who would win fame just because he laughed at it. But the rest of the story shows that neither of them had changed.

In September, Flaubert started on *Madame Bovary*. He was even more determined than before not to let himself be distracted from his work, and he agreed to meet only once every three months. Even then, if the date for a rendezvous occurred while he was in the middle of a chapter, he would put it off. By October La Muse was complaining again. She took up the charge with such energy that instead of protesting Flaubert resigned himself to playing the part of the accused. He had given up the idea of bringing her round to his point of view. "I love you as well as I can—badly, not enough . . . God, I know it, I know it!" He asked her to be content to live in the present, and to take refuge in work. His habits would not change, and nor would his love. That's how it was; there was nothing he could do about it. He had long known what love was really like, and he describes it in a terrible image: "The only encounter is collision. Each accuses the other, while both are trying to hold together their own ravaged entrails." But though both are crippled by life, they can still help each other. Let Louise be philosophical enough not to ask for more.

She gave in, but she champed at the bit. Their letters became for the most part calm and sensible, not so much love letters as, on Louise's part, requests for literary help and advice, and, on Flaubert's, a confidence stretching over several years about the work in progress, his ideas on art and writing, the books he was reading, and his intellectual and psychological discoveries. Unfortunately the seed fell on stony ground: witness La Muse's own writings, which Flaubert and Bouilhet spent a lot of time correcting and improving without enabling her to win the Académie prizes she coveted, or get her plays put on. Flaubert's patience was inexhaustible: he even wrote fashion articles for her, made use on her behalf of personal contacts he would never have dreamed of using for himself, and listened sympathetically to her gossip and intrigues. It seems that in the end La Muse was wounded by some sharper comments than usual on her literary talent. Her love had been denied; she was not going to have her gifts denied as well.

The Break

AFTER THE DEATH of Hippolyte Colet in 1851, Louise thought of

marrying Victor Cousin, the father of her little daughter
Henriette. But either the philosopher got out of it, or Louise
changed her mind. At all events, she turned to Flaubert, and
showed how little she understood the situation by considering
him as a possible husband. This is probably why, with admirable
patience, she toned down her jeremiads. She started trying to
persuade him again to let her come to Croisset and meet Mme
Flaubert. He said he "simply could not understand" why she
went on about it. One day in November 1854 she actually
invaded Croisset. Flaubert was furious, and his mother is
supposed to have had to remind him of the politeness due to a
lady. Louise returned in a rage to Paris.

When Flaubert was in Paris again in March 1855, she tried
to see him for a final explanation. He had her told he was not at
home. At her third attempt he felt it necessary to convey that
he would never be at home to her. This time it was the final
break. Her persistence is all the more strange in that for several
months Alfred de Vigny had been her lover. She did not know
Flaubert knew that, and it never occurred to Flaubert to
reproach her for it. He for his part had been enjoying the favors
of the actress Béatrix Person.

Naive and Clumsy

THE WRONGS were not all on one side in this affair. Flaubert's
love for Louise Colet, though solid and sound, was too reasonable and lacking in panache. The satisfactions she derived from
it gave her no position in literary circles and no assurance
about the future. It was all very well for him to keep saying that
was his character and his way of life, and as he could not
change the first he could not change the second, but she was
entitled to expect he should not invariably put his work before
her. His frankness towards her was sometimes so blunt as to
appall minds less disciplined and hearts less hardy than his
own. He was naive and clumsy, and wounded without meaning
to.

She had forced him to confess his former passion for Elisa.

All well and good; that was the past, and it was a good thing to have things clear from the outset. But there was no need for him to ask her to pass on a letter to Eulalie Foucaud, his former mistress, even if he did let her read it. When she asked him where he had been during the two or three occasions when, in her arms, he had obviously been thinking of something else, it was not very considerate to reply: "I am with no one, I am nowhere, either in my own country or perhaps in the world." When she tried to make him jealous by recounting the bad behavior of the "philosopher" or of Musset, she did not expect to be told to have more respect if not for themselves then at least for their talents, little as he himself might esteem them. His anxiety to keep her from falling into the ridicule she was so prone to, his generosity and serenity and common-sense all suggest he was too detached altogether. A man who is in love is not so invariably controlled. And how could she do otherwise than apply to herself certain of his most profound and unsentimental confidences? Such, for example, as: "I have buried within me a deep-rooted chagrin (*embêtement*), bitter and incessant, which prevents me from enjoying anything and fills my soul to bursting."

Flaubert certainly did not lack emotional delicacy, but was the psychological insight he showed in the novels absent from his behavior in ordinary life? Was he unable to tell when to speak and when to be silent? It is more probable that though in general he was without illusions, he did delude himself about his mistress's emotional and intellectual stature. She wrote prose and verse and called herself an author. Therefore she loved Beauty and wanted to create it. That was enough; for Flaubert, Louise Colet was an equal, and it was as an equal that he spoke to her, though he sometimes had to call her to order: "Art, the only true and good thing in life! Can you compare it to an earthly love? Can you prefer the adoration of a relative beauty to the worship of true beauty?" But La Muse had neither the intelligence, nor the magnanimity, nor a love of Art sufficiently profound, to submit to being called a "relative beauty."

Flaubert's Ideal Love

BUT IT WAS the woman herself he loved—her body, her beauty, her grace. He was sensual and ardent, but he knew love was something more than a physical encounter. He loved Louise as a person, with her virtues and faults, her work, her life, her affections. He felt her disappointments and was glad of her modest joys. If he would not let himself be invaded by her it was partly because art came before love, partly because love as she saw it, at least as far as words went, was an impossibility, doomed to inadequacy and frustration. This ought to be signally clear to a writer, whose job is to judge life and exhibit it truthfully. And this is what Louise Colet ought to have admitted, if she put her vocation before her personal concerns, if she could stand back far enough and rise high enough to forget that she was a woman. But it was to this she related everything—her life and her writing. She proclaimed that she was a woman and proud of it; instead of trying to escape from the fact, she revelled in it. She wanted to make Flaubert, or in other words Art, bend the knee before the Eternal Feminine. For him, this would have been a complete abdication. "I thought at first I would find in you less feminine personality, a more universal conception of life. But no! The heart, the heart! the poor sweet charming heart and its eternal graces . . ." Flaubert rebelled against the rule of the heart, the excuse for every sort of falling away, capitulation, and besottedness. It was weakness, stupidity, a sinking into a vegetal existence. It was respectable; everybody praised it; it swelled the current of the ordinary life that was uncreative and hostile to Art. It made that life, on the whole, acceptable.

The image Flaubert dreamed of, to which he would have liked Louise Colet to conform, was that of a woman endowed with a masculine intelligence, a woman in the matter of love, a man when it came to understanding life and artistic creation. She wanted to convert him to her views; he would have liked to shape her with his own hands. "I should like to make you into something quite apart, neither friend nor mistress. All that is too limited, too exclusive: one doesn't love a friend enough, one is too foolish with a mistress. What I mean is something between the two, the essence of the two feelings put together." In fact he was pursuing a very ancient dream: "In short, what I should like is for you to be a new hermaphrodite, and give me with your body all the joys of the flesh, and with your mind all the joys of the soul." He knew as he said it that it was an impossible dream, and it was not long before he realized it was a particularly unsuitable one to tell to Louise Colet. Then he fell back more inflexibly than ever on his minimum demands. He knew now for certain that what one would like and what life can provide are two different things.

To say Flaubert did not really "love" Louise Colet calls, then, for qualifications. One must remember the ideal which the hermit of Croisset cherished at that period of his life. Matter-of-fact as he would have liked to be, he too pursued a chimera. He and Louise Colet were pulling in opposite directions, and in spite of appearances it was he who strained after the extraordinary and she who tugged towards what might only have been expected. The miracle was that they did manage to go along together for a while.

6

THE JOURNEY TO THE EAST

LIKE ALL ROMANTICS ever since Napoleon's Egyptian campaign, Flaubert had dreamed about the East from childhood. In this as in other matters, imitation preceded personal experience. The dream recurs in countless different forms throughout the writings and correspondence of his youth: the marvels of the cities, the characteristics of the people, the languor or ferocity of the landscape vary with the mood of the dreamer. The East represents the opposite of a "shop-keeper's" civilization: it is liberty, life drunk at the source and savored as an elixir. "*Je suis autant Chinois que Français,*" he wrote to Louise Colet, "I am as much a Chinaman as a Frenchman." And he said of the Arabs: "I love these hard, persistent, lively people, the last example of primitive society, who at their noonday halt lie in the shade smoking their hubble-bubbles beneath their camels' bellies, laughing at our fine civilization and making it tremble with rage."

The young Flaubert rejected the narrow, paltry, Western world, and often thought of going and trying to rediscover the anonymity of primitive life in the seething cities of the Orient or the vast forests of India. He wrote, again to Louise Colet: "I have thought for a long time, and *very seriously*—don't laugh, it's the memory of my finest hours—of going and turning renegade in Smyrna. Some day I shall go and live far away and never be heard of again." The East was the ultimate escape, the ultimate possibility of living according to his heart's desire, in such a way that the self could merge in the All.

For him the East, an image built up out of his imaginings, his reading and his dreams, was Egypt, India, the Jordan and the Euphrates, China, Malaya, and Japan. It covered vast continents, and contained thousands of years of history. It was *l'autre monde*, the other world, immense, unknown, mysterious. Its civilizations, for all their differences, were all truly adapted to man, and adjusted through long practice to his essential needs and permanent desires. All the poets and painters of the nineteenth century had dreamed of the East—and Hugo, Delacroix, Nerval and the rest had not been disappointed when they confronted their dream with the reality. In fact, their art had increased the charms of the mirage.

One reason why Du Camp's standing was so high with Flaubert was that he had made "the journey": in 1844 he had been to Constantinople, returning via Italy only to set out again for Algiers. He told the young Flaubert what he had seen and heard and done, naturally making it all sound as impressive as possible. On the walking tour in Brittany there was plenty of opportunity for Flaubert to ask questions and Du Camp to answer them. Flaubert saw his dream might be turned into a reality.

During the autumn of 1846, he had begun *La Tentation de Saint Antoine*, which did in a sense embody the dream. He had gone through hundreds of books which further stimulated his imagination. He incarnated his fantasies in an orgy of splendor and color, mingling gold with tinsel, mystery with extravagance. For no other reason than to savor as fully as possible his vision of the East, he brought in the Queen of Sheba in person. Although the spirit of God is strong enough in Saint Anthony to make him resist her charms, the hermit's creator, pulling the strings, could have imagined no greater happiness than to yield.

Difficulties

DU CAMP WAS TO RETURN to the East on an official mission. Why should not Flaubert go with him? He would be a fool not to take such an opportunity. Not only would it make his fondest dream come true, but it would also get him out of the baneful atmosphere created by the early death of Alfred Le Poittevin, the break with Louise Colet, and his brother-in-law's madness.

Flaubert's nervous attacks had started up again; he needed a change of air.

The two friends sounded Mme Flaubert on the subject. Flaubert hesitated to leave his mother alone for months, perhaps years, with his little niece Caroline, whom her father, Emile Hamard, threatened in his lucid intervals to take back to live with him. Mme Flaubert did not think her son's health was equal to a life of adventure in strange lands. Flaubert managed to get round the first obstacle, and applied to Dr. Cloquet, who had been his companion in Corsica, to help him get round the second. To Mme Flaubert's surprise, the medical verdict was that to recover his health her son ought to spend some time in a "warmer climate."

Another obstacle was *La Tentation*, which he had begun two years ago and meant to finish before he left. The journey was put off. Finally, on September 12, 1849, full of self-confidence, the young author summoned his friends Du Camp and Bouilhet to Croisset to hear his masterpiece. As we know, their verdict was that it was unpublishable and he ought to throw it on the fire. His friends, whose judgment he trusted, were categorical and not to be shaken. Flaubert yielded and put his manuscript away. He was free to leave.

One can imagine the mood in which he went. The setback over *Saint Antoine* called in question his whole future, his fundamental ability as a writer. Also he had come round again to thinking it would be impossible to leave his mother. Du Camp pressed him, and a compromise was found. Mme Flaubert was to go with her son as far as Paris, and from there take little Caroline on to stay with Flaubert's great-uncle Parain at Nogent. This would make the break less abrupt. In Paris Flaubert and Du Camp gave a farewell dinner to Bouilhet, Cormenin, and Théophile Gautier. Flaubert was still hesitant and melancholy, and though it was now too late still kept wondering if he ought not to stay with his mother. However, on October 29 he and Du Camp left by coach for Marseilles, and on November 4 they embarked there for Alexandria. They stopped off at Malta three days later, but it was on

November 15 that Flaubert first set foot on the soil of Africa.

Visions of the East

HE WAS DAZZLED. In Alexandria and Cairo and during the voyage up the Nile, he found towns and landscapes he had imagined a thousand times, and discovered them to be as he had thought, only now not "vague" but tangible and clear. The reality more than came up to his dream. He was astounded by the seething, colorful mass of humanity into which he was plunged—by their dress, customs, manners and way of life. He set down details which would have escaped a less practised eye. His notebook recorded shapes, colors, sounds, sensations just as they occurred, without comment or development. He was accumulating material for later.

But he could not always prevent feeling breaking through. When the Pyramids came into view he spurred his horse into a gallop and flew along uttering wild inarticulate cries. As they stood before the Sphinx: "It bent on us a terrifying gaze. Maxime had gone pale, I was afraid I'd turn giddy, and tried to master my emotion." Then they both "tore off again, dashing along like madmen through the rocks."

The voyage up the Nile held another adventure in store for him. He was to remember all his life the feelings it aroused in him. We see its echoes in *Salammbô* and *Hérodias*.

First a typical episode at Kenek. Flaubert and Du Camp went walking in the dancing-girls' quarter—not merely in search of local color: already in Cairo and elsewhere they had allowed themselves plenty of amusement. They met one woman who reminded Flaubert of "Mme Maurice" (Elisa Schlésinger), but he did not wish to tarnish her memory. Various women laid hold of him and tried to drag him off, but, characteristically, "I forbade myself to b—— them, in order to preserve as well as I could the melancholy of that recollection. So I went away." In this incident the young man still in love with Elisa joins hands with the writer who wishes to keep a certain emotional quality intact in order to describe it better when the time comes.

Kuschiuk Hanem

BUT A FEW DAYS LATER, at Esneh, he was eager enough to experience a kind of pleasure which the setting and the person concerned had made him look forward to with enormous expectation. He describes the encounter as if it were a vision or apparition. "We entered a house with a little courtyard and a staircase leading up opposite the door. On the stairs, facing us, bathed in light and silhouetted against the sky-blue background, stood a woman, wearing pink trousers and nothing around the upper part of her body but a thin mauve veil." The vivid, detailed vision engraved itself on his memory for ever.

The "almehs," as such women were called, were in the first place professional singers and dancers, and it was this sort of entertainment that the two travellers were offered to begin with. "She asked us if we would care for a little *fantasia*"—and one dance followed another until it was dark. Flaubert then tells us no more about Du Camp, but gives an account of the night he himself spent with Kuschiuk Hanem, a night full of "nervous intensities and reminiscences," of violent pleasure and tenderness, and of Biblical memories. "I thought of Judith and Holofernes sleeping together." For Flaubert, Kuschiuk was not just a nameless woman: already he loved or wanted to love her. "What a gratification it would be to one's pride if one could be sure of leaving a memory behind, sure she would think of you more than the others, sure you would remain in her heart!" At last, tender and reluctant, he left her.

Flaubert described her as a "tall, spendid creature, with a whiter skin than most Arab women," with huge black eyes, black brows, wide nostrils, strong broad shoulders, and full breasts shaped like apples. Although the dances she performed had come down through the ages, she was neither solemn nor shy: she put on Flaubert's tarbush, climbed on his back, and got up to all sorts of pranks. She seemed to be the mistress of the house, and the most important of all the women there.

Flaubert came back to see her on the return journey seven weeks later. But the original thrill gave place to disappointment. This time she was not waiting for him at the top of the stairs, "her torso bare, lit up by the sun." She was tired and seemed to have been ill. She recognized her guest, danced for him again, and attempted a joke about his big moustache and tiny mouth. He left her, saying he would come back next day, but did not. It was all over. "All that has come out of it is an infinite sadness. . . . It is over, I shall never see her again, and her face will gradually fade out of my memory!" Her face might fade, but not the recollection of a "privileged moment," at once happy and melancholy. In Constantinople Flaubert was seized with a sudden longing to see Kuschiuk Hanem again. Back in France, he could not prevent himself talking of her to Louise Colet, who made no secret of her jealousy, and of her contempt for casual love-making. He could not persuade his mistress, and he could not persuade himself, that his meeting with "*la petite princesse*" had been just a casual encounter.

The Money-changers in the Temple

FLAUBERT AND DU CAMP and their party arrived in Palestine on July 19, 1850. By August 9 they were in Jerusalem, where Flaubert, a great Bible reader, was surprised to feel no emotion. It was a Moslem holiday and the streets were empty and abandoned. "Jerusalem strikes me as a fortified charnel-house. The old religions rot away there in silence, you walk on excrement, and all you see is ruins. It's tremendously dreary." The Holy Sepulcher was "bedaubed and bedizened, and got up for exploitation, propaganda and business." There was no solemnity about the place; even a believer would find it impossible to concentrate his thoughts amid all the shouting and quarrelling between the rival sects. The crowning touch was a full-length portrait of Louis-Philippe on one of the walls. "So, grotesque," Flaubert apostrophized it, "you are like the sun, dominating the world with your splendor, your light gleaming even in the tomb of Jesus!" He felt "cold and satirical." But when a Greek priest blessed a rose and gave it to him, he was moved and would have liked to have faith. But he could not.

"It had been one of the bitterest moments of my life. How sweet it would have been for a believer!" But what did believers do here? When he went later to the Mount of Olives he saw two Capuchin friars getting drunk "in company with two very charming persons whose white breasts were naked and clearly visible." All was ridiculous and grotesque, but he, an agnostic, felt like weeping rather than laughing.

He went to see other holy places. The Dead Sea reminded him of a lake, the Jordan at one point of the river Touques at Pont-l'Evêque. There was a pleasant diversion when pistol-shots were fired at their party on the outskirts of Nazareth. Flaubert galloped off in pursuit, sabre in hand, inwardly fancying himself as a "smart *cuirassier* of the Empire," as usual appraising his own deeds with cool objectivity. One evening in Jerusalem, after dinner with the French consul, he heard someone playing a Beethoven sonata, and was reminded of his "poor sister," the little salon in Rouen, and Miss Jane, his sister's governess, bringing in a glass of sugar and water. "A sob filled my heart." All night he lay remembering—and having nightmares about— the past.

Disappointed, homesick, forever falling into despondency, he was only stirred to enthusiasm by the ruins of Baalbek. "The stones seem to be deep in thought." He stayed there for two days, walking about alone in the sun and the wind, intoxicating himself with history.

Art is not a Lie

THEY GAVE UP the idea of going on to Persia because of lack of funds, and landed on October 4 in Rhodes. There they had to stay in quarantine, and Flaubert occupied himself tidying up his notes, bringing his correspondence up to date, and planning three novels. One was to be called *Une Nuit de Don Juan;* another, *Anubis*, "the story of a woman who wants to be loved by the god," is at once a resurgence of his old "oriental tale" and a foreshadowing of *Salammbô;* the third was set in Flanders and was to show "a girl who lived with her mother and father and died a virgin and a mystic." He toyed again with the idea, already discussed with Bouilhet, of a *Dictionnaire des Idées reçues* (a dictionary of "received ideas, or clichés"). The Austrian Lloyds ship *Asia* took them to Constantinople, where they landed on December 12.

Flaubert's first reaction to things was usually enthusiasm; his second withdrawal, disappointment, depression. In Constantinople he ran true to form. He drank in the picturesqueness, the colors and the smells, the marvels and the dirt. He went to see the Seraglio, and Saint Sophia and the other mosques. He got to know various people: Edouard Delessert, son of the former prefect of police; M. de Saulcy, a member of the *Institut;* Baudelaire's stepfather, General Aupick, who was French Ambassador at the court of the Sultan. The General was very jovial and familiar: "He kept slapping Maxime on the back and calling him a devil of a wag." A letter from Croisset made Flaubert depressed and sarcastic: his mother told him his oldest friend, Ernest Chevalier, had got married. Flaubert was very bitter about him—"married, established, and still a magistrate into the bargain," doomed to become a "nice fat respectable bourgeois," and a champion of "order, the family, and property." He predicted the worst possible fate for the traitor: "As a magistrate he is a reactionary; as a husband he will be a cuckold. And so, passing his life between his mate, his children, and the depravities of his profession, this fine fellow will have fulfilled in his own person all the conditions of humanity . . ." He wrote all this to his mother, thus warning her off any plans she might cherish for getting him "settled." He left Constantinople "deathly depressed": he had lost a friend, and shut the door of the East behind him.

Greece and Athens cheered him up again. His "mind took in the antique in gulps"; he felt "Olympian"; he cried out in admiration at what he saw. "The sight of the Parthenon," he wrote to his mother, " is one of the most moving things I have ever experienced. Whatever they may say, Art is not a lie." Antiquity had been turned into "something cold and un-unbearably naked": Flaubert told Bouilhet what it really looked like, describing the golden hue of the Acropolis, the intense vitality of the sculptures and bas-reliefs, a charming gesture here, a powerful fragment of torso there. His admiration deepened into a sort of religious emotion: "It wouldn't have taken much to make me pray." These were the real holy places for him—Eleusis, Delphi, Marathon, Sparta, the Peloponnese. Sometimes it rained, sometimes he had to sleep in stables, he was eaten alive by fleas, but none of these things mattered. Enjoyment gave him an access of energy which made him mingle with wandering minstrels, indulge in jokes not always very refined, and learn from a guide who had been a prisoner of the Turks how to whirl like a dervish. He did so, letting out piercing shrieks and frightening the whole neighborhood. But by the time the visit to Greece ended at Patras, he was experiencing the usual reaction and "half-dead" with boredom.

By now it was February 1851. His mother was to come and meet him in Italy, but before that he wanted to see Naples and Rome as he had wanted to six years earlier—without family or mentor, alone. Du Camp was going straight on to France.

Flaubert had a "delightful" stay in Naples. He was attracted not so much by the bay and the city and the surrounding countryside, all steeped in literary associations, as by the antiquities in the museum—their richness kept him awake at night. In Rome he felt "even smaller than I did in the desert." He explored the Vatican, was enraptured with *The Last Judgment* and Michelangelo, and wrote more paeans on the immortality of art. Yet just as not everyone can become Pope, so not every artist can become Michelangelo. Still, "the lowliest friar may be as worthy of respect as a cardinal," for he serves the same God and shares in the same grace. So it is with even the humblest artist: he is the servitor of the finest religion in the world. Even the Romans, so heavy and plodding in their borrowings from the Greeks, can be admired: Flaubert allows the intention to be taken for the deed.

The Stranger in Saint Paul-without-the-Walls

IN ROME, by the church of Saint Paul outside the city walls, he saw "a woman in a red blouse" leaning on the arm of an old woman. She was pale, with dark eyebrows and a "broad red ribbon bound into the hair in the nape of her neck and falling down over her shoulders." At first he was stunned, then as feeling returned he was filled with "rage as sudden as a thunderbolt" which seized him "in the belly." "I felt like hurling myself on her like a tiger." One has only to look at a portrait of Elisa Schlésinger to see whom Flaubert was reminded of by this white-browed apparition with pupils so clear they seem to stand out, and with a shadow of down on the upper lip.

Flaubert does not actually mention Elisa in his account of the meeting, but it is clear from its shattering effect that his first great love was not dead. He had "seen" Elisa again in Egypt, and he "saw" her once more in Rome; he bore her image within him, and projected it everywhere. He was beside himself at the thought of losing the stranger of Saint Paul-without-the-Walls for ever. He had to restrain himself from "throwing myself at her feet and kissing the hem of her gown." He immediately made wild plans, such as going straight to her father to ask her hand in marriage, or introducing himself into the house by pretending to be a doctor, or, less circuitously, by simply practising "magnetism" on her! Of course he did not put any of these schemes into practice. He preferred his familiar bitterness to problematical joys, and returned to his hotel in despair. "Already her features are fading from my memory. *Adieu! Adieu!*" He enjoyed suffering. And this new memory would enrich his dreams, and in some form or other find a place in his work.

Mme Flaubert arrived, and mother and son visited Florence and Venice together: Flaubert was now less keen to note down his impressions. After a détour via Cologne and Brussels, he was back again in Croisset in June 1851. He arranged his travel notes, still with something of a thrill, and took up again, not very hopefully, the liaison with Louise Colet. Then he pulled down the lid of his tomb and on September 19 began *Madame Bovary.*

Confrontation

THE TRIP TO THE EAST had lasted slightly less than two years. It had cost a lot of money. And Flaubert returned from it physically changed. Though still under thirty, he was prematurely aged: he "looked the worse for wear," he had lost most of his hair, and he had acquired a paunch. He had contracted syphilis either at Esneh or Beirut. He said he was experiencing the first symptoms of a "humiliating deterioration." He had been continually anxious, too, about his literary future; he was still suffering from the blow over *Saint Antoine*. He had written to Bouilhet from the East: "Yes, I'm getting old. I feel as if I were good for nothing. As regards style, I'm afraid of everything. What am I going to write when I get back? That's what I never stop asking myself."

Du Camp said that throughout their journey Flaubert always seemed to be thinking about something else, and was often quite indifferent to what was in front of his eyes and what he had come so far and with such enthusiasm to see. Du Camp shows him as frequently apathetic, plunged in lassitude and *ennui*, thinking about Croisset and his mother and Normandy. Du Camp even gives the reason for Flaubert's state of mind: "He was overwhelmed by the mortification of his *Tentation de Saint Antoine*." But Du Camp was perhaps mistaken in saying that for Flaubert "all the temples, all the landscapes, all the mosques seemed alike." For Flaubert's notes are as clear, precise, and vivid as engravings. They firmly seize a gesture, a pose, a moment in some scene, a detail of some landscape, a fleeting sensation. They are the work of someone who is a careful observer and who knows that his future imaginings will be based on this reality. An ordinary "reporter" like Du Camp, camera in hand, may well have found it impossible to understand how such an objective observer of reality might at the same time have taken what he saw as the starting point of long reveries and inner journeys which were anything rather than the apathy they seemed.

Admittedly Flaubert did spend a good deal of time pondering

the future. He had rejected the common way of life and set himself apart in order to depict it better. Now he could not help wondering whether he had made a mistake. His gifts were not so convincing that his friends did not challenge his first serious attempt to display them. Perhaps he himself was completely mistaken? But no, he felt he was right, and that though he might have made a false start he knew what he was aiming at. The fool's bargain was not his but the world's, the one he had shrunk from because he knew that if he made it he would be lost forever. To get established, marry, have a family, exercise a profession, would be to surrender to the common fate. The fact of wanting to be an artist was sufficient justification for refusing the yoke.

> *Tu peindras le vin, l'amour, les femmes, la gloire, à condition, mon bonhomme, que tu ne seras ni ivrogne, ni amant, ni mari, ni tourlourou. Mêlé à la vie, on la voit mal; on en souffre ou en jouit trop.* (You will be able to depict wine, love, women, and glory on condition, my friend, that you are neither a drunkard nor a lover nor a husband nor a redcoat. You can't see life properly if you're in it; it gives you too much pleasure or too much pain.)

During the journey he came to believe more firmly than ever in this creed, and informed his anxious bourgeois mother of the fact. The life he proposed for himself might seem abnormal, he agreed. But "I don't give a hang for the world, or the future, or what people think, or getting established, or even for literary fame." The artist was a "monstrosity, something outside nature," and Flaubert had resigned himself to that fact.

The trip to the East confirmed him in his vocation. The novelty of strange sights and contacts with unknown civilizations only brought him permanently face to face with himself, and enabled him to measure more thoroughly his own origins, past and habits—everything that went to make up his inmost being. His discovery of new aspects of a world so far from home led him to the discovery and reinforcement of aspects of himself as yet imperfectly known to him. He could cram all of himself into an instant, be at the same time in Athens, intoxicated with what he saw, and also thinking of "old Mme Leblond's inn at Pont-Audemer." The sights actually in front of him evoked, indirectly, visions long shut away in his memory. Of old Mme Leblond's inn he wrote: "How hot it was! And the flies! I can still hear the harness of the cart-horses jingling in the dusty courtyard." The process worked by contrast. It was in the desert that he was most likely to think of the water-meadows of Normandy, misty and lush. It was under a broiling sun he realized he was "a man of the North." Although Du Camp's story that as they were visiting the second cataract of the Nile Flaubert suddenly exclaimed, "I'll call her Emma Bovary!" is for various reasons impossible, the anecdote testifies to Flaubert's evident preoccupation. What Du Camp could not see was that his friend's preoccupation did not prevent him reacting fully to what was before his eyes. Flaubert was in fact recording everything in minutest detail—the smallest patch of color, the subtlest line, anything which might later enable memory to find its bearings. He was registering, for future use and by the intense light of vision, the exact circumstances of time and place. At the same time he was sharpening his senses. In short, he was behaving as a writer, for whom "travelling is serious work".

Du Camp's "Misrepresentations"

Du Camp, in his *Souvenirs littéraires*, says that Flaubert made the journey more or less like a sleep-walker, and some critics deduced from this that Flaubert's account of it did little more than copy his friend's notes. Du Camp wrote: "Gustave Flaubert who had travelled through Egypt, Nubia, Palestine, Syria, Rhodes, Asia Minor, and Constantinople without zest or curiosity, came to life as soon as he set foot on the soil of Greece. Memories of the antiquity he knew so well awoke in him . . . every evening he made notes, which he had not done before, except occasionally in Egypt . . ."

If this had been the truth, Du Camp might have been congratulated on achieving so "Flaubertian" a style that Flaubert, himself felt unable to improve on it, but when Flaubert's own *Carnets de Voyage* were published these assertions were swiftly disproved. A few details apart, the *Carnets* corroborate the *Notes de Voyage* (at which Du Camp's aspersions were aimed). The attitude and approach and often even the phrasing is the same, and the *Carnets* also relate episodes, such as the night with Kuschiuk Hanem and the encounter in Rome, which only happened to Flaubert himself. Yet further disproof of Du Camp's claim is provided by Flaubert's letters from the East to Mme Flaubert and Louis Bouilhet, which were published a few years after the *Souvenirs littéraires* and often reproduce the *Notes* word for word. Presumably even Du Camp would not have maintained that he dictated Flaubert's letters.

Flaubert, back home again, used Du Camp's notes in the same way as he had used the notes they had made between them on the trip to Brittany. They served him as reminders. If any part of what he wrote is attributable in any way to Du Camp, it is probably the part which interests us least—descriptions of buildings, topographical detail, external circumstances, the "tourist" aspect of the journey. All the impressions, reflections, longings, and reveries are unmistakably Flaubert, even though some of them may have been triggered off by factual details provided by Du Camp. There can be no doubt on the matter.

It was perhaps only human that when Flaubert was dead, Du Camp should have envied his fame and tried to get a share in it for himself, and posterity judged him harshly and dubbed him a "false friend." Flaubert was less severe, on the whole, though during their long companionship in the East he came to see how little they had in common. Not many months after their return, Flaubert was drawing away and telling the co-editor of the *Revue de Paris* and the lover of Mme Delessert that one should distinguish between a "man of letters" and a "writer." The differences between Flaubert and Du Camp were not so much of temperament or character as of values.

7

THE GENESIS OF
"MADAME BOVARY"

B Y THE BEGINNING OF 1853 Flaubert had finished the first
part of *Madame Bovary* and started the second. It was to
take him until 1856, another three years, to complete his
task and one of the great novels of the nineteenth century.

There were few external events in Flaubert's life during this
period: he lived almost in seclusion, entirely devoted to his
work. He went on seeing Louise Colet about once every three
months, either in Paris or in Mantes. She was eager for academic
honors, and he corrected her writings; she edited a women's
magazine and he wrote a fashion article to appear in her name.
Their relations grew gradually more and more embittered until
the final break in March 1855.

Flaubert had fewer nervous attacks now, but he still suffered
from long spells of apathy and depression which cannot be
fully accounted for by the difficulties he had to struggle with in
his work. In August 1854 he complained of mercury in his
saliva and thought of consulting Dr. Ricord, the great specialist
on syphilis. At the end of 1855, with *Madame Bovary* almost
completed, he installed himself in Paris for the winter, in his
pied-à-terre in the Boulevard du Temple. He devoted 1856 to
publishing his novel, first in instalments in the *Revue de Paris*,
then in book form. He also re-worked *La Tentation de Saint
Antoine*, extracts of which were published by Théophile Gautier
in *L'Artiste*.

After Louise Colet, his chief and then almost sole correspondent was Louis Bouilhet. He and Flaubert had been at school
together, and Bouilhet had later become one of Dr. Flaubert's
pupils, but he abandoned medicine, and earned a meager

living as a "crammer" in order to devote himself to writing. Flaubert's first letter to him is dated August 15 1846, a month after Le Poittevin's marriage. Flaubert and Bouilhet were the same age, they shared the same interests, they had the same artistic ideal. They were as close as brothers for twenty-three years, until Bouilhet's death in 1869. Each submitted his work to the other. In particular, every line of *Madame Bovary* had to run the gauntlet of Bouilhet's criticism during the latter's weekend visits to Croisset. Flaubert regarded him as his literary conscience; he was tirelessly vigilant and ruthlessly exacting. When he decided to go and live in Paris at the end of 1853, Flaubert approved for Bouilhet's sake but missed his friend sadly.

There was never any coolness between them. *Madame Bovary*, when finished, was shown to Bouilhet for further alterations and improvements before it was finally transcribed and sent to Maxime Du Camp at the *Revue de Paris*. Flaubert, for his part, made himself Bouilhet's advocate with all his acquaintances in Paris, and helped him get a play put on at the Odéon. When the piece, *Madame de Montarcy*, was a hit, Flaubert was as pleased as if the success had been his own. He had in fact largely contributed to it. There was no envy or jealousy on either side. There have been few literary friendships to rival it. Each respected the other's personality; they helped each other unstintingly and in complete confidence; nothing was too much trouble to make the "*l'œuvre*" as it should be—perfect. It may be said that one had genius while the other only followed the beaten track; one was an innovator, the other was merely gifted. And Bouilhet is only remembered today because of Flaubert. Yet without this stern judge, this purist and perfectionist, the author of *Madame Bovary* would have lacked the self-confidence that makes bold experiment possible. Bouilhet's "permission" to go ahead was an invaluable encouragement. The masculine element in this couple was not Flaubert, but the poet who wrote *Melaenis*.

A Change of Course

It was Bouilhet who first pronounced the verdict on *Saint*

Antoine. And even according to Maxime Du Camp it was Bouilhet who suggested that Flaubert should tell the story of Eugène Delamare. Flaubert, after having reflected at length on his disappointment during his travels in the Middle East, agreed that his friends had been right to "amputate" the cancer of lyricism, and took on the "bourgeois" subject of the Delamares as a penance. He had come to see that *Saint Antoine* really was lacking in rigor—"it's the string that makes a necklace, not the pearls"—and that he had failed to keep himself separate from his hero. But with a subject not of his own choice, one which in fact was so far from his normal interests as to fill him with repugnance; with a main character an adulteress of the *petite bourgeoisie* driven to suicide; and therefore with a plot of no grandiose metaphysical significance—here he was in no danger of being carried away by his own temperament. The project presented no risk as far as overall conception was concerned, nor was Flaubert in this case likely to confuse himself with his main character: the whole problem would lie in the execution. Flaubert needed such an "exercise" to show what he was made of as a writer and as an artist, and it was as an exercise that he regarded it. If it was successful, he would be able to embark on two works which really mattered to him: a *"grand moderne"* in which he would take it out of mankind in general and his age in particular, and the famous "oriental tale" he had spoken of to Bouilhet and Louise Colet. To him, writing *Madame Bovary* seemed like performing acrobatics or doing a trapeze act. He disowned in advance what could only be foreign to him, "all calculation and tricks of style". But in spite of the disgust he sometimes felt with his task, he devoted himself to finishing it, to perfecting it, to mastering it.

He was not entirely new to this sort of writing. In the last fifteen years he had often switched from one manner or source of inspiration to another, passing from historical narrative to romantic tale, from romantic tale to personal confession, from *Novembre* to the first *Education sentimentale*. And although into the latter, his first real novel, he put much of himself— memories, feelings, ideas, preoccupations, even an exposition of his artistic ambitions—at the same time he produced a work which in tone, construction, style and conception was quite different from the novels being written by his contemporaries. This is not to say that the first *Education*, shorn of its personal confessions and assertions and asides, would make a work comparable to *Madame Bovary*. But it does belong to the same family, and Jules's declarations about art, when developed, lead to an aesthetic which leaves far behind the author of *Novembre*, and perhaps even the still somewhat uncertain author of the first *Education* itself. When he embarked on his penance, Flaubert broke with the line of *Saint Antoine* only to resume one he had tried before and which was no less personal to him than the other.

To live for fifty-three months with a book, dragging it page by page out of the void, or in other words out of oneself, this, even though the author has to drive himself to the task, cursing and lamenting, is bound to change the writer himself, bound to make him see in a new light the material he has had to wrestle with so hard. The provincial girl for whom he had felt so little sympathy at first and whom he had difficulty in bringing to life until he had launched her into the world and characters of the novel, ended in being so consubstantial with him that he could say, "*la Bovary, c'est moi.*" He became attached to his story because it was tangible, and dazzling, proof that an "exercise" could produce a creation; and also because this creation showed that the principles he had laid down for himself were valid and his method of applying them sound. *Madame Bovary* tested an aesthetic hypothesis of which the terms had not yet been subjected to experiment; it demonstrated a bold new method the details of which Flaubert arrived at as he went along. Both the hypothesis and the method derived from a view of the artist and the work of art which would have remained barren had it not been for this venture of Flaubert's. Flaubert wanted to be more than just an emancipated follower of Balzac. And indeed he laid the foundations and supplied the model for a way of novel-writing which his successors left almost unchanged for fifty years.

The letters of 1852, and those spread out through 1853 to 1856, which are often lectures in aesthetics to *La Muse*, rounded out with confidences and with the reflections arising out of difficulty encountered and overcome, show how Flaubert's hypothesis and method developed in parallel with the work itself. He does not reveal secret recipes for masterpieces. He shows a way, what he calls *la ligne droite*, "the straight line", and puts up safety-barriers on either side. What the writer must do is take the "straight line" and burrow into the work "like a mole", deeper and deeper, without looking right or left, until he emerges into a reality hitherto hidden by words, conventional sentiments, and ready-made ideas, and buried beneath tons of literature.

It is a long and difficult enterprise, with an ambush at every crossroad. Flaubert did not think genius was necessary, but he did think a writer must have a "zeal" which precluded minor indulgences and easy solutions. Just as the work should manifest "a sustained energy running from one end to the other and never flagging," so the unremitting will of the artist should be applied to search and discovery. Without this heroic concentration there is no salvation. It is this which enables even those who consider themselves without talent or genius to produce great works. "How can one not believe that, with 'application,' time, fury, and sacrifices of all kinds, one will eventually achieve something? No, it would be too silly!" Success, though partly a heaven-sent gift, is even more the consummation of unwearying labor, persevered in to the point of suffering.

Writing Coldly

FLAUBERT BROKE WITH the tradition of the artist as someone inspired, the mouthpiece of mysterious forces whose oracles he merely translated. "Let us beware of that kind of overheating called inspiration, which often has more nervous emotion in it than muscular strength." If ever he felt himself in "exceptionally good form"—"my forehead is burning, sentences crowd in on me"—he began to worry immediately: "I know these masked balls of the imagination, from which one returns sick at heart and exhausted, having seen nothing but sham, having uttered nothing but foolery." He mistrusted anything which was not the result of deliberate, vigilant, considered attention, solely preoccupied with the end in view. "Everything should be done coolly, deliberately. When Louvel set out to kill the Duc de Berry he drank a glass of fruit juice, and he did not miss. This is a comparison poor Pradier used to make; I was always struck by it. It is extremely instructive for anyone who can understand it." To Louise Colet, singer of emotional turmoil, he said: *"Il faut écrire froidement"*, "One should write coldly." And again: *"Ce n'est pas avec le coeur qu'on écrit, c'est avec la tête* (It's not the heart one writes with, but the head)." Imagination, feeling, the senses, all had to be controlled calmly if words were to be found to do justice to their intensities. Art is not translation, always inadequate and far from the original; it is re-creation and creation. Diderot's paradox about rendering the sublimity of nature with sang-froid is valid for the writer as well as for the actor.

Impersonality

To "WRITE COLDLY" was to trample down one's own passions, which are too closely dependent on temperament, mood, and circumstance. It was to choose, in complete lucidity and without prejudice, nothing but the means most suited to the end. In this way the writer could concentrate his whole force on the one point which mattered. In this way that force could overthrow obstacles and make new discoveries: a particular nuance of feeling, the significant detail in some ordinary fact, the inner springs of a character. It was only by forgetting oneself that one could give life to others, and make reality solid and immediate. Art is not a monologue by the author. Nor is it a mere dialogue between him and reality. It is reality brought to life and made to speak for itself.

Louise Colet was uninterested in all this, and indeed seems not to have understood a word of it. Did not what she wrote come out of herself? What would remain if she left herself out, if she said nothing of the warmth of her feelings and the workings of her soul? What else should she sing of but what she felt? Flaubert was trying to lead her into pastures which didn't appeal to her at all. He lost patience, and resorted to crude comparisons: "*Il ne faut pas faire de son œuvre le pot de chambre de ses humeurs* (One should not use one's work as the chamber-pot of one's moods)."

She accused him of having no "feelings," of being a "monster," and assuming airs of superiority. But he could be refractory too. Hadn't she ever understood a word he'd written? "Didn't you see that all the irony with which I've attacked feeling in my works was simply the cry of someone who's been vanquished?"—in other words, of someone with passions, who lives and suffers, who struggles every day against despair, and seeks compensation in the ideal. But does that mean one has to surrender to emotion? No. Though anger or despair or emotional disarray may be strong enough to set the mechanism of creation in motion, they are not sufficient to keep it going. Creation goes beyond them, uses them as a springboard to something higher. Then the cry of the vanquished changes into the cry of the victor. The artist is liberated from his dependency on the common condition, and attains the impersonality and impassivity of a god. Flaubert does not deny that individual lyricism may be a form of expression. But only if it is "strange, wild, and so 'intense' that it becomes a 'creation' . . ." He will not budge from this. "As for saying feebly what everyone feels feebly, no."

Nature

ART, LIKE NATURE, has its own permanence, its own "evidence," its own necessity. It is impervious to changes of time, climate, fashion or country. It is another nature captured in words, sounds or marble, and, like the nature which surrounds us, pursues its own imperturbable revolutions. Death follows life and day succeeds night, and nothing men can do can greatly affect the rhythm or the cycle. And Homer, Rabelais, Michelangelo and Shakespeare are also eternal and implacable: they have the weighty and ineluctable presence of natural phenomena.

> *Les très belles œuvres . . . sont sereines d'aspect et incompréhensibles . . . Elles sont immobiles comme des falaises, houleuses comme l'océan, pleines de frondaisons, de verdure et de murmures comme des bois, tristes comme le désert, bleues comme le ciel.* (All really fine works . . . are serene and incomprehensible . . .They are as motionless as cliffs, as rough as the sea, as full of leaves and greenery and murmurs as the forest, dreary as the desert, as blue as the sky.)

Did their creators seek to act on their contemporaries, to please or touch them, to move them to laughter or tears? These were merely secondary ends: what they were really trying to do was rival nature by the same means as those which had moved them themselves.

> *Ce qui me semble, à moi, le plus haut dans l'Art (et le plus difficile), ce n'est ni de faire rire, ni de faire pleurer, ni de vous mettre en rut ou en fureur, mais d'agir à la façon de la nature, c'est-à-dire de faire rêver.* (It seems to me that the highest—and the most difficult—thing in Art is not to make people laugh or cry or lust or rage, but to act as nature does, and give food for dream.)

Man should be touched by Art at the innermost and loftiest point of his being, where he confronts the fundamental and insoluble problems. He has the same feeling before great works of art as before nature—the feeling of a harmonious and incomprehensible organization shaped for ends which escape him. Like nature, they both foster and satisfy his longing for the infinite.

To act as nature does is not only to set aside one's passions, feelings, and intentions good or bad; it is not only to become impersonal and impassive. It is also to open oneself to the world and allow oneself to be penetrated by it. Or, conversely, to break through appearances in order to enter into and identify oneself with things. In Flaubert the two processes sometimes operated simultaneously. "We must absorb the object and let it circulate in us, and reproduce itself outside without our having an inkling of understanding of this marvellous chemistry." It was a form of participation in or communion with what eludes the limited vision of the individual—the very metaphysical causes and ends of the universe. When Flaubert said that by contemplating a pebble he could enter into and become wholly it, this was yet another way of attaining the infinite. In every instance, it was a matter of "no longer being 'oneself', but circulating throughout all the creation of which one speaks." When he had just written the scene in which Emma yields to Rodolphe for the first time, he said:

> *Aujourd'hui par exemple, homme et femme tout ensemble, amant et maîtresse à la fois, je me suis promené à cheval dans une forêt, par un après-midi d'automne, sous des feuilles jaunes, et j'étais les chevaux, les feuilles, le vent, les paroles qu'ils se disaient et le soleil rouge qui faisait s'entrefermer leurs paupières noyées d'amour.* (Today, for example, man and woman simultaneously, lover and mistress at the same time, I rode through a forest on an autumn afternoon under yellow leaves, and I was the horses, the leaves, the wind, the words they spoke, and the red sun which made them half-close their love-drenched eyes.)

He attained the ubiquity of a god who was at the same time the priest of a vaster religion: that by which all the elements in the universe, even down to its invisible atoms, are held together through fine, imperceptible links patiently forged anew by the artist. The artist is in his work like "God in the universe; he must act by similar methods." When Louise Colet expressed satisfaction at the progress she had made under Flaubert's guidance, he revealed the key to the mystery: "You have simply acquired 'Religion', and as you revolve within it you have risen. I believe that if one always looked at the sky one would end by having wings." To become an artist one must learn to possess the world, to merge into it while keeping it under constant observation.

To Live as a Bourgeois and Think as a Demi-god

LOUISE COLET thought Flaubert deluded himself and idealized his function as a writer. She was sarcastic about the "god" who "lived as a bourgeois" in a quiet backwater and was incapable of leaving his mother's apron-strings. She compared him in her mind with Manfred and other romantic heroes, with Byron himself, and (nearer at hand) with Musset and *his* autobiographical hero, Rolla. What a vast distance there was between these grand fictional figures and those who created them, and that icy ideal of calculation and labor!

Flaubert saw he had to clear up another confusion—in this case, between the personal life of the artist and the creations of his pen. From the point of view of art it is not Musset's nights of debauch that matter, but what he was able to derive from them. Could Louise say what sort of men Homer and Shakespeare were? They are immortal, though they have come down to us without any personal apparatus. Flaubert did not deny that having been born into a bourgeois age he was obliged to live as a bourgeois. But both the way of living and the age repelled him. He believed he had eliminated the influence of his age on his art by dividing his life into two parts: the common condition to which he belonged in spite of himself and from which he turned away—"*vivre ne nous regarde pas* (living does not concern us)"—and, on the other hand, the existence which brought him into contact with great creative spirits, the "colossi" who "filled him with awe." To live like a bourgeois was a sad necessity. To think like a demi-god was the duty of the artist, who could overcome the bourgeois within by irony, "*blague supérieure*" or derision, the rejection of vulgar sentiments and interests, and by pointing out the grotesque side of existence. The artist could triumph over the bourgeois by eschewing all the latter's nonsensical notions: he "should have neither religion nor country, nor even any social convictions". He was born for the loftier function of "judging" life, "that is to say, painting it."

Judgment demands a clear vision, which must not be blurred by memory or nostalgia or any over-emotional entanglement. In August 1853, when he went back to Trouville to rediscover his "beloved ghosts," Flaubert decided that self-pity was yet another form of indulgence harmful to what he was trying to do, and he thereupon said "farewell for ever to the 'personal,' the intimate, and the relative." He abandoned his old project of writing his memoirs in order to explain himself and avenge himself on his age. That sort of thing was a weakness, unworthy of one whose work alone should speak for him. As he said to Bouilhet, in a phrase that calls Rimbaud to mind: "*Avec la Bovary finie, c'est l'âge de raison qui commence.* (With Bovary finished, the age of reason begins)."

Scientific Art

THE "AGE OF REASON" which Flaubert meant to enter by rejecting everything which so far, in the novel, "and I would go farther and say in literature in general, except perhaps for two or three men," had only been "exposition of the personality of the author," coincided with a fundamental change in ideas, feelings and philosophical conceptions which was coming about as the nineteenth century turned towards new gods.

Although the fashion in literature was still for effusion—sentiment, mood, tears, blood—Balzac had recently shown that the novel could be something else. It could be a detailed and living study of social types—their manners, way of life, interests, ambitions, the adventures consequent on their position in society, and that society itself. Out of this realization that others exist independently of the novelist and that they are more interesting to depict than the novelist himself, Flaubert made a system. The great writers of the past argued in his favor—Homer for the ancients and Shakespeare for the moderns. And what poet and playwright had done, the novelist too might attempt. Flaubert was unconsciously expressing the aspirations of an age in which the lead passes from poetry and literature to science and the scientist.

He was born at the dawn of the industrial era and of practical, concrete truth. Literature, in order to maintain its position, needed more than ever to contribute to a knowledge of man which was constantly being expanded by the revelations of all the physical, natural and human sciences. It was the age of Geoffroy Saint-Hilaire, Lamarck, Darwin, Cuvier, *The Origin of Species* and the theories of the evolutionists. After the *idéologues* came the economists and Hegel; after them, on the one hand Michelet and on the other Marx. The *Communist Manifesto* had just been published when Flaubert embarked on *Madame Bovary*. It was based on a new conception of history and gave a philosophical and economic basis to the class struggle. The mists of sentiment, religiosity, good intentions and divine will dissolved before a dazzling new light shed on both the mysteries of society and of a human nature conceived of in predominantly biological and historical terms. "History and natural history—they are the two muses of modern times," wrote Flaubert. He often repeated, "We live in an age which is above all historical"; in other words, in the midst of the relativity into which ideals had fallen. Man too had fallen from the pedestal on which religion and philosophy had placed him, and no longer quite took himself for a creature specially chosen. He was conscious that his destiny now weighed even heavier than before. The great change was that instead of being content to measure the consequences, he wanted to know the reasons.

The semi-divinity which Flaubert attributed to the artist had less to do with the claims of the romantic poet than with the new ambitions of the naturalist, the historian, and the biologist. While the artist's function was to create beauty, he could no longer, without making himself either ridiculous or suspect, issue his truths from Mount Sinai, present himself as seer or prophet, or set himself up as the leader of nations. For Flaubert, Lamartine the author of *Graziella* was no better than Lamartine the paltry politician; he was ironical about Hugo too, though he admired him as a writer. The real job of the poet, the novelist, and the artist was to mark out the limits of their own field, acquaint themselves with their new role, and add to knowledge by the means appropriate to their calling. Of course, they did not come within the narrow limits of utilitarianism, and this is what saved them. Art towers above the useful: its gratuitousness is necessary to man, and as indispensable as the air he breathes.

Relationships

THE FIELD OF THE NOVELIST is the largest and most complex of
all: it is the "human soul," whose mysteries are reborn as soon
as they are penetrated; it is life, whose ends and origins are
obscure. It is not for the novelist to ponder on explanations of
either the soul or life. Generations of thinkers have devoted
themselves to these subjects, practically without result. There
is no more a first truth than there is a last; it may be that everything—things, beings, life itself—is an illusion. Flaubert,
earnest disciple of Montaigne, declared:

> *Le doute absolu me paraît être si nettement démontré que vouloir le
> formuler serait presque une niaiserie.* (Absolute doubt seems to me so
> clearly demonstrated that it would be almost foolish to try to
> formulate it).

Late in life he said to Maupassant:

> *Il n'y a de vrai que les "rapports," c'est-a-dire la façon dont nous
> percevons les objets.* (Nothing is true but "relationships," that is to
> say the way we perceive objects.)

If nothing is sure but what comes within the scope of the
senses, reason and experiment, life and the "human soul"
have to be treated as complex, mysteriously organized assem-
blages of facts.

Does this include love, pity, tears, and all the other things
which take place, sometimes fleetingly, in the heart and mind?
"I maintain," wrote Flaubert, somewhat uneasy nevertheless
because the first part of *Madame Bovary* was so devoid of event,
"that 'ideas' are facts." The series of psychological states through
which Emma passes—her dreams, her *ennui*, her vague ambitions—develop out of one another after the same fashion as
they were born, fought against, divided up or added together
in her, causing, deep down, greater or lesser dramas of which
her actual conduct is the result. Seven or eight years earlier, in
the first *Education*, Flaubert had said:

> *Ce qu'ils sont maintenant, ce qu'ils font, ce qu'ils rêvent est le résultat de
> ce qu'ils ont été, de ce qu'ils ont fait, de ce qu'ils ont rêvé.* (What they

are now, what they do and what they dream, is the result of what they were, what they did and what they dreamed before.)

Thus decreed the law which Flaubert was the first to apply in all its rigor—the law of psychological determinism.

Mastodons, Crocodiles

WAS ONE TO REGARD Emma's conduct as scandalous, as Napoleon III's judges were soon to do? Or does she really arouse pity? Was she to be imitated or condemned? Was the book immoral or edifying? Flaubert's contemporaries were astonished that the author himself did not take sides, but systematically abstained from letting the scales tip one way or the other. Their surprise is the best possible tribute to the soundness of his intentions and his success in carrying them out. Just like a natural phenomenon, his book is open to various interpretations; it "gives food for dream." He constructed it by the methods of the scientist: observation of fact, accumulation and juxtaposition of data, minute and scrupulous description of every phase of the experiment. And he succeeded in doing what he himself had thought almost impossible, what might enable art to take a "huge step" forward: "to treat the human soul with the impartiality employed in the physical sciences."

Flaubert's *"impartialité"* was that of someone who deliberately stands outside his own experiment so as to avoid falsifying its results; of someone who, because the field of the experiment is the human soul, might be tempted to judge or appraise or give his own point of view. But in the sphere in which Flaubert was operating, it was as "inept" to introduce moral ideas as to try to prove anything whatever.

> *Ce qu'ont de beau les sciences naturelles: elles ne veulent rien prouver. Aussi, quelle largeur de faits et quelle immensité pour la pensée! Il faut trai... r les hommes comme des mastodontes et des crocodiles.* (The great thing about the natural sciences is that they don't try to prove anything. As a result, what breadth of data and what huge scope for thought! One should write about men as if they were mastodons or crocodiles.)

And of Emma Bovary as of a little provincial adulteress logically driven to suicide. "Poetry is a thing as precise as geometry."

Finding the Method

FLAUBERT DOES NOT SAY that poetry, art, and literature are indistinguishable from the sciences. The objects of the scientist and of the artist are as different as their intentions, as different as the facts they are concerned with, even though one may borrow the other's methods. Artistic and scientific observation are two quite distinct things, and the experiment conducted by the artist on the basis of the material he has accumulated takes place very largely in his heart and brain. He "imagines" and invents, only occasionally touching ordinary reality for inspiration or the verification of his theories. What he invents must have the same solidity and "truth" as that which comes within the scope of the senses; it acquires them by a "method" comparable to that of the scientist.

Flaubert did not claim to have invented this method. But he believed he had come close to it through a similarity of attitude—an attitude of impartiality, non-intervention, refusal to judge or draw conclusions. The artist should limit himself to "representing" life; art should be "expository." "*Ne blâmons rien, chantons tout, soyons 'exposants' et non discutants* (Let 'us blame nothing and sing everything; let us be 'expounders', not discussers)."

Psychology is not physiology, but the method which consists in tracing causes from effects and then verifying the consequences if the former does apply to human behavior. "Induction is as valuable as deduction": by dint of following, in either direction, the links in the chain of strict determinism "we can now see the truth about whatever relates to the soul." "*Tout ce qu'on invente est vrai* (All that is invented is true)" and "*pauvre Bovary, sans doute, souffre et pleure dans vingt villages de France, à cette heure même* (poor Bovary is no doubt suffering and weeping at this very moment in twenty villages in France)." There is no phenomenon so particular and unique that, if studied methodically and in depth, with the object of revealing simultaneously "what is on the surface and what is beneath," does not lead to a general truth. At this point the umbilical cord is cut between the creator and his work. It goes without saying that the creation takes its place in the world of literature and art; but it also takes its place in the world of man's knowledge of himself. "*Madame Bovary*," said Flaubert, "is above all a work of criticism, or rather of anatomy." It was so both by its construction and by its result.

Discovering Laws, as in Mathematics

BY REFUSING TO REGARD the "soul" as a separate realm from behavior; by according psychological data their full value as facts, with causes and consequences amenable to demonstration and study; by re-establishing the unity of man's being which religion, ethics and philosophy had all done their best to break up, Flaubert also corrected a discontinuity which reigned at that time in the novel. Lamartine's heroes and heroines are in love. Do they sleep together? To Flaubert the question was at least as important as debates on matters of "soul": "the word 'soul' has made people say nearly as many stupid things as there are souls!" To put it more generally, what pride or fear prevents us from applying to man himself the laws observed by the physical sciences with such positive results? Is not man too a product of nature? "And before studying nature, should we not study its products, and know its effects in order to be able to trace their cause?" What is there to be learned from sciences which remain shut up within themselves, criticising philosophy from the point of view of philosophy, history from the point of view of history, "whereas we ought to place ourselves above all that from the outset"? For Flaubert there was no contradiction between mind and matter, and "if the moral sciences had, like mathematics, two or three basic laws at their disposal, they could make some progress. But as it is they grope in the dark, coming up against contingencies and trying to erect them into principles." In every field Flaubert wanted to see established the attitude of the observer, the experimenter, the scientist. Then, when the same laws were observed in every domain, it would be possible to understand society as a whole and to foresee its future with certainty. Flaubert dreamed of some "Cuvier of Thought," who would be able to reconstruct "a whole society" out of a line of poetry just as well as out of "a pair of boots", and who could "predict to the day, to the hour, as is done for the planets, the return of the same manifestations. So that we should be able to say: in a hundred years' time we shall have another Shakespeare, and in twenty-five years such and such a kind of architecture."

"Dazzling Psychic Suns"

FLAUBERT REGARDED himself as a product of his age, and the literary genre which he wished to establish as the result of a necessary evolution. He was constantly preoccupied, either with misgivings or with exaltation, with the future. He was anxious that men might lose their love of the beautiful and turn instead to the useful, reduced to terms of self-interest. This was the obvious tendency of industrial society. He was hopeful in so far as a synthesis might be possible between the beautiful and the useful, science and art. Since art was becoming scientific, why should science not become artistic? He saw them joining "at the summit after having been separated at the base." Once they supported one another, cooperating and keeping in step in obedience to the same intellectual laws, "no human mind can now foresee upon what dazzling psychic suns the works of the future may unfold." A strange prophecy on the part of a skeptic and pessimist who had regarded his work as a sufficient pretext for turning his back on the world.

In fact, Flaubert was very much alive to the new possibilities glimpsed by his own age, and his despair may have been a form of furious impatience at the danger that these promises might not be realized, that the future might be compromised by stupidity and complacency. He was tortured by the fact that he lived in an age which was the end of one world and the beginning of another—an age of decadence. He himself was torn between the old type of man, so in love with the beautiful that he made a religion of it, and the innovator establishing an art-form which claimed all the seriousness of science. Thrown back on himself, groping his way "in a corridor full of darkness," all he could do was turn to his vocation. Feeling himself necessary to no one, all he could do was "go up into his ivory tower" and grow drunk on his dreams, "like a nautch-girl among her perfumes." But *Madame Bovary* proves that this withdrawal was in no sense a defection.

8

"MADAME BOVARY"

FLAUBERT STARTED *"la Bovary"* in September 1851, in doubt and uncertainty.

Eugène Delamare, to whom Bouilhet and Du Camp had drawn his attention, had been a student under Dr. Flaubert and known to the Flaubert family. He had practised not as a fully qualified doctor, but as an *officier de santé*, a sort of local medical officer. His first marriage, to a woman older than himself, soon left him a widower, and he took as his second wife a young woman called Delphine Couturier, who was unfaithful to him, contracted debts without his knowledge, and died leaving him a small daughter. Delamare himself died a few months later. They had lived in the village of Ry, near Rouen, and theirs was a recent case which had been in the local news at the time when Flaubert was reading the *Tentation* to his friends.

That was the canvas on which the author was supposed to set to and compose his work—with facts, characters, and places supplied to him in the same way as they were supplied to the author of *Le Rouge et le Noir* by a *fait divers* read in the *Gazette des Tribunaux*.

The strange thing is that whereas, in the case of Stendhal, the novel caused the real-life incident to be forgotten, *Madame Bovary* fostered a mythology maintained right up to our own time by a crowd of "witnesses", commentators, local experts, and even serious Flaubert specialists. People who lived in Ry said they had known Emma. They pointed out the house she was supposed to have lived in, her grave, M. Homais's pharmacy, the *Lion d'Or*. Flaubert was praised for having "invented nothing". The fiction led people in all good faith to reconstruct fact: places, men and women, and events were all remodelled in accordance with a picture so convincing that it was unimaginable they should be otherwise, and as if the work itself gained in force from being furnished with such "proofs."

Flaubert, far from being flattered, did his best to nip the legend in the bud. *"C'est une histoire totalement inventée,"* he wrote, "It's an entirely made-up story." To those who even then were wasting their time searching his novel for factual allusions, he replied: "If I'd made any, my portraits would not have been such good likenesses: I would have been aiming at individuals, whereas in fact I was trying to reproduce types." So vehemently did he deny his point of departure that he said, without self-contradiction, both *"Madame Bovary, c'est moi,"* and "My poor Bovary is suffering and weeping at this very moment in twenty villages of France."

The story of Delphine Couturier was only one small factor. Neither her name nor that of her husband occurs in Flaubert's notes, though as his *"scénarios,"* or outlines, show he liked to "name" the people who inspired his characters. Nor is there any reference to MM. Jouanne or Mallard, who are supposed to have served as models for Homais. The Abbé Bournisien, Mayor Tuvache, and the merchant Lheureux are such common types one might well imagine oneself to have met them, in Normandy or anywhere else. When it was asked whether Yonville-l'Abbaye, in the novel, really did correspond to the village of Ry, it was pointed out that Flaubert's own map of the place, with streets, houses, and public buildings, proved it. And then a local expert showed that in fact it depicted Forges-les-Eaux, where Flaubert had spent a few weeks with his mother and niece in order to elude his mad brother-in-law, Emile Hamard. On the other hand, Yonville was not a spa, and the surrounding country was not like that round Forges. Whom was one to believe?

About Delphine Couturier, Du Camp himself knew little. She was neither rich nor beautiful; she was said to have "suffered from nymphomania"; she died at the age of twenty-seven; but there is no proof at all that she committed suicide.

When Flaubert included his heroine's suicide in his first outlines, he attributed it to disillusion in love. He had not yet
thought up the fatal mesh of debts, the headlong course from
which there was no escape. It was as if he followed the unfolding
of events as he recreated them, detecting as he wrote what
interested him most—their psychological motivation. It is the
reader who at a later stage transforms likelihood into certainty.

Other Possible Sources

IN 1947 MLLE GABRIELLE LELEU, then librarian of the municipal
library in Rouen, discovered among the Flaubert papers a
document which caused consternation among those who
had maintained that there was a strict parallel between
Delphine Couturier and Emma Bovary. It is an illiterate
manuscript entitled *Les Mémoires de Madame Ludovica*, which
tells of the wild doings of Louise Pradier, the young wife of the
sculptor. The writer, probably a maid, describes how her
mistress took lover after lover, and how, having got into the
habit of contracting debts and signing notes of hand by virtue
of a power of attorney extracted from her husband, she
suddenly found herself threatened with the bailiffs. In a panic
she, like Emma, went and asked help of her former lovers, and
when they refused thought of throwing herself in the Seine. But
things ended more happily for her than for Emma: husband
and wife separated, and Louise went on to other adventures.

The fact that Pradier and his wife were his friends must have
lent these *Mémoires* an added interest for Flaubert. After the
marriage broke up, he continued to see Louise Pradier and
probably enjoyed her favors. There would have been oppor-
tunities for long conversations about the diabolical piling-up of
debts; he could have witnessed and shared her desperation. It is
a curious fact that while Emma is carried away by hearing
Lagardy sing in the theatre at Rouen, and next day gives
herself to Léon Dupuis, Mme Ludovica is similarly affected by
the tenor Mocker, and gives herself the next day to Charles
Puis. There is more than one coincidence of this kind. And yet

Flaubert no more plagiarized the story of Louise than he did that of Delphine.

The character of Emma Bovary owes something to still other models. One of these is the famous Mme Lafarge, who had recently poisoned her husband, and whose *Mémoires* (published in 1842) showed her to be romantic, flirtatious, unfulfilled, and a dreamer. She was married to a clod who kept her shut away in the country. Her decision to do away with him may have had something in common with the impulse which made Emma, on the point of being found out by her husband, ask her lover if he has his pistols. Like Emma, Mme Lafarge was caught in the mesh of her own plotting and lying. But she chose to kill her husband rather than herself.

This catalogue of sources leads to the common-sense conclusion that Flaubert, like every other novelist, took his material wherever he found it and used it in accordance with his own purposes. It is strange that he should have been denied this right, and regarded instead as a minute recorder of local gossip. Emma is made up of all the women he had known; of those, like Mme Schlésinger and Louise Colet, that he had loved; and—why not?—of those he had imagined. He took more or less from each as the consistency or "logic" of the character of Emma demanded. In this sense, Emma is his, his own creation. If more than one woman reader recognized herself in Emma, it was not because of Delphine Couturier or Mme Ludovica. The same is true of Homais, the Abbé Bournisien, Tuvache and Binet, all made up of countless traits arranged by the creator to form a unique character which would go on giving the illusion of life long after all the models from which it was taken were dead.

A Question of Style

THE LETTERS TO Louise Colet tell us the story of this creation almost day by day. It was a long and difficult process, less because of the subject itself than because of what Flaubert wanted to make of it. More than once he cursed the "mediocrity" and "vulgarity" of the story he had to tell, so "bourgeois" and typical of "scenes from provincial life." For him the whole difficulty consisted in endowing this trivial subject with the appeal and nobility of a work of art.

He aimed at doing so in the first place by a rigorous method of composition in which each part "flowed" naturally from the others. He labored to make these links and transitions as varied as possible. He also sought after a general "tone," which he wanted to be the color of "the mildew of the soul." At the same time he wanted to be "impersonal," and to give a glimpse of "an attitude of lofty mockery (*blague supérieure*)" which corresponded to his sense of the grotesqueness of existence. But might not irony detract from the truth and pathos of the situations? Was he not in danger of turning portraits into caricatures? And how was he to interest the reader in Emma's fate if he made her into a provincial simpleton? All the questions presented themselves simultaneously, and he had only one weapon with which to answer them. It was style that had to carry the whole book and make it hold together. It was style that would make it a work of art, whatever the subject, the situations or the characters. It does not matter, he wrote to Louise Colet, that Boileau is not so great as Shakespeare: he will endure just as long because he said perfectly what he had to say.

Style is more than a way of writing, more than the result of the writer's deliberate choice. Convinced that "there is no idea without form and no form without idea," Flaubert saw style as the actual manifestation of the subject, situations, and characters; there could be no distinction between form and content. If one holds to "the idea," the object delivers itself up with the word which denotes it, through a process which nevertheless requires of the author "frightful labor and fanatical and devoted perseverance." While his past and present detractors see Flaubert as a mere fiddler with words, he was really engaged in alchemy: "*Le style c'est la vie, le sang même de la pensée* (Style is the very life and blood of thought)." It is not surprising that when he was describing Emma's poisoning he himself experienced the symptoms, including vomiting and the taste of arsenic.

While obliged to use prose, already a too familiar servant of thought and feeling, Flaubert wanted to endow it with the strength and dignity of verse. He wished it to be harmonious, rich, vivid, and articulated like a living organism; beautiful in form and aspect, and speakable. It had to conform to the requirements of what he called the *"gueuloir"* ("jaw"). Any sentence which did not fall within the natural rhythms of breathing was ruthlessly rejected as a deformity. For Flaubert there was a necessary correspondence between the object, the word which denoted it, and the vocal utterance. A false note implied a defect in one of the three elements, which had to be detected and remedied. "No one," he exclaimed proudly, "has ever had in mind a more perfect type of prose than I." In fact he bettered the instruction of the masters he himself had chosen—La Bruyère, Montesquieu, Voltaire—and achieved the "blank" writing Camus aspired to.

This single object, the novel, because it contained all other objects, demanded an effort and application which often had to be super-human, and which left Flaubert harassed, sick of his subject, and in a state close to despair. But he never doubted the necessity of his task. "I shall either be conquered or conquer," he wrote to Louise Colet. With this second major attempt his fate as a writer, in other words his life itself, was at stake. Fortunately, he found unparalleled delight whenever, at last, he succeeded in writing a sentence or a paragraph or a page to his satisfaction. When that happened he would exult and offer thanksgivings: "It's a delightful thing to write, and instead of being oneself to circulate all through the creation one treats of." As an example of his power to "make himself feel things (*se faire sentir les choses*)," to lose himself completely in his creation, he describes to Louise Colet the boundless world of sensation inspired in him by the scene in which Emma first yields to Rodolphe.

At Work

BEFORE HE STARTED WRITING he "did some planning," that is, sketched out in note form the course of events and the movements, relationships, and emotions of the characters. This stage of the work corresponded to what he called the "conception," which for him was of cardinal importance (he often alluded to Goethe's "all is in the conception"). The different parts of the plan gave rise to "*scénarios*" or outlines, still fairly laconic, and the scenarios were developed into drafts written out freely and at more length. After this, as is shown in the versions published by Mlle Gabrielle Leleu and M. Jean Pommier, Flaubert would go over these drafts as many as ten or so times, usually tightening up and cutting, and never thinking the time wasted if at the end of the day he had safely set up a sentence or a paragraph, or more rarely a whole page, which would then have to run the gauntlet of the "*gueuloir*." Sometimes the over-all flow of a part, chapter, or scene would demand the elimination of one of these laboriously produced pages. This entailed another sort of torture: when the individual stones of the edifice were so minutely fitted to one another, how could you remove one without danger of a whole wall collapsing? The only solution was to go back and start again. Flaubert's desire for perfection sometimes made him so strict that he decided the best thing was to let the machinery run, to "slacken the joints," to loosen the verbal stays in which Emma seemed to be stifling. To give the impression of naturalness and facility, Flaubert had to perform acts of virtuosity.

The work he expected to take eighteen months—the time it had taken him to write the *Tentation*—lasted nearly five years, and even then he was not satisfied with the result. Even though Bouilhet had given it his imprimatur, for Flaubert the book showed "more patience than genius, and much more labor than talent." In his opinion the writing, on which he had spent every effort, was still not irreproachable. In short, he wrote to Bouilhet, "It has been a great miscalculation, and it would need a deafening success to drown the voice of my conscience, which cries out 'Muffed it!'" But the success was to be deafening indeed.

The Vicissitudes of Publication

IN MAY 1856 HE SENT his manuscript to Du Camp for the

Revue de Paris. The estrangement which had existed between them since 1852 did not prevent them doing one another a service when the occasion warranted.

Maxime congratulated Gustave. But on July 14 he sent him an embarrassed letter. He did not go back on what he had said, but he thought the book was too dense and that it would gain essentially from being freed from "a mass of superfluities." Flaubert need have no fear: Du Camp had at his disposal a specialist who "for a hundred francs" would turn *Madame Bovary* into "something really good." He would cut the chapter about the wedding, shorten the agricultural show, and prune most of the episode about the club-foot.

Flaubert was furious. He rushed to Paris to plead against the proposed amputation and then waited. The August number of the *Revue* announced the publication, but misprinted the author as "Faubert," the name of a well-known grocer. It was a bad omen, but in spite of everything *Madame Bovary* saw the light in the October number and the five which followed.

A new difficulty arose when the secretary of the review cut the scene in the cab. Du Camp explained to his friend: "The scene is impossible, not for us, who laugh at it, not for me, who am responsible for this issue of the review, but for the court of summary jurisdiction, who would condemn us outright." Various other cuts were proposed in the latter part of the novel, and in a note to the reader of the *Revue*, before the final instalment, Flaubert declined to accept responsibility for the text which followed, and asked that it be considered "only as a fragment and not as a whole."

The fears of Du Camp and his two co-editors, Laurent Pichat and Louis Ulbach, turned out to be well-founded. Their precautions back-fired, and only succeeded in attracting the attention of the authorities. The cuts merely awakened morbid curiosity. What could have happened in the scene in the cab? The *Nouvelliste de Rouen*, which had obtained permission to serialize the novel in its own columns after it had begun to appear in the *Revue de Paris*, took fright and discontinued publication. Flaubert was advised, first unofficially, then officially, that he was going to be prosecuted. The *Revue de Paris*, which was of a liberal tendency, had already had two "warnings"; this gave the authorities a good opportunity to silence it for ever..

The Trial

FLAUBERT WAS horror-stricken. What he had feared most of all was a *succès de scandale* which would detract from the dignity of an art practised as a sort of priesthood. But this was much worse—the court of summary jurisdiction! Then he suddenly remembered that he belonged to a good bourgeois family, one of the most respected in Normandy, and that he was the son of the famous Dr. Flaubert. At that moment he reconciled in his own person two realities—art and the bourgeoisie—which he had always considered mutually exclusive.

He had representations made to the Empress, who calmed his fears. He went to see Lamartine, whom he did not know and did not much like. He alerted all his most prominent and influential contacts. Either the Empress's reassurances must have been empty, or else her efforts were in vain, for on January 29, 1857, Flaubert, Laurent Pichat, and the printer appeared before the judges of the *VIth Chambre de Police Correctionnelle*, and had to listen to the venomous nonsense of Pinard, the public prosecutor. Maître Sénard, whom Flaubert had briefed to defend him, was a former president of the National Assembly and had been Minister of the Interior under the Second Republic. His defence lasted over four hours, and demanded not only acquittal but also apologies. Just over a week later, on February 7, the verdict was announced: all three of the accused were acquitted, but they were not awarded costs. The judge declared that the indicted work deserved a "severe reprimand," and drew Flaubert and his companions' attention to the fact that there were "limits which even the lightest literature should not transgress." Flaubert reprimanded! Once again the law did not miss the opportunity to make itself ridiculous. It was to repeat the process with Baudelaire a few months later, and with Proudhon the following year.

Flaubert had signed a contract with Michel Lévy for the publication of *Madame Bovary* in book form. The author's fee was only eight hundred francs. The trial took away all Flaubert's desire for publication. He procrastinated and tried to find a compromise, suggesting an edition with wide margins in which he would restore the passages cut by the *Revue de Paris* and would comment, with quotations, on those singled out for reprobation by the public prosecutor. But the publisher, anxious to profit from the unexpected publicity, was in a hurry. The book appeared in April 1857, dedicated to Maître Sénard (it had been dedicated in the first place to Bouilhet), and the whole edition of fifteen thousand copies was sold in a few days. Other editions were contemplated.

Critical Response

THE BOOK GOT A BAD RECEPTION from the critics, who, though often in a subtler manner, reproached it—and sometimes its author—for the same things as had been brought forward at the trial.* The novelist was blamed for the crudeness of his descriptions, the lack of what today would be called a "positive hero," and for Emma's immorality. Above all, everyone would have preferred the author to praise and condemn, to take sides. Whereas what was usually absent, and what gave *Madame Bovary* both its novelty and its power, was the application of the "scientific" attitude to human life and behavior, the transposition into the novel of the "method of the natural and physical sciences," the determinist approach to events, situations, and character.

Sainte-Beuve saluted Flaubert's "talent" and praised his ability as a creator of landscapes and "speaking" characters. But he "would have sometimes preferred the details of certain descriptions to be carried less far . . . I should also have liked, though I cannot quite say how it could have entered into your composition, to see some character just as true as the others but with feelings that were gentle, pure, deep and restrained. It

---

*J-G Prod'homme: *Vingt Chefs-d'œuvres jugés par leurs Contemporains* (Stock, 1931).

would have been a respite . . . " In short, he was accusing
Flaubert of harshness. But Sainte-Beuve did recognize that the
book was "completely impersonal," and that this was "a great
proof of strength." He went on to say that Flaubert, "the son
and brother of distinguished doctors, wielded the pen as others
wielded the scalpel." The expression has caught on, but although
the comparison is apt, it only calls attention to one, and that the
most obvious, of Flaubert's gifts.

The reservations quoted above are from a private letter from
Sainte-Beuve to Flaubert, but when, in May 1857, he wrote an
article on *Madame Bovary* in the official paper, *Le Moniteur*,
this attention to a beginner, from such a critic and in such a
place, made a considerable impression. It called forth certain
angry replies. In *L'Univers*, Léon Aubineau declined to mention
either the title of the book or the name of its author: "There can
be no criticism of this kind of book . . . labored, vulgar, and
culpable . . . Art ceases the moment it is invaded by filth." He
rejoiced at the "sort of administrative sanction" which had
caused Sainte-Beuve to leave *Le Moniteur*, which in fact he had
left for quite different reasons.

Charles de Mazade, in the *Revue des Deux Mondes* considered
that "M. Flaubert imitates M. de Balzac," and that his was a
"talent which so far has more of imitation and virtuosity in it
than originality."

According to Paulin Limayrac, in *Le Constitutionnel*, Flaubert's
art was "second rate." He leant towards "realism," which was
"nature without light." It was to be hoped that his brush with
the law would teach him a lesson.

Nestor Roqueplan, in *La Presse*, called the book "charming,"
but this was beside the point. A critic by the name of Deschamps
considered that Sainte-Beuve's ambiguous praises gave nothing
away, and went on to point out a couple of dozen solecisms he
had found in the novel: "The author is not without talent, but
he does seem to be without learning, or friends candid and
enlightened enough to point such things out to him."

Similar remarks on the style were made by Cuvillier-Fleury,
editor of the *Journal des Débats* and later a member of the

Academy. He gave only "a few samples of bad style," but could have quoted "handfuls." He considered the "affectation of the language" sorted ill with the "harshness of the drawing." The characters, he said, were "draped in the cast-offs of romanticism." He prophesied: "If Madame Bovary lived to grow old her future would be that of a second-hand clothes dealer."

M. de Pontmartin, comparing Flaubert's novel with one by Edmond About, said that "M. About is the bourgeoisie and M. Flaubert is democracy in the novel." *Madame Bovary* was "the discontented democracy's unhealthy exaltation of the senses and the imagination." Unfortunately it was impossible to make out what side the author came down on, but "we take it upon ourselves to say that realism is and can only be literary democracy, and *Madame Bovary* is proof of it." Over-abundant proof into the bargain: the book could "easily have done without a couple of hundred pages, or in other words a couple of thousand descriptions."

In *Le Figaro*, Jules Habans wondered whether "M. Flaubert really meant, when he took up his pen, to write the novel we now have before us." He admitted he had "first-class talents," but maintained that he was "not a writer."

Barbey d'Aurevilly, on the other hand, said *Madame Bovary* broke away from the "literature of imitation . . . based more or less on Balzac or Stendhal." He praised "the constant and indefatigable narrator," the "unwavering analyst," the "describer of the minutest subtlety." Unfortunately, though, a machine made "in Birmingham or Manchester out of good English steel" could have done the job just as well. Flaubert was "a man of marble" who had written *Madame Bovary* "with a pen of stone, like a savage's knife." He was neither moral nor immoral: he was without feeling. But at least he was an artist, an "entomologist of style", whose only mistake was to have "lost" himself, to have been "swamped," in trivialities.

Did Flaubert catch the ear of the young? Of some of them, but not all. Some would later become his followers, but Granier de Cassagnac, for example, though not denying the

author's talent, compared his book to "a huge heap of dung."
Duranty, who championed realism, found in *Madame Bovary*
"neither emotion nor feeling nor life," but at the most "great
arithmetical power."

Only two great writers, one celebrated, the other as yet
unrecognized, did Flaubert justice immediately. Victor Hugo
wrote from exile: *"Madame Bovary* is a work!" Baudelaire saw
the nature of the difficulties the writer had had to overcome to
apply "a racy, colorful, subtle and precise style to a banal
subject," and to express "the most passionate and turbulent
feelings through the most trivial story . . . "

Unfounded Reproaches

FLAUBERT HAD A LOW OPINION of the critics, who were also to
belabor him over *Salammbô*, *L'Education sentimentale*, and *La
Tentation de Saint Antoine.* And one can hardly disagree with
him when one looks at the conspiracy of stupidity, malice, and
blind complacency yapping at the heels of Emma Bovary.
Flaubert was right not to pay undue attention. Criticism is
only a reflection of public opinion, naturally against anything
which upsets its slothful view of things.

But this means that criticism has at least a sociological value.
The impact and originality of *Madame Bovary* can be seen
through the bitterness of the criticisms directed at it.

There is no need to waste time on the accusation of "immorality." Such a charge was typical of an age of great and
gilded courtesans which would only tolerate them in literature
if they were consumptive, or secretly of noble origin, or the
victims of evil influences. A little provincial, the wife of a doctor, who experiences the acutest emotions of love with her first
lover and the delights and perhaps perversions of the flesh with
her second, giving herself to both impetuously and without
remorse, was certainly beyond the pale. The author ought to
have condemned such "guilty" loves outright. Emma does kill
herself, and dies tragically, but that was not a sufficient
punishment: she has no death-bed regrets for what she has
done, no repentant reflections. Her death is dictated by events,

by the concatenation of circumstance, or, as Charles Bovary says, by "fate." She was punished by life, but for morality to be safe she ought also to have been punished by men, by society, and by the author.

Disturber of the Peace

YET AT THE SAME TIME Flaubert was accused of being "cruel." In other words, of having organized his picture around an implacably rigorous chain of events, and characters who all, with the exception of Emma, convey the most wretched opinion of the human race. Although his love for Emma is touching, Charles Bovary simply emanates mediocrity. Homais, a pompous ass, has a kind of intelligence which makes him odious. The Abbé Bournisien is obviously a lost shepherd, impervious to anything spiritual. Rodolphe is a cheap seducer, Léon weak and a coward, Lheureux a scoundrel. And this whole provincial society, with its limited horizons and petty feelings and thoughts, is a picture of stupid self-satisfaction.

How could Emma Bovary, who has the courage of her sensuality, do other than try to escape from such a world through her naive dreams, her romantic yearnings bred on trashy literature in a convent school, and her longing for a life of luxury, which was for her inseparable from refinement of feeling? Her dreams may have been conventional, her desires mere insipid idealism, her appetites may have found no outlet but adultery, but at least she rose above her environment to the extent of rejecting the awful materialism of a society that was greedy, cowardly, and dense. So life takes her back by the scruff of the neck and drowns her. Only one person escapes the general condemnation, and that is the boy Justin. And he is the instrument of the gods, who supplies the poison. There is no concession to sentimentality, humanitarianism, conventional ideas, or to the philosophy and morality which present man as a chosen being. Flaubert painted a Hell—the hell of the provinces, and of a doomed humanity. He was a disturber of the bourgeois peace.

Real and Ideal Life

HENCE THE ACCUSATIONS of "materialism" and "realism."

Through an examination of human and social relations in a society supposed to be ordered, civilized, and progressive (and, into the bargain, enjoying God's blessing), he exposed the interests, appetites, and instincts by which men are really motivated. He was less interested in their mental ideals than in their actual behavior, and showed how, even when, as in the case of Emma, their intentions are not at all sordid, they can lead to the ruin of the individual and the destruction of all around him. Instead of the life which everyone assumed to obey an imposed moral and religious code, Flaubert showed a life which did without any reference to values. Charles Bovary practises medicine like a beast of burden. Homais aspires to politics for the honor and glory it will bring (not neglecting, however, to give secret consultations for the sake of his purse). Bournisien ministers to his flock as if they were a herd of cattle. Binet's whole object in life is making napkin-rings. And these are the leading lights of the place. The others are scarcely more than animals. The doctor's wife, who longs to know a better kind of existence, is doomed to scandal and suicide. By her aspirations even more than by her conduct, she disturbs an "order" in which success is reserved for the crook (or clever business man) Lheureux, and the *Légion d'honneur* bestowed on the departmental dabbler in politics. Flaubert not only held a mirror up to the society of his age. He also produced an X-ray photograph.

"Ideas are Facts"

THE ACCUSATIONS of "materialism" and "realism" also applied to his method. An indefatigable describer, he stuck to the facts, and reduced to facts which could be rendered in words feelings and instincts, the whole psychological world vaguely associated with the "heart" or the "soul" and with an ideal human nature in which the body was of minor importance. When Flaubert declared that "ideas are facts," he meant to reunite in a single whole the planes of imagination and dream and everyday life, breaking the sacrosanct dichotomy between body and soul. Emma's conduct is as much the product of her old girlhood dreams as of sensuality frustrated by marriage, convention, and environment.

The springs of behavior lie in various, apparently incompatible realms, but Flaubert restores them to a living, complex, puzzling synthesis, made up of "forces" varying only in amplitude and strength. They simply mark out a field of investigation, and no one of them deserves special or preferential treatment. Whether visible or imagined, whether arrived at through divination or induction, whether they belong to description or to analysis, all have descended from the empyrean of categories to endure the level scrutiny which separates them out and reconstructs them according to the laws of life.

An Ever-open Path

HENCE THE MULTIPLICITY of details, the diversity of colors, and the endless descriptions. Flaubert's descriptive zeal, his mania for what Barbey d'Aurevilly called "trivialities," aim at capturing a life which is perpetually changing, and open every moment to different and perhaps contradictory explanations. In this way the writer, instead of speaking "off" and by allusion, to a certain extent catches reality in the net of words, and instead of presenting the secondary world of language offers the actual reality of the world in which his characters live. All Flaubert's labors were in fact directed to the one end of making words merge into the things for which they were the signs. "*Plus le mot colle dessus, et disparaît, plus c'est beau* (The more closely the word fits, the more it disappears, the better)," he wrote.

His aim was not so very different from that of his junior, Mallarmé. For him as for Mallarmé, language "nothings" (*néantise*) the thing it designates, and must be "nothinged" in its turn for the thing to emerge in its primal freshness together with the unique expression which reveals it. For Flaubert there is no discontinuity between mind, to which language belongs, and matter: between reality and the expression of reality. "Style" is a mediation, an ever-open path leading to and from both worlds. The only condition is that, for the necessary transformations to take place, the novelist must be sailing in sufficiently deep waters. He describes himself as "skimming before the wind over the smooth waters" of his creation.

The ferment below the surface only reveals itself in tiny details, appearing and reappearing with subtle modifications in different permutations and combinations. Everything seems the same, and yet all is changed, as in drawings where the alteration of a single stroke produces a completely different design. This art of "retouching" is a sort of writing "from the life"—life apprehended as it passes, ceaselessly analyzed and ceaselessly synthesized again. The passage of time is measured by this art, rather than by the round of the seasons or the succession of events. Balzac and Stendhal were still to a large extent in the tradition of the *"récit"* or personal narrative. Flaubert was working in a material which already anticipated Proust.

A Technique of Description

THANKS TO A TECHNIQUE which, as we have seen, he perfected in his travel notes, the facts Flaubert described always comprehended more than the facts themselves. He had no use for a description whose only object was to set the scene for, or provide an intermission in, the plot. For him, description must accord with events, situations, and people, upon all of which it acted, preparing the one, throwing light on the other, and enabling the plot to develop without direct reference to the "story." The famous cap of the schoolboy Charles Bovary, which is described in minute detail, tells us more about its owner than a long psychological analysis; it even acts as a symbol of his fate. It is by describing the forest and a clearing that Flaubert "tells" of Emma's first adultery, and by following a cab on an endless drive through the streets of Rouen that he conveys the second.

Description, while forwarding the narrative itself, also does much more. It supplies a sort of "sub-narrative" which forms a quiet accompaniment to the story, providing it with backgrounds, exits, and outlets on to new and sometimes strange horizons. It creates a "depth" beyond the reach of mere observation.

It does so by the use of image, metaphor, and sustained simile, which break up the natural inertia of objects and incorporate them into a moral or spiritual world in which they take on new significance. Conversely, the psychological world finds its correlative in the material world: Emma's loneliness is expressed by a fire left burning alone on the steppes; her half-suppressed desires are conveyed by a quivering of the nostrils which allows her to "breathe in the coolness of the ivy round the capitals of the columns." The abstract speaks to our senses through the suggestive power of images; and through the same power the concrete—a village street, a pasture, a morning sky—insidiously evokes feelings, desires, and values. Finally, description arrives at its effects by a certain subtle and voluntary distortion similar to that which gives Vermeer's paintings their strange charm. It is amusing that Flaubert should be accused of "realism" when he was the first to conjure up the total world of mingled consciousness and fact, through sensible appearances and with the aid of poetic language.

Madame Bovary owes its unique richness to all these different kinds of discourse operating harmoniously at different levels. There is the discourse of events, which can be reduced to a commonplace and touching "story." There is that of human and social relationships, full of irony and pity, which plunges us into the grotesque side of existence. And lastly there is that sort of song, new at the time, which links our sensibility and perhaps even our unconscious to realities which are inexpressible—nature, ever-changing yet imperturbable; the life-wish and death-wish of a disintegrating society; the murky depths of aimless, mediocre, pretentious minds, attracted by such lures as eternal love, happiness, security, wealth, honor and fame, all the things that lend people whose desires and needs are sadly limited an imaginative life which itself is sadly narrow.

"Un chant désesperé"

IF WE TODAY are still alive to the virulence of Flaubert's accusation against mankind, we are yet more so to the elements in his work which, by means of "a mysterious chemistry," fuse subject and object and enable the most secret subjectivity to issue forth in general truths. We are able to hear that *"chant désesperé,"* that song of despair, which tells of man's incurable solitude, his inability to live, his fundamental failure. But for this it is not enough to read the signs on the paper. From time to time one's eyes must leave the page, and the reader must cast off from words to ride the waves of modulation. Then new countries open up, countries with the shifting shapes and indeterminate colors of our dreams. Black is not quite black, but rather grey-green, grey-blue, or dove-grey intensifying to purple. A single bird flies through the air, or a butterfly, which aspires to sun and light but falls back to the ground with broken wings. By looking up to watch its flight, the stick-in-the-muds of Yonville-l'Abbaye have added a few inches to their stature. They will have uneasy consciences at going on living in the same old way. The wife of the medical officer will have given them "an extra bit of soul" (*un supplément d'âme*).

Flaubert's contemporaries, their ears deafened by the trills of romanticism, were not ready to hear this subtle song, and preferred to see Emma as a trollop rather than as the female Quixote she really is. They were rather like the inhabitants of Yonville-l'Abbaye itself—fond of gossip and over-ready with moral indignation. Then, for fifty years, *Madame Bovary* was put away in a glass case with other *objets d'art*—a relic saluted with awe by writers, who admired its challenge; a tedious masterpiece for the general public. But now its purgatory seems to have ended, and Emma is back among us in her eternal youth.

9

THE WORLD AND THE DESK

W HEN *Madame Bovary* appeared in book form its author was thirty-six. He was forty-three when he began *L'Education sentimentale*. In the meantime he had published *Salammbô*, a strange work at once epic and romantic, full of noise and color, arousing much criticism but establishing its author's fame. Flaubert was no longer the young man who ten years before had proudly rejected Du Camp's offers. He made long visits to Paris, frequenting literary circles and minor actresses, appearing in society and even at court at Compiègne. He was still the same demon for work, the same high priest in the agonizing service of art, but he was now a bear who allowed himself to be wheedled, and although Croisset remained his hermitage and laboratory he no longer shut himself away there so aggressively from his contemporaries.

At least, that is how it seemed. In fact, Flaubert had not changed. He was still the same restless, unsatisfied creature, subject to unbearable *ennui*, to whom art offered still the same outlet for his rebelliousness, and ever-fresh food for his insatiable desire to possess the universe in a phrase. His standards as a writer were even higher than before: he took longer to embody the frail and fleeting dream who is the daughter of Hamilcar than he had done to create the sensual and chimerical Emma. Flaubert was not one of those who think that because they have become famous they have "arrived." Although he now had more of a social life than before, he reserved the better part of his strength, time, and ambition for communing with his own creations, for the kind of converse in which he was himself, fully and without disguise or pretence. The only real pleasure in his eyes he found in "the throes of art;" as we have learned, it was a masochistic pleasure. He had not acquired self-confidence: he had contracted habits.

To begin with, he rejected the public image of himself which had been created by *Madame Bovary*, the trial, and the generally hostile criticism which greeted the novel. He refused to be regarded as a sensational writer and a latter-day follower of Balzac. He made huge cuts in *La Tentation* and wanted to publish it, but the extracts which Gautier obligingly published in *L'Artiste* met with such a cool reception that he gave up the idea, on the pretext that he did not want to risk another trial and perhaps a prison sentence. In fact, he had realized that the work was not yet ready for publication. In May 1857 he wrote: "I know now what it lacks. Two things: first, a plan; second, the personality of Saint Anthony." And as this was "a book that mustn't be muffed," for which the author needed "time and yet more time!" he put it away in a drawer again and returned to the idea of the "oriental tale" which he had written about to Bouilhet during his travels in the East. "*Anubis* would be the story of a woman who wanted to be loved by the god." After having spent so much time on a vulgar subject and the description of bourgeois manners, he wanted to return to his old loves—sumptuous, glittering phrases and the "great machine" of antiquity. *Carthage* (the original title of what was to become *Salammbô*) emerged as a new incarnation of the world Flaubert had already conjured up in *La Tentation*.

> *Je vais pendant quelques années peut-être vivre dans un sujet splendide et loin du monde moderne dont j'ai plein le dos.* (I am going to live, for several years perhaps, in the midst of a splendid subject far from the modern world, which I'm thoroughly sick of.)

"A Way of Living"

Madame Bovary had earned Flaubert accusations of realism and triviality, but this new venture was undertaken not to surprise his readers so much as to return to what Flaubert considered the essential function of literature and the practice of literature: the right to lead a life which has nothing in common with ordinary people's lives. The book was to bear the marks of artistic creation, but not merely as a beautiful, self-sufficient object which owes its characteristics only to the skill, observation, imagination or even genius of the author. In order that it should draw, release or force the reader from his everyday life, the author must have felt and experienced the urgencies involved. To those who failed to see that *Madame Bovary* was not so much a picture of manners as a cry of revolt and a call for help, Flaubert repeated that cry and that call, though with no more hope now than then of being understood: "Few people will guess how sad one had to be to undertake to revive Carthage! It's a wilderness I was forced into out of disgust for modern life." He was making an important revelation when he said: "A book has always been for me just a way of living in a certain environment." One might add that literature was a way of living absolutely.

The *ennui* and world-weariness which oppressed Flaubert grew greater rather than less with success and the passage of time. The writing of *Madame Bovary* had plunged him right into the "nauseating odors" which rise from the scullery of life; the book's success was based on a maddening misunderstanding. His "poor Bovary," the pathetic creature who had gradually silenced his own irony, and to whom as the pages piled up he came to lend his own heart, overflowing with love and throbbing with the wounds of existence, had been "dragged through the courts by the hair, like a whore." Flaubert's rebelliousness grew tinged with bitterness and sadness. He took up his yoke again having had proof of the enormous rottenness of the world he hated, and with a sharper sense than ever of having nothing in common with it.

> *Pour ne pas vivre, je me plonge dans l'Art, en désespéré; je me grise avec de l'encre comme d'autres avec du vin.* (In order not to live I plunge desperately into Art; I intoxicate myself with ink as others do with wine.)

What he did before by choice he was now compelled to do, and he realized what the rejection cost him.

> *Je ne vis pas, j'escamote l'existence, c'est le seul moyen de la supporter.* (I don't live, I juggle away existence. It's the only way to bear it.)

The Boredom of Literature

FOR SOMEONE WHO DECLARED "despair is my natural state," literature must have possessed a necessity it did not have before. After he was grown up, writing was never easy for Flaubert, but on the whole the pleasures had made up for the pains. The observer and the *voyeur* that are in every novelist found many sources of satisfaction, and the creator was often lifted out of himself by sudden gusts of enthusiasm. By throwing himself into *Carthage*, this time a subject which was to his taste, which he had chosen himself and been incubating for a long time, Flaubert hoped to enjoy these privileged states once more. He probably did experience them again without needing to say anything about them, as he had done to Louise Colet in the case of *Madame Bovary*. But although he was no longer engaged on a "task" or an "exercise," pleasure is not the predominant strain in his letters to Feydeau, Duplan, and Bouilhet. Once again we find him sweating and straining, struggling in the "throes of style," cursing the millstone round his neck. He is no longer fretting against the subject: it is literature and art he cries out against, their often insuperable difficulties and the obligation to overcome them. Tied to the necessity of uttering, he had reached the point where there is no longer any loophole. From being an object of cajolery, art has become a single, exacting mistress. Or worse: an evil he loathes but in which he is taking up his abode.

> *La littérature m'embête au suprême degré! Mais ce n'est pas ma faute; elle est devenue chez moi une vérole constitutionnelle; il n'y a pas moyen de s'en débarrasser. Je suis abruti d'art et d'esthétique et il m'est impossible de vivre un jour sans gratter cette incurable plaie, qui me ronge.* (Literature bores me utterly! But it's not my fault. With me it's become a sort of constitutional pox, and there's no getting rid of it. I'm stupefied with art and aesthetics, yet I can't live one day without scratching at the incurable wound that's eating me away.)

Of course, one must not be misled by the strong metaphors. Flaubert wrote to his correspondents at the end of long, heart-breaking nights of work, when he was tired, often right at the end of his tether. And although his nervous illness had not given him any real trouble for years, he experienced longer and more frequent periods of depression—one in the autumn of 1859 lasted three months—when he had an acute sense of nothingness, helplessness, and the destructive power of time.

> *Je vais chaque jour me détériorant, et la confiance en moi, l'orgueil de l'idée, le sentiment d'une force vague et immense que l'on respire avec l'air, tout cela décline peu à peu.* (I deteriorate day by day, and my confidence in myself, my pride in thought, the sense of some huge vague force that one breathes in with the air, all this is gradually declining.)

His manner of living and poor health had something to do with such feelings: he suffered from rheumatism, attacks of boils, and perhaps also syphilis. He said himself that he suffered from the *maladie noire*, mechancholy: "I had it for eighteen months when I was young, and it nearly killed me." He wrote this in October 1858, and the mood remained more or less constant until *Salammbô* was finished. After that he allowed himself a few weeks' rest, and went to Paris for a breather.

A Second Flaubert

THIS STATE OF MIND would seem highly unpropitious for literary creation if Flaubert had not been inhabited by another personality which, either in the long term or the short term or both, always triumphed over the side of him which was melancholy, depressed, and ailing. It is impossible not to think of the character Proust speaks of in his essay *Contre Sainte-Beuve*: the personality the writer slips into as soon as he takes up his pen and moves through his creation, that "more him than himself" whom the reader gets to know through the work, the mover of mountains, the magician. Also the man who could write to his friend Feydeau, after perfunctory condolences on the approaching death of the latter's wife: "You have and will have some fine pictures to look at, and you'll be able to make some fine studies!" For at such times "the mind has an extraordinary sharpness." Novelist speaks to novelist in sincere friendship.

While writing *Madame Bovary* Flaubert was "like one possessed." It was a long time before he took fire over *Salammbô*. He went through libraries of material, assimilating a hundred ancient books about Carthage in order to "cram himself with his subject" and trying to force inspiration to come. In vain. He would have to go to the actual places and breathe the air his characters had breathed two thousand years before. When he got back from Tunisia he no longer thought, as he had in May 1857, merely of "cooking up something loud-mouthed and glittering" which would prevent the critics from making any comparisons with Balzac. He had entered into possession of his characters, of their thoughts and feelings and even of the unknown language they spoke. They now inhabited him and he was going to live with them, celebrating this new union with one of those bold images in which his correspondence abounds:

> *Un livre est une chose essentiellement organique, cela fait partie de nous-mêmes. Nous nous sommes arraché du ventre un peu de tripes, que nous servons aux bourgeois.* (A book is something essentially organic, it is a part of ourselves. We have torn out a bit of our own innards to serve up to the bourgeois.)

He could say this the more freely because since, according to him, an author must be impersonal, no one could recognize him in his work. The novelist would be lifted up on the shoulders of a man "weary and exhausted to the marrow of his bones," who "thought eagerly of death," and whose existence no one would suspect. "When people read *Salammbô* they will not think, I hope, of the author."

A Third Flaubert

THE LETTERS, by revealing the Flaubert of every day, both before and after the task, might make us forget Flaubert the hero and Titan, existing in his creation like "God in the universe." The Letters cannot show us the metamorphosis which took place every day when he sat down at his desk and rejoined his companions for the next stage of the "long journey."*

*He wrote to the Goncourts at the beginning of July 1862: "For me a book to write is a long journey . . .!"

The correspondence gives only an intaglio portrait, though it is useful for throwing into relief the portrait which emerges from the work.

God also manifests himself invisibly, of course; in this instance in ways of which Flaubert himself was unconscious. The reader of *Salammbô* detects a certain eagerness in the description of horrors, which come thick and fast towards the end of the book. The reader of the Letters is startled by certain revelations, and would very much like to know what lies beneath the irony, the doubtful jesting, the over-emphasis. If he knew all the reasons which led Flaubert to write *Salammbô* he would suspect the existence of another, unavowed motive which may have triggered the whole process.

Flaubert declares, for example, that he is not aiming at "the truth." For him, that is not "the first condition of art," and he doubts whether the object of "fictions" is to "discover" it. This was a surprising admission on the part of a novelist who had been called a "realist" and shocked people by his "medical approach". But in *Madame Bovary* he had aimed at depicting at least a certain psychological and social truth. And in *Salammbô* he meant to do the same. He refers, in fact, to two different "truths": that of everyday life, of the commonplace, which he refuses to depict because it is devoid of artistic interest ("I cannot bring myself to write such platitudes, popular as they are at present"), and that which belongs to metaphysics and which it is vain to pursue (it is foolish even to want to settle such questions). What remains is something between the two, the knowledge of man and nature, attainable on the one hand by art and on the other by science. Until art has taken over the methods of the sciences, the truth of art must be first and foremost the truth of the artist. Thus does Flaubert maintain the royal prerogatives of the imagination.

But of an imagination which is exercized within certain limits—in the case of *Salammbô*, those of historical verisimilitude. As he is dealing with an unknown or little-known civilization, these limits are vague and flexible. It was for this reason he chose it. At the same time as he escapes into another world and

a new "*manière de vivre*," he can unburden his heart and vent
his spleen about the world in which he lives, his contemporaries,
and mankind in general. "All that emerges from this book is
an immense disdain for humanity," he wrote to Amélie Bosquet,
and it was with a ghoulish laugh that he embarked on "*la
grillade des moutards* (the roasting of the brats)." To Mme
Jules Sandeau he announced: "*J'éventre des hommes avec prodi-
galité. Je verse les ang. Je fais du style cannibale* (I'm disembowelling
people right and left. I'm shedding blood. I'm writing in
cannibal style)." It is as if he were trying to revenge himself
for some denial of justice; all his bitterness has turned to
aggression. It is particularly striking in what he wrote to
Feydeau: "Let's be fierce . . . Let us pour eau-de-vie on this
age of sugar and water. Let us drown the bourgeois in a brew
eleven thousand degrees strong, and burn his gizzard, and make
him howl with pain." So to the man suffering from the
"*maladie noire*," and to the writer enthroned impersonally in
his work, we must, if we want to understand Flaubert, add
this third and somewhat terrifying personality. It is this one
which gives tone to the other two.

The letters written during these years reveal the secret
Flaubert, and hint discreetly at the sort of reading he indulged in. For pleasure, not because of the needs of the work
in progress. They were authors, therefore, with whose thought
or feeling he found himself in sympathy, from whom he
unconsciously derived inspiration and imaginative stimulus.
In fact, there is only one of them. Flaubert refers constantly
to Sade, affectionately nicknamed "*le Vieux*," the Old 'un.

"The Great de Sade"

FLAUBERT HAD BECOME acquainted with Sade when he was
very young, had procured copies of his works (circulated
clandestinely then as some still are now), and was so steeped in
him that he nicknamed his friends after his characters—
Cardoville, Saint-Florent, Président de Blamont, Minski, and
so on. The works of the "Divine Marquis" had an immediately

tonic effect on Flaubert: "I braced myself up, *au débotté* as Villemessant says [*i.e.* immediately on arrival], by reading the second volume of *La Philosophie* [*dans le Boudoir*], again with renewed pleasure." He read Sade aloud to groups of friends. To Gautier, whom he was inviting to Croisset, together with Feydeau and Saint-Victor, he promised as an inducement: "I shall contrive to get my guests a complete De Sade! There will be volumes from it on the bedside tables!" He probably did not have to look far for a complete set.

Flaubert's liking for Sade, and his habit of constantly referring to him, partly to provoke and partly out of long custom, had finally irritated the brothers Goncourt. One is not surprised to find them announcing the fact in their *Journal* and affecting astonishment at it. They speak of "a mind haunted by de Sade, to whom he returns as to a delicious mystery and sin." As if to emphasize the link with *Salammbô*, they go on: "Flaubert has chosen Carthage for his novel about antiquity, as the site of the most degenerate civilization ever known, and according to himself he has written no more than two chapters in six months: a mercenaries' feast and a boy's brothel . . . " After *Salammbô*, Sade's influence on Flaubert was still visible enough for an ill-disposed critic to see it in *L'Education sentimentale*, seven years later.

Flaubert told Sainte-Beuve he was not a "disciple" of Sade. He could scarcely do less. Some years earlier he had said he did not envy Sade his laurels. We may believe him. But we should also remember the young man who vowed he would be a "demoraliser," and saw this as an opportunity of throwing a few "truths" in the face of the age. He had forgotten Byron, but Sade was still with him. He had never found a better incarnation of revolt.

And, although he denied it, he may have owed him more besides. Who was it he invoked on the death of Bouilhet, his dearest friend and spiritual brother? "One has to try to be a 'philosopher and wit,' as the great de Sade used to say. But there are times when it isn't easy . . ." He found in Sade a lesson of virility and courage. Though he knew him as the author of scandalous works which only people like himself could really appreciate, he also valued him for a moral and philosophical attitude which could serve as an example and model.

The Need of the World

BUT ONE MUST AT ONCE point out the limits in the relation between Flaubert and Sade. Flaubert like to call himself a man of "every excess," and was certainly strongly attracted by a genius who was a sort of incarnation of excess; he was influenced by him, and, to a certain extent and in some circumstances, shared his philosophy of life. But for him there was no question, as there was with Sade, of installing himself in absolute egoism and totally denying all morality, belief, and civilization, all the values slowly acquired by the human race in order to moderate the effects of the laws of biology and of the blind struggle of appetite. For Flaubert the world might indeed be a jungle, and society mere "banditry"; life might indeed be a bitter farce, and his desired role in it, consciously or unconsciously, that of a "demoralizer"—just the same, there were all sorts of barriers preventing him from falling into Sade's lofty solitude and cutting himself off from the rest of humanity.

The age he abhorred, the contemporaries he detested, the life that was a burden to him, the universal stupidity he depicted and denounced—he could not withdraw from them without cutting himself off from his own roots. Unlike Sade, he was not a *grand seigneur* of the eighteenth century; nor had his character the same degree of organization as Sade's. At forty as at sixteen, he was still in search of his own "identity"; but he had found a way of gathering together the various divergent forces within him, and it was this which now constituted his self-affirmation. He wanted to impose on the world not his personality but his work; and he wanted his work to be impersonal and without visible connection with himself, a mirror in which he alone could see his own reflection. Just as a woman needs her feminity, so he needed this detour in order to have the world at his feet. The conquest was undertaken by one whose sensibility was extremely delicate, whose nerves were always raw and often on the verge of giving way. It was not without cause that his doctor described him as "a hysterical old woman", and Flaubert's declarations of love for such "proud males" of literature as Shakespeare and Goethe support that comment rather than otherwise. By writing Flaubert adopted a "way of living." Sade, conversely, had tried to impose his.

When Flaubert conjured up the civilization of Carthage, a civilization so foreign and far removed from every point of view, he was escaping in spirit but not in fact. He still had in view his own age, his contemporaries, mankind. He offered the men of his own time a foil for their thoughts, feelings, and views on life, and it did not matter how much they were shocked or astonished so long as they responded. The paths he followed in *Salammbô* may have been more devious, but they corresponded to the same relationship between him and the world as the short cuts of *Madame Bovary* or the avenues of *L'Education sentimentale*. He needed the world in order to oppose it. The world was his object, the "others," *les autres*, his constant preoccupation.

Art as Religion

NOR, IN THE WORLD OF VALUES, did Flaubert sweep away everything but his own ego. Though he himself was an atheist, he was one of a more moderate kind than Sade, and regretted that anyone should be "without religion"—that is to say, without a sense that everything in the universe is linked together in harmony, as in a dynamic system where all the forces balance each other and the whole both depends and acts upon the part. Though the why-and-wherefore of this system may be unknown to us, man is nevertheless a part of it. He cannot set up as an isolated and independant monad. Like Baudelaire, Flaubert lived in a universe of *"correspondances,"* He always remained a Spinozan.

Art, because it restored the links broken by modern life and industrial society, was also religion, a supreme and unique religion, the only one remaining and avowable. The artist, imitating the methods of nature and constructing a "second

nature," restored mankind to the cosmic setting gradually lost
to it through the disintegration of belief. In place of these
numerous, over-simple faiths, now dead or dying, art offered a
new religion which itself demanded saints and martyrs. "*Il
faudrait des christs de l'Art*," as Flaubert said: "Art needs its
Christs." He strove to become one. We are a long way now
from Sade.

Flaubert among his Peers

It was in the years 1857-1864 that Flaubert made his official
entry into literary society, and through that came to rub
shoulders with the great. Though Bouilhet remained dearest to
him, he widened the circle of his friendship to include Feydeau
and Duplan, whom he also made his confidants. For years he
was the faithful, attentive, helpful correspondent of Mlle
Leroyer de Chantepie and of Amélie Bosquet, who wrote to
him after the publication of *Madame Bovary*. He made important
revelations to them both about his work and about himself.

In Paris, where he now spent the winter, Flaubert saw
Sainte-Beuve, the most celebrated critic of the time, and, in
spite of certain limitations, the most important; Théophile
Gautier, a poet and writer he had long admired; Baudelaire;
and the young Goncourt brothers. They used to meet either at
the offices of *L'Artiste*, for which Gautier wrote, or at the house
of Madame Sabatier, "*la présidente*", in the Goncourts' apartment, or in Flaubert's study in the Boulevard du Temple. Later
came the "*dîners Magny*" held at the restaurant of that name,
and attended also by George Sand and Turgenev. Everywhere
Flaubert created an impression with his height, his vehemence,
the extravagant and paradoxical things he did and said, and
his love of art. He used to declaim speeches from great authors
and demonstrate passages of particular beauty. "He is very
tall," wrote the Goncourts, "broad-shouldered, with fine big
prominent eyes under slightly puffy lids, full cheeks, a shaggy
drooping moustache, and a mottled complection with patches
of red." Then they describe him in action. "When he gets
excited his eyes start out of his head and he is all aglow, his

arms outflung like Antaeus, his chest and throat emitting fragments of the *Dialogue de Scylla et d'Eucrate*,* a din which he flings in our faces like the roar of a lion." When pressed, he would use his extraordinary gifts as an actor to imitate "the idiot of the salons":

> He borrows a coat from Gautier and turns up the collar. I don't know what he does with his hair, his shape, his face, but there he is suddenly transformed into a terrific caricature of stupidity. Gautier, seized with emulation, takes off his frock-coat, and, dripping with perspiration, his big behind bouncing nearly down to his knees, does the dance of the creditor, and the evening winds up with gypsy songs, wild airs for which the strident note is marvelously struck by Prince Radziwill.

Among his friends, then, Flaubert was far from indulging the melancholy side of his nature. These outbursts were a recreation for him. "I am not naturally merry," he wrote to Feydeau. "As low, farcical, or obscene as you like, but gloomy nonetheless. In a nutshell, life gives me a good pain in the ass (*la vie m'emmerde cordialement*)." Taine, who also knew him, says "he is a primitive, a dreamer, and a '*sauvage*,' "† and he was struck by the strange nature of Flaubert's imagination.

> His mind is a photograph. He can imagine the smallest crack in the parquet as clearly as the dimensions of the room. . . . If he should see an advertisement for a concert in the street, it will so stick in his head that when he comes home it will prevent him from doing anything else for the rest of the day. . . . Above everything he has a feeling for appearances, for nature: "It does not rest me—it consumes me." He is absorbed by it . . . He has wearied his mind, squeezed it like a lemon so that he has become as nervous as a woman, he who is so strong and sinewy. . . . What is striking is the curious state of his imagination—powerful, strained, morbid.

---

*The Goncourts should have written: *Dialogue de Sylla et d'Eucrate*—the title of a short dialogue by Montesquieu (1722), in which Sulla defends himself after having surrendered the dictatorship.—Tr.

†"*Sauvage*"—literally "wild" or "untamed," but said of people who are shy, retiring, or unsociable. Compare Jane Austen, on herself, letter of May 24 1813: "I should like to see Miss Burdett very well, but that I am rather frightened by hearing that she wishes to be introduced to *me*. If I *am* a wild Beast, I cannot help it. It is not my own fault."—Tr.

Women

"LIKING, AND ABLE, TO PLEASE," wrote Du Camp, "he had a certain coquetry with women, who were interested by his strangeness." He showed this coquetry—and also, no doubt, for he was shy by nature, a good deal of *gaucherie*—in the salon of *la présidente*, though the atmosphere there was far from strait-laced. Madame Sabatier ("Apollonie") received writers and artists, bolder, it is true, in word than in deed. Flaubert played the role of a discreet admirer, no more. He experienced neither the imaginary happiness nor the torments which Apollonie inspired in Baudelaire.

In fact, Flaubert was more attracted by women less sedately placed in society—*demi-mondaines*, actresses, the somewhat volatile companions of artists. He sought only pleasure from Esther Guimont, now getting on in years, and from young Mlle Lagier, whose ears and cheeks both had long forgotten how to blush. He seems, however, to have had a real passion for the beautiful Jeanne de Tourbey, acknowledged protégée of the director of the Porte Saint-Martin Theater, and later Mme de Loynes. In unpublished letters which M. Jacques Suffel has been able to consult,* Flaubert calls her his "angel," and says he thinks of her till he howls and nearly dies. It is clear from his description that she allowed him into her dressing-room; it is less certain that she admitted him to her bedroom. Albert Thibaudet supposes that he was disappointed of this favor, and that he characteristically made up for his discomfiture and lack of boldness by giving Hamilcar's daughter the "delicate, luminous, oriental and mystical face" of Jeanne de Tourbey.

It was after the publication of *Salammbô* that Princess Mathilde, niece of Napoleon I and cousin of Napoleon III, asked to be introduced to him and gradually admitted him into her circle. Much later, after the royal family had been over-taken by misfortune, a kind of *amitié amoureuse* grew up between them. But Flaubert never went beyond the bounds of respect,

---

*Flaubert (Editions universitaires, Paris 1958).

even though, very late in the day, he did show a glimpse of his true feelings. For the time being he went to the Tuileries and was made much of by great ladies, who asked him to sketch Salammbô's costume for a forthcoming ball. "It was then," wrote Du Camp, "that he went in for being elegant and well-dressed. We used to tell him he was like an elderly Almanzor, and he used to joke about it with us." But Du Camp need not have bothered to bring Flaubert back to earth. He was sufficiently awkward and out of place in this comedy of appearances.

Honors

HE FELT EVEN MORE ill at ease at Compiègne, though it was with some satisfaction that he obeyed the Emperor's summons to Court: it was from Compiègne that the order to prosecute *Madame Bovary* had been issued. But finally he could not contain himself.

"One evening," wrote Du Camp, "in the private circle of the Empress, someone spoke slightingly of Victor Hugo. I don't know whether the words were meant sincerely, or if they were merely an attempt at flattery. But Gustave Flaubert spoke up, and in no uncertain terms: 'Just a minute! You're talking about someone who's the master of us all, and his name should only be pronounced hat in hand.' The other insisted: 'But you must agree, Monsieur, that the man who wrote *Les Châtiments* . . .' Flaubert, with terrible rolling eyes, cried: '*Les Châtiments!* There are some magnificent lines there! I'll recite them if you like!' It was thought better not to carry the experiment through: the discussion was interrupted, and one of those present made haste to turn the conversation."

The anecdote is typical, and shows one of Flaubert's most likeable traits. He was not one of those whose honors go to their heads and make them trample underfoot their artistic ideals and independence.

10

SALAMMBÔ

S*alammbô* was always the most disputed of Flaubert's works, and even today there are conflicting opinions about it. As soon as it was published it provoked surprise and controversy, and it is still criticized for its picturesque barbarity, violent colors, apparent gratuitousness, and unrelentingly high-flown style. Some people are astonished if anyone claims to recognize in it the author of *Madame Bovary* and *L'Education sentimentale*—just as if Flaubert's greatness did not reside in this renewal, in each of his works, of inspiration and form.

Although *Salammbô* conjures up, with enormous luxury of detail, a lost civilization, it is not a "historical novel." Flaubert took certain major liberties with the facts; he arranged and modified the characters concerned, inventing some entirely and changing the identity of others. He did not use the events he described to draw a moral or depict a "special type", as Chateaubriand had done with Cymodocée and Velléda (*Les Martyrs*, 1809). Nor did he aim, as Michelet or Augustin Thierry had done, at "historical reconstruction."

He had not tried to write a psychological novel, either. His characters are broadly drawn, with simple motivations that preclude dramatic dilemmas, and although Salammbô is an incarnation of the eternal feminine she does not occupy a predominant place in the book. She does not have the solidity of Emma Bovary or even of Mme Arnoux. Her individual adventures merge into a general story and are largely subordinate to it. The psychology of each character depends on the part he or she plays in the plot, even on his or her race or color. Such rivalries or conflicts as there are arise principally out of political or social motivations.

Théophile Gautier was the first to find the most appropriate

description for the book: he said it was an "epic." At first it had
a success as a curiosity, and it has always been a favorite with
the general public (there have been as many editions of
Salammbô as of *Madame Bovary*). But it was not very long before it
fell into disrepute with those who claimed to be more dis-
criminating: they found it too showy, too full of frippery and
gratuitous horrors, too lavish of decorative effects. Only now
can one see more clearly the nature and importance of what
Flaubert was trying to do, and the strange success he achieved in
doing it. The time for the rehabilitation of *Salammbô* has only
just come.

"It Seems to Me I've Always Existed"

WE HAVE SEEN THE CIRCUMSTANCES in which Flaubert began
writing it in May 1857. He was weary of the "bourgeois" world
in which *Madame Bovary* had forced him to live for four-and-a-
half years. The revenge he hoped to take with *La Tentation* had
hung fire. So he meant to translate into fact the "Oriental tale"
of which he had dreamed so long. After his minute and an-
atomical description of French provincial manners in the
nineteenth century, he wanted to give his imagination elbow-
room, and to live in other places, at other times, among other
men.

Flaubert, like many of his contemporaries, had felt *le frisson
historique*, "the thrill of history." He was readier than any of
them to escape in time and space from the limits of his ego and
of his age. As he wrote later to George Sand:

> *Il me semble que j'ai toujours existé, et je possède des souvenirs qui
> remontent aux pharaons. Je me vois à différents âges de l'histoire, très
> nettement, exerçant des métiers différents et dans des fortunes
> multiples . . . J'ai été batelier sur le Nil,* leno *à Rome du temps des
> guerres puniques, puis rhéteur grec dans Suburre où j'étais dévoré des
> punaises. Je suis mort pendant la Croisade, pour avoir mangé trop de
> raisins sur la côte de Syrie. J'ai été pirate et moine, saltimbanque et
> cocher. Peut-être empereur d'Orient.* (It seems to me I've always
> existed, and I have memories going back to the Pharaohs.
> I can see myself quite clearly at different ages in history,

exercizing different professions, and with many varying
fortunes . . . I have been a boatman, a *leno* in Rome at the
time of the Punic wars, then a Greek rhetor in Suburrum
eaten alive by bugs. I died in the Crusades from having eaten
too many grapes on the coast of Syria. I've been pirate and
monk, mountebank and coachman. Perhaps an eastern
emperor . . .

His ability to "make himself feel things" extended to bygone
ages, continents he had never visited, conditions as different as
they possibly could be from those he had chosen for himself.
Even when he was still at school he had lived in communion
with the Greeks and Romans, the men of the Middle Ages and
the Renaissance. The people he admired were always strange or
striking, always somehow exorbitant: Nero, Heliogabalus,
Savonarola, Lorenzo de' Medici.

Why Carthage?

THE "ORIENTAL TALE" was to have been set in the times of
the Pharaohs, but he renounced Egypt for Carthage. Why
Carthage? Practically nothing was known of the ancient
Phoenician colony which became the rival of Rome; it had
disappeared almost without trace. But as it had been part of
the Mediterranean East where he had spent two years storing
up sights and scenes, he could laugh at archaeology and rely
instead on the vast reservoir of memory and the free flight of
his imagination. At liberty to organize his subject as he pleased
within the broad framework of historical reference, he might
be able to create a work of art which, even more than *Madame
Bovary*, "would hold together by the sheer inner force of style."
In the course of the writing other purposes also came to him,
but he molded and subordinated all of them to his main object.

It was probably Michelet and his history of Rome which
were at the root of the enterprise. Flaubert had read and made
notes on the book as a schoolboy; it had haunted his dreams.
He had been thrilled by its vivid account of the "inexpiable
war," in which, after the defeat off Sicily which ended the First
Punic War, the Mercenaries attacked exhausted Carthage in

order to exact payment for their services. It was a savage and cruel war in which neither side gave quarter, and it ended in the massacre of the Mercenaries.

Michelet follows Polybius's account closely. Polybius witnessed the revolt, and puts forward a psychological portrait of the Carthaginians—"a harsh and dreary people, sensual and avaricious, rash but without heroism," with an "atrocious religion teeming with frightful practices." The last sentence of his account was especially evocative to the young Flaubert: "Even in the bloodthirsty world of Alexander's successors, even in that age of iron, everyone, Greek or Barbarian, was horrified by the war of the Mercenaries."

Polybius's conclusion was no doubt in Flaubert's mind when, before starting on *Salammbô*, he consulted his friends Gautier and Feydeau: the first had recently published his *Roman de la Momie*, and the other was interested in archaeology. Both of them thought the subject capable of much development in view of the simultaneous vagueness and precision of the historical element. As to the psychological element, that could be worked up by inventing the adventures of Hamilcar's daughter, who according to Polybius was promised by her father to the Numidian chief Naravasus "on condition that he remained faithful to the Carthaginians." How was she to manage to "make herself loved by the god"? This was where Flaubert the poet came in: the story must have a symbolical side while at the same time reflecting accurately what was known of Carthaginian religion. Although Flaubert was not aiming at "historical reconstruction," he still wanted to conjure up the fundamental implications of a civilization which disappeared completely more than two thousand years ago.

Not surprisingly, he started by reading all that had been written about Carthage: for him this was more than a way of mastering the subject—it was to live with and in it. "For a book to exude truth," he wrote to Feydeau, "you have to be crammed up to the ears with your subject." In five months he "ingurgitated" more than a hundred books, ancient and modern: first Polybius; then the *Periplus* of Hanno, the only Carthaginian text to have come down to us; then all the writers who have ever made reference to Carthage, in general or in particular— Appian, Diodorus of Sicily, Cornelius Nepos, Pliny, Athenaeus, Plutarch, Xenophon, Justus Lipsius, Strabo, Silius Italicus, Livy, and even Saint Augustine. To fill out his knowledge of the Semitic peoples he also consulted the eighteen volumes of the Cahen Bible. Further details of all kinds he culled from a couple of dozen books by modern historians, geographers, archaeologists and ethnologists.

He made a series of plans, scenarios, and sketches for the lay-out of the story. The title changed from *Carthage* to *Les Mercenaires* to *Salammbô*. The name of the heroine herself was Pyra, Pyrrha, Hanna, Sallammbô, and Sallambô, before taking on its final form. On September 1 he began to write the first chapter. It is a Balzacian description of the city, the various districts and alleys, the surrounding country, the sea which borders it on three sides. He wanted to be "at once rapid and rich," but could not bring it off. He was convinced he was on the wrong track, and fell ill. Then he decided to go and seek inspiration on the spot.

Understanding One's Characters

WHEN HE RETURNED from Tunis on June 12 1858, after two months' exploration, he wrote to Feydeau: "I must tell you *Carthage* has to be completely done over, or rather done. I'm scrapping everything: it was absurd, impossible, false. I think I shall hit the right note. I begin to understand my characters and to be interested in them." His main difficulty was to depict his protagonists so as to prevent them from being "*mannequins*," or dummies, to differentiate them and give them a general psychology without attributing to them anachronistic feelings. They had to be brought close to the reader in order to arouse his interest, but the author had to respect their own truth, which resided in many factors which were unknown or merely surmised. But now he knew how to set about it, just as, after having gone to gaze at the sites, the landscapes, the sea and the desert at various hours of the day and night, he now had the atmosphere and setting at his command. He knew too that the tone must be one of relentless "ferocity."

Then, just as with *Madame Bovary* but this time for even longer, there began the months and years of toil, and the daily plunge into "the throes of style." Shut up at Croisset, "out of the light of day," Flaubert led a life which he himself described as "*farouche, extravagante*." He knew precisely what he wanted to do, but the difficulties of execution sometimes seemed insurmountable, and the "right note" impossible to find. He was walking a tight-rope between the real, which he could only imagine, and "the makeshift of being 'pohetic' "— *i.e.* of falling "into all the familiar old tricks, from *Télémaque* to *Les Martyrs*." Writing to the Goncourts, he said:

> *Pour être vrai il faudrait être obscur, parler charabia et bourrer le livre de notes; et si l'on s'en tient au ton littéraire et françoys, on devient banal.* (To be accepted as true one would have to be obscure, talk gibberish, and plaster the book with foot-notes; if you stick to being literary and really French, you're banal.)

He was afraid of repetitiveness, of too much similarity between situations, and the slowness of the action; the reader might find the soldiers' excesses wearisome, and the heroine "deadly boring." "I have to find a middle course between the inflated and the real." In short, "It may be very fine, but it may also be very foolish."

In May, when he had just finished writing the chapter on "The Aqueduct," he considered the book sufficiently far advanced to read what he had done so far to his friends, and to give them a summary of what remained to be done. The Goncourts at least were not favorably impressed. "*Salammbô* is not up to what I expected of Flaubert. He sees the East, the East of antiquity, in terms of the bric-à-brac of Algiers." After a dutiful word of praise for the author's "effort" and "endless patience," the *Journal* unleashes a cruel Parthian shot: "Mathô is really no more than an operatic tenor in a barbaric poem." There is no mention of Hamilcar's daughter, the priestess of Tanit who offers herself to the leader of the Mercenaries in a scene reminiscent of Judith and Holofernes. The authors of *Les Maîtresses de Louis XV* had a lighter way of "bringing history to life."

The last chapters, the most prodigal of horrors, were written comparatively fast—in a year. Flaubert, carried along by a fury which made him "wade through entrails," and a vision Surrealist before its time, seemed to have reached the utmost heights of the horrible in the "roasting of the brats," when the gigantic articulated figure of Moloch crams living infants one by one into his white-hot maw of brass, where to the sound of savage music they turn at once to smoke. But a little further on we come to the cannibalism in the defile, and the last chapter of all, with the interminable torture of Mâtho and the sudden death of Salammbô, seems straight out of a nightmare.

A Cold-blooded Hallucination

IT IS "very fine" or "very foolish" according to whether or not one yields to the magic of the writing, whether or not one enters into the vision of the writer. It was unlike anything Flaubert's contemporaries were in the habit of reading, and to all appearances a thousand miles away from *Madame Bovary*. The meticulous observer of reality had transported his readers into the midst of a hallucination described in cold blood. When the manuscript was finished, it was as if he was emerging from a dream. He wrote to his niece: "My heart bounds at the sight of my writing." He was frightened by what had issued from his pen, and anxious to see the new face of his other self as it would be revealed to him by the critics and the public. In spring 1862, when he was due to deliver the book, he held it back for a further revision, claiming it would be better to delay printing because *Les Misérables* was about to be published: how could the public be expected to be interested in Hugo and himself at the same time? Then, with good reason, he declined to have anything more to do with the publisher of *Madame Bovary;* got the brothers Duplan to look for someone else; and finally came back to Michel Lévy. He rather surprised everyone

by the firmness of his financial conditions: 30,000 francs down
and no argument. A stranger condition was that the publisher
had to undertake to publish without reading the manuscript:
"He must buy my name and nothing else."

After months of bargaining in which Ernest Duplan acted as
go-between, the contract was at last about to be signed, with
more modest financial arrangements, when the unlucky
"fils d'Israël" (Lévy) took it into his head to bring out, in
addition to the ordinary one, an edition with illustrations.
Then Flaubert saw red, and said something which threw light
on his whole approach to the book: "A lot of use it was going
to all that trouble to leave everything undefined, just for a
money-grubber to come along and destroy my whole dream in
his idiotic hurry." In a letter to Sainte-Beuve in which he
replies to some cantankerous objections, he makes himself
plainer still: "I wanted to fix a mirage by applying to antiquity
the methods of the modern novel." Dream, mirage, vision—
that is how *Salammbô* has to be approached.

Critical Reception

SAINTE-BEUVE, by the mere amount of space he gave to it in
his three articles in *Le Constitutionnel*, emphasized the importance
of Flaubert's latest book. But he did not like it, and pronounced
it a failure, for reasons which relate chiefly to his own pre-
judices, his own ideas as to what a "historical novel" should be
and what the author of *Madame Bovary* ought to have written.

He began by declaring that "one cannot reconstruct the
civilization of antiquity" and restore it to warmth and life.
Flaubert certainly tried, he even tried too hard, poring over the
details of his book instead of regarding it "as a whole." (This
is a new version of Barbey d'Aurevilly's criticism of *Madame
Bovary*, that the author tended to get swamped in "trivialities.")
Sainte-Beuve's objection hits at the subject itself: he did not
see the point of conjuring up a civilization which had disappeared so completely that it was only of interest through its
connection with Rome. If one was going to describe the rivalry

between the two empires and the two different kinds of people, Rome should have been given pride of place. Sainte-Beuve thought it strange that someone should want to bring to life again a civilization which instead of being refined and artistic was mercantile, military, and bloody, and that through what was only a minor episode in its history. Carthage no longer meant anything to anyone.

He found the psychology of the characters arbitrary, crude, and overdone. Salammbô was monotonous and lifeless. Her behavior was illogical, like that of the rest of the Carthaginians. What was their reason for "massacring" the Mercenaries? He suspected Flaubert of enjoying describing horrors and of having "a touch of sadistic imagination." His display of learning called for a glossary. As for the general tone of the work, it was in keeping with the style—high-flown, over-emphatic, would-be classical, "strewn with pebbles of every color and precious stones." In short, while there was something "grandiose" about it, Flaubert's venture had failed. However, "the execution showed power," so things were not as bad as they might be; Flaubert was thus dismissed with a few compliments as consolation. Never had Sainte-Beuve tried so hard to conceal his hostility, and never had it emerged so clearly. But at least he was fair enough to append the author's telling reply to his *Causeries du lundi*.

In Guillaume Frœhner Flaubert had to deal with an adversary less well equipped for the struggle and yet more dangerous. He was a native of Baden, an archaeologist, an expert, who had been appointed by Napoleon III to be director of the Museum of Antiquities. In an article commissioned by the *Revue contemporaine* he attacked Flaubert's documentation, pointing out mistakes and inadequacies and inventions, and, by means of labored pleasantries, crushing the novelist with the weight of his own scientific superiority. Flaubert was sure of himself and accepted the challenge. He declared that he "had no pretentions to archaeology," but proceeded to catch the expert out on his own ground. Frœhner was up in arms, but Flaubert's sarcasm annihilated him and won over those who enjoyed a laugh.

But, in general, the critics went along with Sainte-Beuve. They mocked at what to them was an incomprehensible enterprise; some very mean ones recalled the case against *Madame Bovary*, and went out of their way to furnish ammunition for a renewed onslaught by the public prosecutor. The chapter called "In the Tent" was accused not only of "bad taste" but also of "eroticism." "Obscenities" were discovered in the "Serpent" scene. One particularly knowing critic said that if Salammbô died from having touched the mantle of Tanit, "after having read the book one knows how to take the hint."

Flaubert, however, was unmoved by the carpings of journalists. He found ample compensation in the reactions of his equals. Once again Baudelaire was his champion. "*Ce que Flaubert a fait, lui seul pouvait le faire,*" he wrote in a letter to Poulet-Malassis, "What Flaubert has done only he could do. . . ." In different words, Hugo, Michelet, Berlioz, Fromentin, Manet, Leconte de Lisle, and George Sand all expressed the same admiration. Théophile Gautier distinguished himself by a very pertinent article not motivated by friendship alone. He showed that "Flaubert, in writing *Salammbô*, has not gone beyond his own nature"; ιo read such a work was "one of the most violent intellectual sensations one can experience." Although this was not the unanimous opinion of the Court and the Town, at least the Empress liked the book so much she read on until far into the night; her husband was greatly intrigued by all its engines of war. For a ball in the Tuileries, Madame Rimsky-Korsakov decked herself in the transparent veils of Hamilcar's daughter. Galvanized by such lofty examples, everyone who was anyone in Paris became enthusiastic over the young Carthaginian and her brawny lover. Show business did not let the occasion slip: there were revue sketches and parodies on the topic. As Sainte-Beuve elegantly put it, "Flaubert comes out of it a bigger noise than ever."

A Hundred Years On

A CENTURY AFTER its publication, *Salammbô* is still young enough to find favor with the public, but the reasons for which most critics admire it today are somewhat different from those put forward by its original admirers.

We are less impressed than they were by the *artisteries* or "arty bits" which Flaubert deliberately flourished throughout. We tend to be put off rather than attracted by this aspect of the book: the famous "visions of art," so dear to the age in which it was written, are what have dated most in *Salammbô*. It does not bother us if some of the details about Carthaginian customs have been found to be inaccurate; we are only moderately glad that archaeologists have confirmed the soundness of Flaubert's general approach. What interests us is the fresh *tour de force* performed by the author of *Madame Bovary*, and his use of what he calls "the methods of the modern novel" to "fix a mirage."

We know what these "methods" were, according to Flaubert. They aimed at depicting in depth 19th-century man and his world, by means of observation, documentation, rigorous ordering of facts (facts being taken to include ideas, feelings, and passions), and an exact correspondence between language and its subject. These methods were applied to a reality of which art, that "second nature," offered a meaningful equivalent. Through the particular they hoped to attain a general truth, and even some incontrovertible certainties.

On the face of it, this looks a very unlikely apparatus for a writer who decided to turn his back on his own age in order to give form to his dreams, rebellions, and longings, and who took refuge in Carthage as others might in a Trappist monastery. The reality he was addressing himself to, his knowledge of which was gathered from books which themselves often differed from one another, did not permit of tangible certainty. The fact that the places, landscapes, and skies concerned are all still there is not enough to give the reader the thousand and one links he needs with the story he is told and the sights and peoples displayed before him. Though Flaubert did not include a single feature of manners or behavior for which he could not give the source, and though all the characters are consistent both in themselves and with their setting, only Flaubert himself actually knows that the reality he is trying to depict exists. This reality is something quite other than assemblage of information or learning; and he is the only one who knows it because he created it and is inhabited by it. He was opposed to "historical reconstruction," and he himself reconstructs nothing: he creates and brings to life the thing of which he speaks. With even more reason than of Madame Bovary, he might have said, "*Salammbô, c'est moi.*"

He had to make people believe in the existence of what he described as if it were before his eyes, to moor his vision to points of reference recognizable to everyone, so that it would seem that the objects, events and men he depicted could not have been otherwise. Unless it was to remain merely subjective and poetic, the truth of the novelist had to approach and even merge with a truth that might be called scientific.

The First Objective

THAT WAS the first objective, and Flaubert may be said to have achieved it. He had "made himself feel things" so well in the case of Carthage and the war of the Mercenaries, he had transported himself so completely into another form of human life, with its customs, beliefs and ways, that the recent discoveries of science have illustrated his intuitions. Steles have been found bearing the sign of Tanit which he described, and the "tophet" containing the skeletons of children sacrificed to Moloch. Flaubert would not have been surprised by this. Had he not said that the artist could not be mistaken, once he had attained a certain familiarity with the secrets of nature, the organization of the universe, and the mechanisms of the mind? "Induction is as good as deduction. . . . All that is invented is true." It was Sainte-Beuve and the Goncourts who were mistaken in impugning the truth of Flaubert's presentation of the East of antiquity, with its glaring colors like "Algerian bric-à-brac," and the pitch blackness of white marble seen in the violent rays of the sun. Flaubert's vision rested on an observation and recollection of sites and landscapes which had

given him an intimate knowledge of the reality he described—
that society steeped in blood and perfume on the mysterious
soil of Africa. Except that, while he was still obeying the laws
of the greatest verisimilitude, he was now *creating* his reality:
the author of *Salammbô* was the same as that of *Madame Bovary*.
His aesthetic theories had not varied: he still aimed at impersonality, objectivity, and the attainment of a general truth
through the accumulation of particularized detail.

How Does One "Fix a Mirage"?

THE SECOND TASK he set himself was attaining objectivity on the
basis of a "dream" or "mirage," which he wanted to "fix,"
as if this was not at all impossible and there was no question of
the realities involved being contradictory. *Salammbô* was to have
both the precision of a diagram and the evanescence of a dream.

He was helped in this by going right back in time, and to a
dead civilization as strange in itself as in its passing. But that in
itself was not enough for him. "*Je veux faire quelque chose de
pourpre*," he wrote to the Goncourts: "I want to do something
purple . . ." Just as in *Madame Bovary* he sought to create the
sensation of "certain mildews of the soul," so here too he aimed
at creating a general atmosphere, in subordination to which the
details would be chosen, placed, organized, and if necessary
invented. The reader had to be drawn into a vortex of blood,
sun, gold, rubies, gorgeous stuffs. Let there be crimson con-
flagrations and scarlet rain!

Flaubert succeeded in "fixing" his mirage by his way of
treating facts, situations, characters, and even the city of
Carthage itself, down to its separate days and nights, which
every time they are dealt with seem to engross his whole
attention and have all the lights concentrated on them. All these
elements he treated as components which echoed and balanced
one another, creating a dual sensation of vividness and of
dream. Precision is only a decoy when, as in the Mercenaries'
feast, the battle of the Macar, the siege of Carthage, or the
death-agony of the Barbarians in the defile, the reader gets lost

in the composition of the armies, the mixture of races, the engines of war, the sequence of what is taking place, and sometimes the topography. The wealth of precise detail is designed to have exactly this effect, just as are the hundreds of strange names strewn throughout the book: they are there for their color and evocativeness, to act as stepping-stones to dream. The city of Carthage, so often described, grows larger or smaller as required, sometimes swarming with alleys, sometimes reduced to a few palaces on an Acropolis which itself rises at varying heights into the sky. This exact reality is in fact a shifting one, taking on different aspects at the author's will. It is a city of dream, a construction of clouds. The same is true too of the most humble objects. "Show me the fellow who can draw a Carthaginian chair or Salammbô's robe," exclaimed Flaubert, who admitted having used all his art "to leave everything indefinite." The vagueness he meant was the vagueness into which the forms of a dream dissolve, the vagueness which enables dream to take flight. As for "purple," that is everywhere, even in Mâtho's tent: "Moloch, you burn me . . ."

Human Disdain

ANOTHER OBJECTIVE was that of trying to ally the gratuitousness of the work of art with intellectual, emotional, and philosophical preoccupations. As for the gratuitousness, there was no doubt Flaubert intended that: "The flag of my Doctrine will be borne flagrantly this time, I can tell you that! For the book proves nothing, says nothing; it is neither historical, satirical nor humorous." But Flaubert also wanted to put into *Salammbô* his love for the Orient of antiquity and the hatred for his own age which had soon grown into a disgust for the whole of humanity.

> *C'est la une Thébaide ou le dégoût de la vie moderne m'a poussé . . . de ce livre ressort un immense dédain pour l'Humanité.* (It is a wilderness I've been thrust into by disgust for modern life. . . . The book emanates an immense disdain for the human race.)

But how could a book that wasn't trying to prove anything take on the significance which Flaubert meant it to have? It did so strictly through the methods of art, without a single opinion, judgment, complaint or cry of revolt being uttered. The painting itself speaks to us through the choice of strokes, figures, and colors. It tells us that men are narrow, selfish, cruel, ambitious, and blood-thirsty. All they think about is massacring one another, even if their civilization perishes in the process, as Carthage did. It is the lesson that was taught by Sade. And before the dreadful picture Flaubert's contemporaries drew back in terror. In the twentieth century we have reasons for thinking he did not paint it too black.

What Is Carthage to Us?

So MANY OBJECTIVES aimed at and achieved culminated in a supreme victory: the victory which, thanks to words, Flaubert won over those other words which for every writer form, up to his advent, the great discourse, unique and ever repeated, of literature. "Everything is a matter of style," because "style is the flesh and blood of thought," the narrow personal channel through which it must pass and from which it derives its form. The critics of 1860 accused Flaubert of having "brought nothingness to life." But is this not the secret ambition of every great writer? Is it not this which gives Flaubert's venture the element of the "grandiose" which Sainte-Beuve reluctantly recognized? In the end, what do we care about Carthage?— the poem exists, which by the evocative power of words and the "marvelous chemistry" of its muscular and racy style, at once subtle and solid in its strength, translates both a boyhood dream and the dream of a fully-fledged master, taking revenge by his mastery alone on "the modern world." It is a dream we have all had at some time of our life—of another world, a different humanity, which may for all we care be even more intolerable and ferocious than our own, than our own contemporaries, our own here and now.

Salammbô may be regarded at the same time as the estuary in which the great drive of Romanticism found its outlet, and the source of many other streams, including Mallarmé's *Hérodiade*, Symbolism, and Valéry's *La Jeune Parque*. Flaubert's Salammbô, standing there on the threshold of the temple in her priestess's robes and invested with the secrets of the god, remains a witness. No doubt it was inevitable she should be struck down, letting fall the keys of the sanctuary. And as she fell a world died, a dream faded, and Flaubert returned to his *ennui*.

Back to the Desk

THESE YEARS had been full of joys and sorrows, success and labor, long periods of depression and a few bursts of pride, though the latter were always tempered by the same fundamental doubt Flaubert always seemed to entertain deliberately about whatever work he was engaged on and, more seriously, about himself. But there were also two other events which had profound repercussions on his private life. In January 1862 he learned that Elisa was in a mental home. In April 1864 his niece Caroline, to whom he had transferred his affection for his beloved sister, married Ernest Commanville, a timber merchant. Flaubert resigned himself. He had expected the marriage, which was to bring down upon him a flood of disasters. The first piece of news was probably one more reason for "plunging desperately into Art." On September 1 1864 he began *L'Education sentimentale*.

11

SENTIMENTAL EDUCATION

SOME BOOKS AROUSE admiration and respect. Others one merely likes and keeps reading over again, building up a sort of secret relationship with them, though they are not necessarily masterpieces. Some excite an initial enthusiasm, but seem strangely faded ten or fifteen years later. It is only rarely that one likes and is impressed by a book to begin with, and then with every reading finds it more and more rich and moving and profound. *L'Education sentimentale* is like that—one of the great novels of its age, and one whose youth never fades.

The beauty here is less systematic than that of *Madame Bovary* with its purity of line; less stiff and showy than that of *Salammbô*. Instead of leaping to the eye, the beauty of *L'Education sentimentale* hides behind what is said or, more often, suggested; it has to be found out.

Flaubert the painter is still there, laying on touch after touch to create a general color. Here it is the greyness of life in all its shades: blue for the voyage up the Seine aboard the *Ville-de-Montereau;* red for the revolution of 1848; ashen for the final scenes. Yet the neutral tone into which both private lives and great public events all fade never calls attention to itself. What one does perceive is a kind of music, already familiar to those who have read *Mémoires d'un Fou, Novembre,* and the first *Education.* It forms part of a great symphony in a minor key, crossing the threshold of skin and nerve to penetrate right to the marrow of our bones. It is more heartrending than the plaints of earlier days, because the cry of despair is now serene.

A Novel of Failure

FLAUBERT USED TO TALK of the "*grotesque triste* (dreary grotesqueness)" of life, as if to exorcize and avenge himself on it rather than succumb to it. But now he speaks of the futility and hopelessness of any attempt to escape: every life is a failure in the long run for everyone in turn, the world rushes only downhill. There is no happiness except in the past, walled up in the memory and impossible to live over again. And a good thing too. "We'd have loved each other so well," say a couple who have never been able to belong to one another, and that could be the summing-up. But Flaubert insisted on making it fiercer still, and what survives of the ruined lives of Frédéric and his false friend Deslauriers, that "best thing" they have in common, is their farcical visit to the establishment of "La Turque."

Like the first *Education*, like *Madame Bovary*, like *Salammbô*, this is a novel of failure. The history of Frédéric Moreau belies both its title and its sub-title, *Histoire d'un jeune homme*. When his "education" is over, the "young man" from Nogent is neither stronger nor wiser nor more hardened than he was before, and when he leaves Paris he is thirty. He uses the next fifteen years to so little purpose they can be dealt wi h in ten lines. It is as if Frédéric were only waiting for the final confrontation with the great unfulfilled love of his youth to realize fully his own failure. Then, going over old times with Deslauriers, he accepts it. Once he was full of ambition and longed for fame, wealth, and love, but he was reduced to the common level by life, circumstance, and his own weakness. Now, in the "idleness of his mind and inertia of his heart," all that remains is for him to live and die a *petit-bourgeois*, existing on unearned income. This is how great designs and ranging thoughts may end. At one time Flaubert thought of calling the book *Les Fruits secs* (literally dried or withered fruit, a figurative equivalent of "duds," "failures").

The Son of Madame Bovary

BUT, IT HAS LONG been objected, Frédéric Moreau never really had any great design, was never really borne along by a splendid ideal. What fate had he then a right to, this "mediocrity" whom even Flaubert himself describes as a "man with every weakness"? He only wants what young bourgeois usually expect and consider their due, without their having to make any effort or show any perseverance. Frédéric left things to circumstance, and the fact that circumstance was unfavorable was enough to make him give up.

Why then does he win our sympathy? Why have so many young men recognized themselves in him? In the first place, he is not so mediocre as all that, either in his desires or in his intentions. He is not out for money—he has, or will have, sufficient—or honors, or for the power attached to high office and such careers, political and other, as dictate public opinion. It is as if as soon as he entered on life he saw the emptiness of what most men strive for. All he wants is to be recognized for what he is, to emerge from the anonymity of the crowd, and to live for himself, freely and independently. It is for this reason he is drawn by the glitter of Paris, rather than in order to read law and become a judge or a barrister. As he dreams of his future in his room at Nogent, or on the boat going back there, or in the country with Deslauriers, he never sees himself as exercising any profession, but following some occupation that lies outside common or garden society. He "thought of an outline for a play, subjects for paintings, future passions"—"he aspired to be one day the Walter Scott of France"—"above all else he valued passion; Werther, René, Franck, Lara, Lélia and others less distinguished aroused almost equal enthusiasm in him." He feels himself to be, and wants to be, an artist, though whether a musician, a writer, or a painter he does not know—he is attracted by every art in turn, sometimes several simultaneously. But the main thing for him is to experience a *grande passion*. "Love," he tells Deslauriers, "is the food, the atmosphere of genius. Unusual emotions produce sublime works . . ." Brought up on Byron, Chateaubriand, Victor Hugo and George Sand, he moves naturally among the great clichés of Romanticism. If he is the son of Madame Bovary, he is a son who has been educated into a "Parisian"; he is a cut or two above his mother.

"The Men of My Generation"

FROM THE VERY FIRST PAGES of the book we know he will fail all along the line, that he will not realize any of his ambitions, and that he will not have the strength or courage for the "grand passion" he aspires to. The symphony's main theme is stated in the opening bars, where the whole story is, as it were, already relegated to the past. "*J'aurais fait quelque chose avec une femme qui m'eût aimé* (I would have achieved something with a woman who loved me)." Deslauriers, who sees the funny side of this precocious world-weariness, laughs, and Frédéric recovers and adopts the only tense suitable for one of his age: the future. But he still comes to the same negative conclusions.

> *Quant à chercher celle qu'il me faudrait, j'y renonce! D'ailleurs, si jamais je la trouve, elle me repoussera. Je suis de la race des déshérités, et je m'éteindrai avec un trésor qui était de strass ou de diamant, je n'en sais rien.* (As to looking for the right woman, I shall not try! Anyhow, if ever I do find her she'll reject me. I am one of the outcasts of fortune, and when I die I shan't know whether the treasure I clasped was paste or diamonds.)

Once again the past encroaches on the future, and while Frédéric succumbs anew to Romanticism to the extent of affecting superiority to his own fate, at the same time he entrenches himself in renunciation, rejection, skepticism. It is not that he is exceptionally lucid about himself. He is too young; that will come later.

At present it is his dreams which see clearly for him and which already come up against reality. The time for grand passions is over. It is 1840, the age of *le roi bourgeois*, the Citizen King.

The practical-minded Deslauriers brings him rudely back to earth: since he has a black coat and white gloves, he ought to take up with M. and Mme Dambreuse. "Think of it, he's got millions! Set yourself out to please him, and his wife as well. Become her lover!" Frédéric is indignant: that is not the kind of success he is after. His friend tells him to remember Rastignac in *La Comedie humaine*. But that is just what he does not want to be. Nevertheless, he does waver slightly and agree that his "despair is foolish." "Forgetting Mme Arnoux, or including her in the prediction which had been made about the other, he could not help smiling." The novel has only just begun and Frédéric is already compromising mentally. He is not a "mediocrity," but he is impulsive and weak. He literally does not know what he wants. So he leaves it to circumstance, and hopes circumstance will prove favorable.

If he were the novel's only interest one might accuse the author of having made things too easy for himself. But Deslauriers is there as a corrective. He is a strong, ambitious character who means to "arrive" and has no scruples to stand in his way. He later tries to supplant Frédéric with Mme Arnoux, to get into the good graces of the Dambreuses, to influence opinion through a newspaper, and to play a part in politics. He does in fact hold office for a while under the provisional government, and makes a "good match," thereby doing Frédéric out of his last chance. But his is a poor success. He is of such vulgar stuff, so steeped in greed and envy, that he overdoes it every time, and transforms into immediate or ultimate defeat all the possibilities of victory purchased by effort and ever-increasing degradation. His wife "runs away with a singer," and he too will die empty-handed.

Others—Hussonet, Cisy, Martinon—are different from both Frédéric and Deslauriers. They find their own level in society, as blackmailers, climbers, dowry-hunters. As lacking in character as Frédéric, they are also without the scruples and delicacy of mind and feeling which at least keep him from being abject. But abjection is too large a word for these air-balloons, these corks on the water. They are no more than foam on the wave which carries Frédéric along, and which he lets toss him from one situation to another, from Rosanette to Mme Arnoux, and from Mme Arnoux to Mme Dambreuse.

The only ones who see farther than their own interests and have some conviction or ideal belong to the "lower classes": Dussardier, a shop assistant whose magnanimity makes up for the simplicity of his ideas; Sénécal, the "mathematics tutor" who is spoken of as "a future Saint-Just." They are both republicans and socialists, Dussardier out of hatred for injustice and warmth of feeling, Sénécal out of cool rationalism. But alas, Dussardier, who believes in the fine words of Lamartine, fires on one of his class brothers in June 1848, considers himself half responsible for this betrayal, and by way of absolution gets himself killed by a policeman during Louis-Napoleon's *coup d'état*. Fate has arranged things well: in the policeman, Frédéric, "staring open-mouthed, recognized Sénécal." The wheel has come full circle, and if Flaubert's only purpose has been to write, as he said, "the moral history of his generation," these parallel destinies all ending in moral, intellectual, or political bankruptcy would be enough to show us why the Prince-President later became Emperor of the French.

A Vast Miscarriage

BUT *L'Education sentimentale* is something very different from a moral history; its essence is to be found elsewhere. And yet Frédéric's unfulfilled passion for Marie Arnoux, the impossibility of its living and growing though everything shows it is requited; the faint-heartedness on one side and excessive reserve on the other which gave rise to so many "*intermittences*," as Proust called them, so many eclipses, so much compromise, frustration and suffering; this unhealthy blighting of what should have flowered—all this would be less comprehensible if it did not take place against the background of an even vaster miscarriage. The generation of 1820, their ears still ringing with the loud exhortations of Romanticism, were reduced to inaction, confronted with a mean and cramping reality. Unable to live their dreams, they settled for dreaming their lives. Frédéric is the incarnation of this generation, and his behavior is typical, almost symbolic. He does not take part in the "February Days," he is merely "present." He enjoys the barricades, the riots, the sight of the people in arms, as a spectacle; the looting of the Tuileries he finds in bad taste. He is so afraid of being duped he will not believe in any change, and declares people will always be the same. When the provisional government massacres the proletarians in June he is at Fontainebleau with Rosanette. After the *coup d'état* he lets it be understood that that was not what he wanted. Most of his young bourgeois friends had thought and acted the same way.

L'Education sentimentale would not possess the virtually inexhaustible richness it has without this political and social backcloth, this tapestry into which the story of Frédéric and Mme Arnoux is woven, this turmoil of events which reveals people as they are deep down—rich men, business men, republicans, artists, and even women of easy virtue. History confirms the accuracy and perfect objectivity of the picture, but that scarcely matters: Flaubert was not aiming at historical reconstruction. The truth he aimed at and attained was larger, more general, more typical. Dambreuse is our contemporary, and so is the sinister Père Roque, and you may pass Sénécal still in the Paris streets today, with his stubble haircut and his pseudo-priestly or professional air. More than one generation since 1820 has had its Days of February and June; more than one has been made up of disappointed dreamers and thwarted climbers. Many an adolescent, reading the *Education*, has learned to make his own self-examination. The truth as brought up to date by Flaubert is valid for all "lost" or "sacrificed" generations, and for all "angry young men."

The Historian's Contribution

SCHOLARS AND CRITICS have asked themselves the not very fruitful question, to what extent did Flaubert get his inspiration from fact, and how far did he put himself into his book?

As regards public events the answer is easy. Flaubert and Bouilhet went up to Paris as soon as the newspapers reported the first demonstrations in February, and on the 24th they were in the neighborhood of the Madeleine. In June Du Camp was in action on the side of law and order. He was wounded and decorated, and related his adventures to Flaubert. In 1849 they both set out for the Middle East, returning in 1851, On December 2 of that year Flaubert was in Paris during the *coup d'état,* and narrowly escaped being knocked on the head. He saw—and we know how far he had cultivated the faculty of observation—the main events he described; he had experienced the actual atmosphere in which they took place. About the things he had not seen he meticulously informed himself, seeking eye-witness accounts and personal interviews for the smallest details, reading complete files of newspapers, showing himself so conscientious an archivist and historian that Georges Sorel has said there is no better "document" than *L'Education sentimentale* for the period it describes.

"Frédéric, c'est moi"

CURIOSITY BECOMES EVEN KEENER in answering the question whether he might have said, with even more reason than for *Madame Bovary:* "Frédéric, c'est moi." But this is a yet more futile question than the other. It is obvious that in spite of Flaubert's theories about the novelist's impersonality his hero is part of himself, represents a projection of his own desires and ambitions, expresses many of his own thoughts, feelings, and disillusions. He created his hero and makes him live for us by reference to the young man he has known most intimately— himself. But are these links between creator and creature a sufficient explanation? For it is equally obvious that Flaubert is not Frédéric, this weak and head-strong character, this wax which takes the form of every situation, this dreamer who pretends not to know about the mire he sometimes walks through. How can Frédéric be confused with him who sat in the silence of his study at Croisset, laboring painfully to create out of his own entrails this anti-image of himself, the man he might have been but did not become, having taken refuge in art? Remy de Gourmont, writing of Stendhal's Julien Sorel, said: "There can only be uncertainty in the relations between a man's life and his work, between his own behavior and that which he imposes on his characters. If it were otherwise novels would only be a sort of memoir, and this is not so, at least in the case of real novelists, although knowledge of the author may make us see that he could not have conceived his works otherwise than as he did." This exactly states the limits within which the question stands some chance of being meaningful.

Elisa's Contribution

PEOPLE HAVE WONDERED how far, in this story of hopeless passion, Flaubert was externalizing some experience of his own. M. Gérard-Gailly, in *L'unique passion de Flaubert* (1932), showed with admirable subtlety and tact what underlies the love-story which is transposed in *L'Education* and which, with differing features, atmosphere, and dénouement, had already been treated in *Mémoires d'un Fou*, *Novembre*, and the first *Education*. Maria, Marie, Emilie Renaud, and Mme Arnoux are all different incarnations of the same woman—Elisa Schlésinger, whom Flaubert had seen on the beach at Trouville as a boy, and who had inspired in him a passion which, whether open or "walled up in a royal chamber," was to last all his life. Whereas in his youthful works Flaubert either told the story simply or embroidered freely on the facts, in *L'Education* he seems to have stuck closer to reality, while magnificently assimilating that reality into the life of literature.

Since Mme Marie-Jeanne Durry published certain of Flaubert's notebooks in *Flaubert et ses projets inédits* (1950) we even have tangible proof that the portrait of Marie Arnoux was based on Elisa Schlésinger. After *Salammbô* he spent more than a year turning over various projects. In collaboration with Bouilhet and the Comte d'Osmoy he wrote a fairy-play called *Le Château des Cœurs*, moved in society, married off his niece, read quantities of old newspapers in the Bibliothèque Impériale (now the Bibliothèque Nationale, and hesitated between various novels, various plays, and a history of official art. One title jotted down in the notebooks catches the eye: *Les Deux Cloportes* (literally, the two woodlice, but the word is also used contemptuously to denote some minor and benighted employee). Another, as Mme Durry says, makes one's heart beat faster. It is *Mme Moreau*, and the whole outline reads as follows:—

Mme Moreau (novel)

Husband, wife, lover, all loving one another, all cowards.
—voyage on the Montereau boat. schoolboy.—Mme Sch.—
M. Sch. me.
—development of adolescence—law—obsession virtuous and
sensible woman (accompanied by children).
　　The husband kindly initiating with women of easy virtue . . .
(evening party) ball at la Presid[ente's]. Coup [*de foudre; i.e.*
falls in love]. Paris . . . theater, champs élysées . . . adultery
mingled with remorse & (fear) (terrors) Ruin of husband &
philosophic. developm. of lover. end a tailing-off. all know
their positions with regard to one another & dare not admit.—
feeling ends of itself—they separate. End: see each other
again from time to time—then die.

This sketch is somewhat different from the plan Flaubert
finally adopted for the novel: adultery actually does occur, and
the affair peters out in mutual indifference. But the importance
lies in the naming of the real people whom Flaubert was to use
as originals for his characters: Mme Schlésinger, her husband,
and "me," the "school-boy" later to become a law-student.

　　After this, Flaubert hesitated and dragged his feet, perhaps
put off by the thought of taking as point of departure an experience which was still close to his heart and in which he was still
too involved. Moreover he had not yet managed to bring out
the "idea"; he had not yet been able to formulate the over-all
conception which would be the story's invisible axis and which
he had always regarded as an indispensable preliminary. "It's
the string that makes the necklace, not the pearls." But he
seems to have achieved what he needed by the time he wrote
to Mlle Leroyer de Chantepie on October 6, 1864:—

> *Me voilà maintenant attelé depuis un mois à un roman de mœurs*
> *modernes qui se passera à Paris. Je veux faire l'histoire morale des*
> *hommes de ma génération; "sentimentale" serait plus vrai. C'est un*
> *livre d'amour, de passion; mais de passion telle qu'elle peut exister*
> *maintenant, c'est-à-dire inactive. Le sujet, tel que je l'ai conçu, est,*
> *je crois, profondément vrai, mais, à cause de cela même, peu amusant*
> *probablement. Les faits, le drame manquent un peu; et puis l'action*
> *est étendue dans un laps de temps trop considérable. Enfin, j'ai*
> *beaucoup de mal et je suis plein d'inquiétudes.* (For the past month

I've been hard at it on a novel of modern manners which will be set in Paris. I want to write the moral history of the men of my generation; the "sentimental" history would be more accurate. It's a book about love, passion; but passion such as it is bound to be now, *i.e.* inactive. The subject as I have conceived it is, I think, profoundly true, but probably for that very reason not very amusing. There is a slight lack of facts and drama; and the action is spread over too long a time. In short, I'm having great difficulty and am full of anxieties.)

The Novelist's Contribution

While, in a later outline, Flaubert notes that "the husband possesses both the girl" (with whom Frédéric has consoled himself) "and his wife," he adds that "it would be stronger" not to have Frédéric go to bed with Mme Moreau, who, "chaste in deed, would eat her heart out with love. She'd have her moment of weakness, but her lover wouldn't notice it or profit by it." This vital change in the relations between the two constitutes an essential spring of the plot, making it possible to sustain it, and explaining why Frédéric plunges into love affairs in which neither his heart nor his mind is really engaged. The modification of plan corresponds to the over-all conception of an "inactive" passion, and makes the story of unfulfilled love particularly poignant. The change derives from the novelist in Flaubert. It is certainly probable that Flaubert never became Elisa Schlésinger's lover, but clearly he was not merely recounting his own experience. It was the novelist, the writer, the artist who said, "It would be stronger . . ." What he is preoccupied by is the work, not making a copy of a reality which, however touching, is anecdotal as far as the reader is concerned.

But not to stray too far from traditional Flaubert studies, we may admit that if Flaubert had not had that life-long passion for Elisa there would have been no *Education sentimentale* as we know it. We are grateful for all the information that has been discovered on the subject: Elisa's visit to Croisset as a woman of over sixty when Flaubert was actually writing the

novel, an occasion which may have suggested the scene of the
lovers' final interview; Flaubert's knowledge of Maurice
Schlésinger, his ups-and-downs in business, and his relations
with his wife; many details, situations, and scenes corres-
ponding to those actually experienced or observed, such as the
shawl episode on the "Ville-de-Montereau", the drive in the
forest of Fontainebleau, the liaison with Mme Dambreuse
(a character probably based, at least in part, on Mme Delessert,
once Du Camp's mistress); even the removals of the Arnoux to
their various houses. But when the early sketches say Mme
Moreau "ends mad, hysterical," it was an intuition of the
future rather than a noting down of past or present reality,
though in 1862 Flaubert had learned that Elisa was temporarily
in a mental home in Germany. What was this "reality," really,
to Flaubert? It was a source of inspiration, a constant support,
raw material. In his desire to "represent life" Flaubert was
more sensitive than anyone to the experiences life offered.
But the most important thing still remained to be done: to
recreate those experiences in writing. We ought to pension off
the common delusion that all the novelist does is transport life
into the novel, and perhaps we only shore up that delusion by
setting up parallels, all more or less hypothetical, between an
author's biography and his work. Sometimes they may throw
light on the work, but more often they tend to substitute for the
complex and difficult genesis of the fiction a set of anecdotes
satisfying only pedantry and curiosity. True, we generally
know almost nothing of the genesis itself beyond what the
author himself chooses to vouchsafe, and his confidences are not
always to be taken at their face value.

Flaubert's Problems

IT TOOK Flaubert five years to write *L'Education sentimentale*,
from 1864 to 1869. The work was long and hard. Though he
complained less than before about "the throes of style," he
experienced, as he had over *Madame Bovary*, moments of
suffering, periods of discouragement, attacks of distaste at

being tied to a "bourgeois subject." "It's about time I amused myself at last," he wrote to George Sand. He meant he would like to treat a more congenial subject, one which would require less research of all kinds, less hunting after details apparently unimportant but which for him had to be absolutely accurate. He had already expressed such a wish to Louise Colet. As the years went by bringing the death of friends, especially that of Bouilhet in 1869, and accentuating the fact that he was old before his time, he entrenched himself more firmly every day in pessimism, and, despite his social life in Paris, in solitude. He did not know the worst was yet to come.

His first concern in writing "the moral history of the men of [his] generation" was to create a truthful work, *i.e.* one that was impartial and objective and did not betray his own sympathies and preferences. This concern derived from his theories about a "scientific and impersonal" art, and a novel which "should . . . remain within the limits of general plausibility." He wrote to George Sand: "Rich or poor, victors or vanquished, I don't accept any of all that"—meaning the exalting of the one and debasing of the other. "I don't want to have love or hate or pity or anger"; he hoped to "bring Justice into Art." Then, he went on, "the impartiality of description would have the majesty of law—and the precision of science."

He had to ask himself whether this concern was compatible with his wider aim of creating a work of art, and with the need to give form to what can only be called the author's opinion on "the things of this world."

On the theoretical plane he met with no answer to the first question. He believed what he was in the process of creating was "something useless, by which I mean contrary to the aim of Art, which is vague exaltation. But with the present scientific demands [*i.e.* his own] and a bourgeois subject, that seems to me fundamentally impossible. Beauty is not compatible with modern life . . . "

This was one of the bees in Flaubert's bonnet. But there is more than one kind of artistic beauty, and while *L'Education* does not observe the canons of classical art or of those of the novel as generally written in Flaubert's day, it is this very fact which lends it its eternal freshness and has made it a universal influence on the modern novel.

As to the "form" to be adopted "to express one's opinion now and then on the things of this world without running the risk of seeming an idiot later," one can only agree with Flaubert that it is "a tough question, *un rude problème*." But to this question he did find an answer. Regarding the things of this world, "It seems to me the best is simply to paint them." Simply? What he did was paint them in his own way, with their good side and their bad, their causes and their effects, with a scalpel for instrument. "Dissection is revenge," or in other words the expression of opinion is revenge, because for a pessimist to dissect men is enough to show they are bad and that life drags us towards the void. *L'Education*, like *Madame Bovary*, was to be a work of criticism, even of social criticism. When Flaubert wrote to George Sand, "I confine myself to showing things as they appear to me, to expressing what seems to me the truth," he added at once, "Damn the consequences!" showing how few illusions he had about what the reactions would be.

It was not the vanquished who were likely to be angry. They are dreamers rather than men of action, and Flaubert was irresistibly attracted to dreamers, and satisfied merely with showing their ludicrous side. But what would be the response to the picture of the frightened and cynical bourgeois at the Dambreuses', the shot fired by Père Roque at the prisoner in the Tuileries, and the murder of Dussardier by Sénécal? He had only had to show the characters as they were and describe the situations in detail to reveal the fundamental significance of the events. The impartiality and objectivity of the description add to its force and make it inexorable. Flaubert's powerful searchlight on events makes even those who, like Frédéric, are apathetic about them, appear different and in this respect less sympathetic.

Heroic Self-restraint

ANOTHER DIFFICULTY was how to insert individual stories into a picture of an age, with its great events dictated by history. First of all there was the love of Frédéric for Mme Arnoux, which with all its vicissitudes and consequences had to run right through the book and make its presence constantly felt. Then there were the adventures of dozens of other characters, which as in real life did not always fall into convenient group- ings and were not sufficiently interesting to hold the limelight. Nevertheless the reader had to feel the presence of Hussonet, Cisy, Martinon, and many other minor figures. And how was Flaubert to confine himself to painting a back-cloth when public events erupted on to the front of the stage and monopolized attention? The author also had to be careful to preserve the over-all greyness of tone he was aiming at.

All these problems Flaubert put to himself and to his correspondents. "Will character-descriptions interest you?" "Historical characters are more interesting than fictional ones, especially when the latter have moderate passions; one is less interested in Frédéric than in Lamartine." "I am afraid lest the backgrounds elipse the foregrounds." And so on. He solved these difficulties by returning to them again and again, making changes like a painter muting his colors and transferring them from places where they catch the eye too much. He had to weave within the framework of his main tapestry without allowing himself any "embroidery" that might unbalance it. "No big scene, no purple passages, no metaphors even." He deliberately held back his abilities as a writer and the resources of his temperament, the whole skill of which a novelist is generally so proud, and by this heroic self-restraint he achieved the perfect work of art which is the *Education*, that long flow of dream, love, and nostalgia, the closest possible image of time which passeth and returneth not.

Publication

In the spring of 1869 Flaubert wrote the last chapters and read the book to George Sand, who liked it. He then, in the course of five sessions, read it to the Princess Mathilde, who also gave it an enthusiastic reception. Flaubert's confidence began to be restored. But as Bouilhet was dying and could not be counted on to look over the manuscript, he turned in despair to Maxime Du Camp. Du Camp was far from enthusiastic: he noted that the book was devoid of subject, plot, and character; the best he could manage in the way of praise was that it was "a kind of *tour de force*," and his conclusion was that it was "interesting." Certain scenes he found "very good," others "impossible." An example of the latter was the scene where Mme Dambreuse, sitting by her dying husband, confesses that she hates him. Du Camp criticized the coarse, idiomatic style and thought it sometimes lapsed into "gibberish." He ended by drawing up a list of 251 indispensable corrections. Flaubert quite rightly "sent 87 of them packing," and himself produced nearly five hundred corrections for the new edition published by Charpentier. As usual with him, most of these were cuts.

Michel Lévy jibbed at the title, but although he had hesitated a long time before adopting the one he had used for the novel shut away in a drawer since 1845, Flaubert insisted on keeping it, adding the sub-title, "Histoire d'un jeune homme". *L'Education sentimentale* was in the bookshops by the middle of November 1869.

Critical Reception

THE CRITICS came down on it at once like a ton of bricks. On November 19 Barbey d'Aurevilly savaged it in *Le Constitutionnel*. He was sarcastic about the time Flaubert had taken to produce the book: the long labor did not surprise him. "It shows a mind which is starkest of the stark, an intelligence which is all on the surface, with neither feeling nor passion, enthusiasm, ideal, insight, thought, nor depth . . . *L'Education sentimentale* completely confirms the intellectual emptiness revealed by *Salammbô*." Having dealt with the author, d'Aurevilly turned to the book. Its main characteristic was vulgarity, "vulgarity picked up out of the gutter from under everyone's feet." Barbey was outraged that Flaubert should have given Frédéric the surname "Moreau," "the name borne by the finest of men, a poet and a hero! He ought to have called him something like Citrouillard, for example, for there is something of the *citrouille* [pumpkin, *i.e.* ninny] in this gentleman." He repeats the accusations already brought against *Madame Bovary*: ". . . the style is description, infinite, eternal, atomistic, blinding description, occupying the whole book and replacing the faculties of the mind."

For Edmond Schérer (in *Le Temps*), "*L'Education sentimentale* is not a novel: it is a narrative of various affairs, it is a book of memoirs. By dint of being realist it is no doubt real, but by dint of being real it ceases to interest." But he nevertheless recognized the virtues of the writer and of the artist. Cuvillier-Fleury did not condescend so far in *Les Débats*. He complained of the realist school's lack of "soul," and of Flaubert's mania for "lowering what is elevated, and extinguishing what shines: science, talent, patriotism, independence, nobility, modesty, honestly acquired wealth, elegance and courtesy, both the greater virtues and the less." The colors of his palette were "filth." In *La Revue des Deux Mondes* Saint-René Taillandier accused Flaubert of having "imitated the style of M. Michelet," and having proffered a series of sketches instead of a picture. His book dealt a "wound to the human race."

We do not know what Sainte-Beuve would have said, for he had just died, to Flaubert's grief. It was partly "for him" he had written *L'Education*—for the author of *Volupté*, for him who had regretted the absence of a "touching" character in *Madame Bovary*. But it may be that he would have joined, more subtly, in the chorus. Fortunately it was not unanimous. In *Le Pays* Paul de Léoni, not one of the big guns but with a better aim, said "the book is serious, vigorous, gripping, and belongs to the family of *Madame Bovary*." He was probably the first to point out, with remarkable foresight, that in Flaubert one should look less for "points of contact with Balzac than for points of contact with Charles Baudelaire." He was also the first to congratulate Flaubert on having "rid" the novel of "all the parasitical elements which enslave thought." He noted that "there is not one word that does not possess its just value . . . and which has not been skilfully adjusted to form part of the general harmony of the book."

A Plot?

FLAUBERT COULD NOT UNDERSTAND why his book was so roughly handled, and showed his surprise. He had counted on his friend Paul de Saint-Victor, who out of kindness preferred to be silent about a book he considered "bad." He applied to his friend George Sand who, with sincerity but not much enthusiasm, produced some public tributes. But the public itself, which had thrown itself at *Madame Bovary* and made *Salammbô* a success, this time hung back. Some of Flaubert's friends even omitted to write and thank him for their copies, probably to avoid the dilemma of either lying to him or up-setting him. The file of reactions to *L'Education* has been discovered, with Flaubert's notes: Victor Hugo sent a "good letter"; Alexandre Dumas a "letter of thanks," followed up by a visit; the Goncourts wrote an "admiring letter," Zola a "superb article." And that is about all. Nothing from Vacquerie, Michelet, Amédée Pommier, Cernuschi, Agénor Bardoux, Sénard the lawyer, Ernest Chevalier, Bataille, Ernest Renan, Feydeau, Arsène Houssaye, Monselet, or even from the Bonenfant cousins at Nogent. This was indeed surprising, and Flaubert wondered, half ironically and half seriously, whether he was not the victim of a "plot." The explanation is simpler than that. His book had been a disappointment. People's minds were not ready for a novel which relegated subject, plot, and character to the background, and resembled neither *Madame Bovary* nor *Salammbô*. The readers of 1869 held against Flaubert the grey tones to which he had confined himself, the unrelieved monotony of the landscape, the lack of conclusion or even end to most of the different actions in the book, the universal mis-carriage of ambition, hope, and feeling, the fog of mute, unweeping despair which enveloped the whole novel. It did not occur to anyone that he had done what he set out to do. Even the well-disposed murmured that his talent had declined. No one liked to mention the fact that on top of everything else the book shocked people by recalling events still fresh in their memories, and at a time when the instigator of the *coup d'état* was still on the throne (though not for much longer).

The Followers

THE NOVELTY and value of *L'Education sentimentale* was only appreciated by young writers, for whom *Madame Bovary* had already been a revelation; by "professionals" who wanted to get out of the rut still kept to by Hugo and George Sand and the by now exhausted path pioneered by Balzac. Many of these young writers were to become followers of Flaubert, or in some cases would-be followers.

Zola declared that *L'Education sentimentale* was "the only truly historical novel I know, the only one which is truthful, accurate, and exhaustive, and in which the hours which are dead and gone are completely resurrected, without any sign of literary contrivance." He went on to say that the bid Flaubert was making in the book was "colossal."

> The very plan of the book made the task more difficult still. Gustave Flaubert rejected any traditional central story. He aimed at life as it presents itself from day to day, with its endless series of small commonplace incidents, adding up in the end to a formidable and complicated drama. There are no long-prepared episodes carefully led up to, but instead the apparent desultoriness of facts, the ordinary round of events. Characters meet and lose sight of each other and meet again, until they have said their last word: nothing but passers-by jostling each other on the sidewalk. It was one of the boldest and most original conceptions, and one of the most difficult to carry out, that has ever been attempted in our literature . . .

And Zola, no less sound as prophet than as judge, concluded: "Of all the works of Gustave Flaubert, this is certainly the most personal, the most vastly conceived, the one which cost him most effort, and the one which will long remain the least understood."

Banville, who became neither a "realistic" nor a "naturalistic" novelist, but was content to be a (now somewhat neglected) poet, had already distinguished himself by writing a perceptive review of *Madame Bovary*, and now sent Flaubert an enthusiastic letter, after having used his theater column in *Le National* to write about *L'Education*. When Flaubert died, Banville pointed out the importance of *L'Education* for the future. In it, he said, Flaubert surpassed himself; in it he showed in advance "what will not exist for a long time yet, that is to say the non-fictional novel (*le roman non romancé,*) sad, vague, mysterious as life itself, and, like life, satisfied with dénouements all the more terrible because they are not physically dramatic."

A Genuine Heir

AMONG THE DISCIPLES—Maupassant, Zola, Huysmans—there soon blossomed many "*éducations sentimentales,*" stories of lives that came to naught. But as Banville foresaw, it was not for "a long time yet," not till after the disciples themselves and the "realist" and "naturalist" periods of the novel, that *L'Education sentimentale* came to be recognized as Flaubert's masterpiece and the masterpiece of the modern novel. Remy de Gourmont called it "our *Odyssey.*" In 1913 a club was formed called the "Friends of *L'Education sentimentale.*" Anatole France in *L'Histoire contemporaine*, and Maurice Barrès in his *Roman de l'Energie nationale*, both tried to continue what Flaubert had done. But they got it wrong, and failed. It was Proust, a better judge than Gide or Valéry, who not only showed that Flaubert's lesson had not been lost but also gave it a magnificent continuation.

What Proust admired in *L'Education* were the "blanks," the empty intervals of months or years which separate the chapters and in which the "plot" unravels and then proceeds again, perhaps in another direction. It is a strange, "lost," stripped time, which has its own value and which passes as it does in life. Proust is the spiritual son of the writer who, sixty years earlier, tried to describe the "*intermittences*" of the heart; and

Proust paid Flaubert a splendid tribute. Talent, he writes, is "a drawing-near of the artist to the thing to be expressed," and "it seems that in other centuries there was always a certain distance between the object and the lofty minds which discoursed upon it." But Flaubert shows at last a successful and perfect fusion between the artist and his object:

> *L'intelligence . . . cherche à se faire trépidation d'un bateau à vapeur, couleur des mousses, îlot dans une baie. Alors arrive un moment où l'on ne trouve plus l'intelligence—meme l'intelligence moyenne de Flaubert—on a devant soi le bateau qui file, "rencontrant des trains de bois qui se mettaient à onduler sous le remous des vagues . . ." Cette transformation de l'énergie où le penseur a disparu et qui traine devant nous les choses, ne serait-ce pas le premier effort de l'écrivain vers le style?* (The intelligence tries to become the vibration of a river-steamer, the color of the foam, an islet in a bay. And then there comes a moment when the intelligence is no longer there, not even the mediating intelligence of Flaubert: before one is the boat steaming up the river, "occasionally meeting floats of timber which would rise and fall in the wash . . ." Is not this transformation of energy in which the thinker has disappeared and which brings before us things themselves, is not this the first effort of the writer towards style?)

Proust puts it in the form of a question, but he is making a statement and a vow of allegiance.

At about the same time the other great renovators of the novel, Joyce and Kafka, were also carrying Flaubert's lesson further, and Faulkner and Hemingway were learning the lesson of the master in the United States. It may well be that all of them were especially affected by Flaubert's least classical novel, the one which was the most audacious on the plane which interested them. And now that the immediate influence of these writers has dwindled somewhat, towards whom have such younger men as Alain Robbe-Grillet and Philippe Sollers turned their eyes, together with the rest of a new generation of French novelists anxious to rid the form of its impedimenta and give the closest possible image of modern "reality"? Towards Flaubert. Towards *L'Education sentimentale*, still a fresh and living fountain-head.

12

FLAUBERT'S POLITICAL AND SOCIAL IDEAS

B Y THE BEGINNING of 1865 Flaubert had been working for four months at Part I of *L'Education sentimentale*. He was plunged in the memories and ambitions of youth; he bestowed them on his hero; it was the moment when Frédéric resembled him most. At the beginning of 1870 the book had been out for about six weeks. The public had not taken any notice and the critics had given it a poor reception. Flaubert felt the setback severely. But before the year was out he found himself confronted with other shattering events which took on for him a symbolic significance. In the defeat of France and the Prussian invasion he saw the end of his literary ambitions and his career. Literature now seemed "something futile and useless." He felt as if it was "the end of a world" and the beginning of another in which there was "no place" for a "*mandarin*" like himself.

The old enthusiasm had been absent already from the writing of the *Education*. It was a sort of balance-sheet of his youth; regret, wistful evocation of the past, and melancholy took an even greater hold on him than before. As the years went by he grew more and more impatient of his contemporaries, his age, and the stupidity that reigned everywhere. He began to identify himself with Saint Polycarp, who complained of the century in which God caused him to be born. His niece had married and gone away; he sank at Croisset into gloomy solitude, his companions an elderly mother hard-of-hearing and an aged servant going blind. Though not yet fifty he already suffered the premature depredations of age. The years 1869 and 1870 were black ones for him. The first brought the deaths of Bouilhet and Sainte-Beuve, whom he had come to respect. The second saw the deaths of Duplan and Jules de Goncourt, Feydeau stricken with paralysis, France broken and invaded. and Flaubert's own habits rudely changed.

After *Salammbô* he had attempted to lead a less cloistered existence. He spent the winter in Paris, where he mixed with artists and writers. He was at almost every important first night, and could sometimes be seen at balls at the Tuileries or the Opera. He had renewed his friendship with Du Camp, to whom he was bound by so many youthful memories. To a certain extent he entered into the spirit of things, which was all to the good as far as his moral and intellectual equilibrium was concerned, though there was no danger of his "identifying" with his social persona. His irony lay in waiting as strong as ever; he took more delight than ever in astonishing people with his outrageous paradoxes, his furies, and his gibes. All this derived from a naivety which abandoned him as soon as he sat down at his desk; from a goodness which was perhaps the basic feature of his character; and from a sense of justice easily aroused. Most people knew that under the "crocodile" skin was hidden a sensitive and affectionate being, and an enthusiast.

Bouilhet, Feydeau, and Duplan

HIS MOTHER and his niece still had first place in his heart, though the links with Caroline had become somewhat strained. Mme Commanville responded less eagerly now to her uncle's affection. Travelling about with her husband and helping him with his business, she had less time than before. In particular, she had not found time to read the manuscript of *L'Education sentimentale*. Bouilhet, for his part, still went on helping his "old reliable," following Frédéric's adventures closely from Paris, Mantes, or Rouen, wherever he happened to be. With *Faustine* and *La Conjuration d'Amboise* he began to emerge as a playwright: the latter ran for a hundred performances in 1866. But this success did nothing to line his wallet, and in

1867 he was appointed Librarian of the municipal library in Rouen. After this he fell into a state of hypochondria, from which Flaubert did his best to arouse him, but he died of albuminuria on July 18, 1869. Flaubert was shattered. In Bouilhct hc lost his spiritual brother, his "literary conscience," his "*accoucheur*, who saw into my mind more clearly than I did myself." The void he left would never be filled. Flaubert devoted himself to the memory of of his dead friend, and to the promotion of his work as poet and playwright.

Charming Feydeau and "little Duplan" were intimate with him and in his confidence. But after the success of *Fanny*, which counterbalanced that of *Madame Bovary*, Feydeau's verve, though still strong, began to slacken. Jules Duplan dabbled first in trade, then in archaeology. Both friends were made use of for *L'Education:* they researched, checked, passed on information. He consulted Duplan about exact details of transport between Paris and Fontainebleau during the Days of June 1848; he asked Feydeau for particulars about the posts of the National Guard in the Mouffetard and Latin quarters during the period he was concerned with. He turned to his friends for information about how to manage Jacques Arnoux's financial affairs and how M. Dambreuse would set about floating his coal-mining company. But Duplan died before *L'Education sentimentale* was published, and by the time it appeared Feydeau was paralyzed.

Princess Mathilde

FLAUBERT'S RELATIONS with Princess Mathilde and George Sand rested on different foundations. They arose out of *Salammbô*, which the princess liked and which "the good lady of Nohant" praised in an article. The princess introduced Flaubert into her circle, which included Gautier, Sainte-Beuve, Renan, the Goncourts, and Dumas the younger. Flaubert was flattered. Although both he and his large body were ill at ease in formal dress, apart from that there was little constraint in a salon where the conversation turned mainly on art and literature, and where feelings and ideas were far from conventional. The princess was clever, sensitive, and cultivated, and the "good giant" amused and touched her. She included him among the chosen few whom she invited to dinner and to her country house at Saint-Gratien. When they were too far away to meet, they wrote to each other.

It seems likely that Flaubert, encouraged by her friendly attentions, came to entertain quite strong feelings for her. But he never plucked up the courage to reveal them. One day he said to her in a letter that women never dream "how timid men can be". So he never ventured beyond the bounds of deference. When the régime was overthrown, he went on writing to the princess in exile, and never missed an opportunity to show his devotion. He went to see her in Belgium, declared he was "her old faithful under any political régime," and when she returned resumed his visits to Saint-Gratien. After his death the princess said he was "without malice, without false susceptibilities, easy to get on with", and explained how the roughness of his language never shocked her, even when one day at dinner he described himself as "an underminer of all government of whatever kind," adding, "I'd like to destroy everything." She went on: "In everything he would pose as a colossus. Whatever anyone else said that was exaggerated, he would go one better, like someone from Marseilles." This side of Flaubert had also been noted by the Goncourts and other witnesses. But perhaps they were too easily taken in by appearances.

George Sand

FLAUBERT MET George Sand in Paris in 1859, but their friendship really began about four years later. He was touched by a letter she wrote to him after an article on *Salammbô*, and he replied by declaring his unreserved affection. His affection for her work was less absolute, though he did not forget he had been fond of reading it at school, and that his youthful dreams had been haunted by her heroes and heroines. He was now repaying an old debt of gratitude. It is likely, too, that he was impressed by George Sand's past as an emancipated young woman whose stormy love-affairs were notorious. But now she was an old lady, though her vitality and zest for writing remained unimpaired. Flaubert looked on her as a "*chère vieux maître*," a "*camarade des lettres*," and a member of the "*troisième sexe*." She was devoid of prejudice, and could be talked to freely and without circumlocution. She came to see him at Croisset; he saw her in Paris, or visited her at Nohant. They had interminable conversations on the subject which interested them both most—literature.

Their two theories of aesthetics were incompatible, and it was not long before they had to agree to differ. George Sand, an impenitent Romantic, could not understand why Flaubert insisted, and at such cost, on hewing out phrases and constructing whole books from which he tried to exclude all personal feeling, all passion flowing from the heart. He replied by expressing his "*répulsion invincible*" for such things, and by setting forth his own principles: "I believe that great Art is scientific and impersonal: the first person who comes along is more interesting than Monsieur G. Flaubert because he is more *general* and therefore more typical." She protested. He explained: "I expressed myself badly when I said 'one shouldn't write with one's heart.' I mean one shouldn't 'put forward one's own personality . . .' One ought, by an intellectual effort, to transfer oneself into one's characters and not assimilate them to oneself. That's the method, at least . . . ." It is like reading the letters to Louise Colet all over again. George Sand keeps hammering away at the same old thing, but Flaubert will not budge. But later, to show that he and his "method" could produce what was touching, he was to tell the story of Félicité, a "simple soul."

They compared their views on many other subjects, including love, the sort of life a writer should lead, the evolution of ideas, the best forms of government, social problems, politics. When it came to love they both spoke from experience, and the bolder and less conventional of the two was not always the former mistress of Musset and Chopin. In particular, Flaubert did not make the eternal division between sexual activity and feeling. "Everything depends on the intensity," he said, meaning on the ability in this as in other spheres to "make oneself feel things." On the choice he had "long since" made between art and life, Flaubert made valuable revelations: "The muse, however cantankerous she may be, gives less trouble than woman. I can't reconcile the one with the other. One has to choose. . . ." For the artist, as we know, love has to stay at the back of the shop. He says it now, as he had said it before.

Political Disagreements

GEORGE SAND PROFESSED advanced views in politics. These were soon to melt away under the Commune, but meanwhile, in the 1860s, she was a feminist, an out-and-out democrat, and even, thanks to Pierre Leroux, the humanitarian with whom she had collaborated in the *Revue indépendante*, a socialist. Flaubert, who since his youth had been against any form of authority, particularly that of the state—he spoke of "the fantastic and hateful being called the State"—was just as skeptical about the virtues of the majority and the progress of society. The idea of democracy based on universal suffrage seemed to him a snare from the point of view of justice and a delusion from the point of view of reason. The people are flattered and tricked by the professional politicians who claim to wield power in their name; in fact, the people do not have even the shadow of power, and never rise out of their miserable condition. At the same time Flaubert's disgust and irony were equally aroused by all forms of personal power and every aspect of tyranny, whether authoritarian or paternalist. The cardboard Emperor ruling the country with a rod of iron seemed to him a figure both hateful and ludicrous; after the defeat, Flaubert, in his letters, demanded that he should be hanged. But the masses only get what they deserve: it was they who voted Badinguet into power.*

*Napoleon III, then Prince Louis-Napoleon Bonaparte, escaped from the fortress of Ham in 1846 disguised as a workman called Badinguet.—TR.

Tyranny and demagogy prop each other up, to the great benefit of the bourgeois.

Flaubert does not use the word "bourgeois" in the same sense as Marx. For Marx, M. Dambreuse would represent "finance capital" and Homais the chemist the urban "liberal petty-bourgeoisie." Their respective economic and political powers are as unalike as their ways of life. Flaubert calls them by the same name because of the way they both feel and think—if it is not putting it too grandly, because of the philosophy of life they have in common. Both believe in the future of the industrial society and its unlimited progress, which will bring happiness for all and substantial profits for some. Both believe in a hierarchy of values, guarded for M. Dambreuse by the clergy and other spiritual authorities, and for Homais by the country's institutions, worthy of honor by definition and irrespective of the régime that happens to be in power. Both worship money, technology and its ally the machine, the sacrosanctity of property, and free trade. They are positivists, patriots, materialists, and conformists. Whether the régime is that of a King, absolute or constitutional, an Emperor or a Republic, it is all one to them so long as it is "strong" and seems to be able to hold the balance between the "excessive" desires of some and the "wild" claims of others. M. Dambreuse only asks it to provide him with the "freedom" to collect his dividends; Homais only the liberty to make his seltzer-water and write articles in the *Fanal de Rouen* in praise of the industriousness of rural workers.

For Flaubert, "bourgeois" does not denote just a sociological category or a social class. For him it means anyone who thinks, feels, and acts in terms of utilitarianism, who rejects the individual in all his humanity and uniqueness in favor of the monster, society; who accepts as just and true the values this monster secretes in order to maintain its own existence as the meeting-place of all illusions, all hard-and-fast definitions of good and evil, all the commonplaces of language, stupidity in all its finery, revered and adulated under the names of general truth, the "wisdom of the nations," and the canons of morality.

For Flaubert the "bourgeois in overalls" and the "bourgeois in a frockcoat" were the same: he hated them both as simultaneously products and promoters of a society which worshipped the Golden Calf only less than its own illusory image of itself, and which dismissed as unworthy of consideration men's individual reasons for living, creating, and dying.

"Down with Words"

POLITICAL PARTIES fight for the right, bestowed by the "ignorant" masses, to rule over them. They can only win their support by descending to the popular level, degrading even farther what the masses think, feel, and desire, promising to satisfy their appetites and fostering their illusions. The slogans on political banners may sometimes be impressive, but their object is to deceive.

They all deserve indifference or contempt. As Flaubert wrote to George Sand:

> *Tous les drapeaux ont été tellement souillés de sang et de merde qu'il est temps de n'en plus avoir du tout. A bas les mots! Plus de symboles ni de fétiches! La grande moralite de ce règne-ci—celui de Napoleon III—sera de prouver que le suffrage universel est aussi bête que le droit divin, quoiqu'un peu moins odieux!* (Every flag has been so besmirched with blood and shit that it's time to do away with them all. Down with words! No more symbols or fetishes! The great virtue of this reign—Napoleon III's—will be to prove that universal suffrage, though slightly less detestable, is as stupid as divine right!)

Flaubert could not forgive either the people (which he loved only "when there were riots") or the political parties of the Second Republic for having capitulated before "Badinguet." "I am grateful to Badinguet, bless him!" he wrote in a fury. "He has restored my contempt for the masses and my hatred for the common people." He did not ask himself whether the "masses" and the "common people" were responsible for their ignorance and their defeat. They were the "herd," the majority, and that was enough. There could be no justice or truth except through the individual.

In order to describe, in *L'Education sentimentale*, the ideas and trends which led to the explosions of February and June 1848, Flaubert studied the works of the liberal, positivist, and socialist thinkers. He knew Lamennais, Auguste Comte, and Proudhon, and found them all either "lamentable" or "comic". He re-read them, and also studied the texts of Saint-Simon, Fourier, and Louis Blanc. It was not enough to "read criticisms and summaries of their work: they have always been either praised or refuted, never properly set forth." From all this reading emerged:

> ... one salient feature which they all share, and that is a hatred of liberty, a hatred of the French Revolution and of philosophy. They all belong to the Middle Ages, their minds are all buried in the past. And what pretentious mediocrities! Seminarists on the spree or bank-clerks with a touch of fever! If they didn't pull it off in 1848 it was because they were outside the great tradition. Socialism is one face of the past, just as Jesuitism is another. Saint-Simon's great master was M. de Maistre, and no one has ever really gone into all Proudhon and Louis Blanc owe to Lamennais. The school of Lyons, which has been the most active, is as mystical as the Lollards. The bourgeois didn't understand any of all this, but they felt instinctively what forms the basis of all social utopias: tyranny, anti-nature, the death of the soul ...

There is no need to point out how partial Flaubert's summary is here. His interpretation, though it has some apparent plausibility, is basically false, but he repeated it often, even going so far as to accuse Louis Blanc and other "utopians" of doing no more than serve up the old dish of Christianity disguised in new sauces.

Vive Voltaire!

WHAT IS INTERESTING is to see what Flaubert meant by the "great tradition," which he regarded as a force of the future and to which according to him Fourier, Saint-Simon, and Proudhon did not belong.

Flaubert saw the source of the traditional current he spoke of in the liberal ideas of the eighteenth century, in Voltaire,

Diderot, and Montesquieu, among the deists, materialists, and atheists, among all those who had substituted the cult of reason for that of the Catholics' God, nature for Providence, man for God's creature, the nation and the law for monarchic power. Flaubert was the son of a doctor and the grandson of a veterinary surgeon who had benefited from the *"biens nationaux"* under the Revolution. He belonged to a class which had been emancipated by 1789, and that for him was the touchstone. "Don't you think, really," he wrote to George Sand, "that since '89 we've just been floundering about? It might be wise to go back for a while to d'Holbach. And what about studying Turgot before we start admiring Proudhon?" On this point Flaubert is so close to the liberal and conservative bourgeoisie who sought to manage both their ideas and their estates with a clear conscience that he did not notice that d'Holbach dispensed with "soul" long before Saint-Simon, and that Turgot's proposed reforms applied to an almost entirely agrarian economy. This was not his only inconsistency: he blamed the utopians for lack of spirituality and at the same time accused them of being Christians unawares. The passion with which he undertook this lone rear-guard action is an expression of the rigid philosophy of a social milieu resisting with all its strength the changes involved by industrialization, the growing importance of manufacturing techniques, and the rise of the proletariat.

The Important Thing

FOR FLAUBERT as for Voltaire—"I love the great Voltaire as much as I detest the great Rousseau"—the main enemy was the priest, master of superstition, professor of obscurantism, traditional ally of authority. "I am revolted by the way all religions speak of God," Flaubert wrote to Mme Roger des Genettes. "What irritates me most of all are the priests, who always have the name on their lips. It's a kind of habitual sneeze with them—'God's goodness, God's wrath, offending against God', that's the language they use. As if God were a man and, worse still, a bourgeois." Flaubert believed that in this respect mankind had not got past the primitive stage, that of the "savage" or "cannibal." Flaubert's image of God was quite different. It resembled that of Voltaire, whom oddly enough he regarded as a "Saint" and whose anti-clerical fanaticism, in spite of all his principles, he admired. He respected the beliefs of Mlle Leroyer de Chantepie, a devout Catholic, but could not help disclosing his hatred for the French bishops who in 1859 backed up Napoleon III in his support of the Pope against the people of Italy. "It's disgusting, this clergy which defends and blesses tyrannies, anathematizes liberty, burns incense only to power, and cringes before what is accepted. I can't help being horrified by all these cassocks made from the draperies of the throne!"

By the first half of the nineteenth century Catholicism was no longer what it had been in the time of Voltaire. It had adapted itself to the times, making itself "social" with Lamennais and "evangelical" with the reformers, but always being careful not to displease whatever régime was in power, and (in particular under Napoleon III) taking advantage of whatever concessions the authorities allowed. Having so many faces, it could both cater for the growing religiosity of the masses reacting against de-Christianization, and countenance the theories of those who regarded Jesus as the first "socialist." A neo-Catholic trend won over various writers and essayists, effected conversions, and passed as a new ideology. Flaubert tirelessly denounced what he regarded as a swindle and what he curiously enough alleged to be the product of the "democratic" ideal. "This is what we've come to," he wrote to Feydeau. "We're absolutely clerical. Such is the result of democratic stupidity." He went on, returning to his own first principles: "If we'd continued along the highway of M. de Voltaire, instead of straying off through Jean-Jacques, neo-Catholicism, Gothic, and fraternity, we shouldn't be where we are today." He suspected the "so-called liberals" of conniving with "*messieurs les ecclésiastiques*." He wrote to George Sand: "Neo-Catholicism on the one hand and socialism on the other have deprived France of its wits. Everything evaporates between the

Immaculate Conception and the workers' lunch-tins." In 1868 he described the opposition as "stupid" for "attacking the empire, or rather the emperor, instead of going for the one really important thing, the religious question." He grew "more and more convinced of this truth: we have become so imbued with the doctrine of Grace that we have lost the sense of Justice." Everywhere he saw adherents of the various religions all equally narrow and fanatical, all equally anxious to put the mind in chains. He saw curious parallels between the old "advocates of the [16th-century pro-Catholic] *Ligue*, and Marat and Proudhon. Whichever way you turn it's enough to make you vomit." He was a complete 18th-century anti-clerical, abhorring equally those who traded in God and those who worshipped the abstract idea of the people. Whether, in the name of their beliefs, they built temples or barracks, it was only to imprison critical intelligence, reason, nature, and all the faculties properly called human.

Justice and Science

THESE DIATRIBES, which barely concealed an astonishing social conservatism, surprised and disturbed George Sand. She was alarmed lest in *L'Education sentimentale* he was going to denigrate the "patriots," those who were on "the same side" as he and she. Flaubert reassured her. His picture was going to be "impartial and objective"; he used the same expression (*"les nôtres"*) as George Sand to indicate what "side," in spite of everything, his heart inclined to. He would not be one to kick the defeated when they were down, and he did not expect the "bourgeois" to appreciate his account of the June Days. In him the man of anger and passion always effaced himself behind the artist, who aimed at being "objective." Moreover, anyone who was sincere and disinterested or had been the victim of injustice appeared to him worthy of respect whatever party he belonged to, and despite what Flaubert himself held to be errors of thought or behavior. He wrote a heartfelt letter to Barbès, the rioter tortured by the police, the condemned man whom they dared not execute: *"J'étais habitué à vous respecter, à présent je vous aime* (I always respected you. Now I love you)."

But George Sand upbraided him. What did he do but destroy, vent his spleen, revel in his own nihilism? Did he think he was the only person to see clearly in a world swept by "a wind of stupidity and folly"? Then he poured it all out to her. "The time for politics is over," he wrote. All parties and all régimes were alike in being behind the times, and Napoleon III's was one of the worst. It had left "our beautiful country" in the mire. There was no longer any point in talking in terms of these representatives of the past. One must look to the future.

> The question lies elsewhere now. It is no longer a matter of dreaming up the best form of government, since they are all the same, but of making Science prevail. That is what is most urgent. The rest will follow of necessity. Pure intellectuals have rendered more services to mankind than all the Saint Vincent de Pauls in the world! And politics will be an eternal foolishness until it is a part of Science. The government of a country ought to be a section of the Institute, and the humblest section at that.

Politics a part of Science! Flaubert was saying the same thing here as Saint-Simon; Marx at this period would have liked to make politics an auxiliary of philosophy. Flaubert cannot be forced into preconceived categories. It took the Commune and the terror it inspired in him to turn him back into a "bourgeois" and "property-owner."

At the time we are concerned with now, the common denominator of Flaubert's feelings and judgments lay in the choice he had made once for all: the decision to be an artist, a creator of beauty. Though he belonged, basically, to the complaining bourgeoisie, and naively blamed the "masses" for "not giving a damn for art, poetry, or style," he was nonetheless always "agin the government" whatever its complection. He was sarcastic about "Badinguet" and his desire for "masterpieces to revive the French—as if it wasn't enough to have revived law and order, religion, the family, property, and all the rest." Earlier, he had written to Louise Colet:

> Have you ever noticed how stupid any kind of *authority* always
> is when it comes to art? These excellent governments, whether
> kings or republics, imagine all they have to do is issue the
> order, and the goods will be provided. They set up prizes and
> incentives and academies, and they only forget the one thing
> without which nothing can live: *atmosphere.*

He went on to say that the only possible atmosphere for
literature was freedom. "What can one say, what can one talk
about now?" He tried to have confidence in the future—"And
then we'll rise again! and day will break once more"—and he
dreamed of the possibility of "liberal minds" forming a "closer
guild than that of all the secret societies." At a time when the
people give themselves over to "bad shepherds," "it is we and
we alone, the educated, who are the people, or to put it a
better way, the tradition of mankind (*C'est nous, et nous seuls,
c'est-à-dire les lettrés, qui sommes le peuple ou, pour parler mieux, la
tradition de l'humanité*)."

A Heroic Honesty

So, DESPITE HIS anarchistic nihilism and his class spirit, Flaubert
had subtle and contradictory opinions on "the things of this
world." But he did not consider it right to express them
in his work. What he wanted, rather, was to cause the work
of art to evoke thought and feeling on its own more lofty
plane, above opinions, ideologies, and beliefs. It was a difficult
task, but the novelist could accomplish it if he aimed at recreating exactly and completely a reality apprehended in its
component elements, or in other words "dissected." It was a
question of "method," and this was the only method capable of
conjuring up the "truth." In it consisted his own "duty,"
morality, and way of "doing Justice." For him, the social
question would be resolved if everyone would simply "be
honest, by which I mean do his duty and not encroach on his
neighbor." He went on: "The ideal society, in fact, would be
one in which every individual functioned according to his
capacities. I do function according to mine, so I'm quits."

One might think Flaubert was letting himself off lightly if his words had not been backed up by his work. That work was fundamentally critical, and as well as calling in question social relationships, it has also, for a hundred years now, caused people to re-examine certain ways of living and being. It is based on one man's pessimistic view of the world, personal meditation and knowledge of life and people, but it transcends the opinions and beliefs of its author. They are no more apparent in it than are Balzac's in *La Comédie humaine*. The writer and novelist has gone beyond the ordinary man in Flaubert, and he wants readers too to avoid making mountains out of molehills. The ideas of a particular age, the problems that age has to solve, the events it experiences, though they may be important or even stupendous, are seen differently by the artist. Through imagination, thought, and his own art, he makes them part of another history in which the values accorded to them by ideologists and fanatics emerge in all their transitoriness. The first characteristic of great art is to be honest, and Flaubert was heroically honest.

13

FLAUBERT AND THE THEATER

ONE OF FLAUBERT'S DREAMS, which went back to his childhood, had been to become a playwright.

We have seen how, with his sister Caroline and his friends Alfred Le Poittevin and Ernest Chevalier, he used his father's billiard-table as a stage, putting on short pieces by established authors or written by himself with the aid of his companions. The review he edited and practically wrote himself, at school, followed what was going on in the theater in Paris and Rouen, providing both information and criticism. When he was fourteen he was reading Shakespeare, and planning the historical dramas he wrote when he was fifteen or sixteen.

While he was still at school he created the character of le Garçon, whom he and his friends would impersonate, but it was Flaubert who threw himself into it the most. He had a talent for mime and acting which he was to make use of more than once in his life. He practised these gifts on his father, who was alarmed by this aptitude; on Bouilhet; on Du Camp, Gautier, and the Goncourts. His precocious ability to "make himself feel things" made him confuse himself with other people, both real and imaginary. In 1839 he wrote to Ernest Chevalier, "Properly directed, I could have made an excellent actor," and in 1846, to Louise Colet: "Whatever anyone says, deep down in my personality there is a strolling player. In my childhood and youth I was wildly stage-struck. Perhaps I might have been a great actor, if Heaven had had me born poorer."

When he was a youth, literary fame appeared to him in the guise of success in the theater, and the dream continued to haunt him for years. At the beginning of his liaison with Louise Colet, he wrote to her: "I'll have a play put on, you'll be there in a box, listening to it, hearing them applaud me." How he would have loved to prove himself to his mistress like that!

He had already written a number of tales, short stories and historical narratives, and also *Mémoires d'un Fou* and *Novembre*, when to Du Camp's astonishment he set to work making a close study of the dramatic works of Voltaire and of his friend Marmontel. The result emerged in 1845 or 1846: *Jenner ou la Découverte de la Vaccine*, a parody "in five acts and in verse" written in collaboration with Bouilhet and Du Camp. Although it remained unfinished, Flaubert talked ten years later of "treating" Feydeau to this work, and he did oblige the Goncourts to read it. During the winters of 1847 and 1848, he and Bouilhet worked out several scenarios, including a panto-mime in "six acts" called *Pierrot au Sérail*, a project he was long to have a soft spot for, but of which only a detailed outline has been found.

He proved and proclaimed his love of the theater in a hundred different ways. After having visited La Scala, he wrote in his personal notes:

> *Un théâtre est un lieu aussi saint qu'une église. J'y entre avec une émotion religieuse, c'est là que la pensée humaine, rassasiée d'elle-même, cherche à sortir du réel, que l'on y vient pour pleurer, pour rire ou pour admirer, ce qui fait à peu près le cercle de l'âme.* (A theater is as holy a place as a church. I enter it with a religious emotion. It is there that the human mind, surfeited with itself, seeks to escape from reality. It is there that people come to weep, to laugh, or to admire, which between them about make up the whole circumference of the soul.)

As a young man he had written, in *Novembre*: "There was nothing I loved so much as the theater. I loved even the buzzing of voices in the interval, even the corridors, which I went along with a beating heart . . . The footlights seemed to me the gateway of illusion. Beyond, for me, was the universe of love and poetry." Jules, in the first *Education*, who resembled Flaubert in so many ways, wanted to be a playwright. And when Flaubert wrote the *Tentation*, he was thinking at first of the stage.

A Different Turning

BUT AFTER 1849 Flaubert's literary destiny took another direction. The reason for this was the setback he encountered with his friends Bouilhet and Du Camp over *La Tentation,* and the subsequent inner redevelopment which led Flaubert to his aesthetic of the novel. He repressed his love of the stage, or else fulfilled it by proxy, giving Louise Colet "technical" advice about the dramas she perpetrated, and helping Louis Bouilhet not only to write his plays, but also to get them put on. In Bouilhet's cause Flaubert went and saw people, pulled strings, attended and sometimes even directed rehearsals. For *Madame de Montarcy* and *Faustine* he abandoned Croisset and his own work in order to be at the center of operations, and—or so he thought—to show the professionals a thing or two. Bouilhet's successes and failures were his successes and failures. Flaubert realized his own dream through the works of his old friend.

But he did not give up his wish to write for the theater himself. In 1852, when he had been working at *Madame Bovary* for several months, he told Louise Colet he had "two or three ideas for the theater" which he would "execute" when he had finished his present book and "the Egyptian tale." When *Madame Bovary* was published the theater of La Porte Saint-Martin wanted to adapt it as a play. Flaubert refused haughtily: "When I write for the theater I'll go in by the front door or not at all." He read and re-read Shakespeare, Aeschylus, Sophocles (whom he wanted to have "by heart"), Aristophanes, Goethe, Corneille and Molière. Beside such giants, what were contemporary writers—Ponsard, Augier, Sardou, Dumas the younger, and the various fashionable authors of light comedy? If he, Flaubert, really set himself to write for the theater, he would have no difficulty in wiping the eye of these fellows, with their creaking plots and crude characters, who took themselves for the practitioners of some mystery. "One of the most comical things these days," wrote Flaubert to George Sand, "is the *arcana* of the theater. It's as if the drama were something beyond the bounds of human intelligence, a mystery reserved for those who write like cabmen." At the same time it was a medium so ossified that a real writer, in his opinion, could easily resuscitate it and distinguish himself in it.

A New Genre: the Fairy-play

HE HAD SCARCELY FINISHED *Salammbô*, in February 1862, when he set out at last to translate his plan into practice. Should he write a modern play, with a bourgeois subject?—like all those "humbugs" he despised? He intended to do better than that— to introduce a new genre, which would be to the French theater what certain plays of Shakespeare were to the English, and what *Faust* was to the German theater. It would be a *féerie*, or fairy-play, but with a symbolic or philosophical meaning, un- folding "in a dramatic form that is splendid and vast . . . We need to get away from the old structures and the old stories." He intended to expound all this in "a long preface" to the projected play, which would be "more important for me than the play itself." In short, it was to be a manifesto.

With his usual patience and tenacity he plunged into the study of the modern fairy-plays which had been written so far. They seemed to him very unimaginative and stereotyped. He could learn nothing from them. He abandoned them, and applied for help to Bouilhet and to the Comte d'Osmoy, who was experienced in these things. All three set to work, but d'Osmoy was soon called away by his wife, who had fallen ill. Flaubert then hesitated between two plans: one in which the fantastic element ran parallel to the realistic plot, and another, which on Bouilhet's recommendation he eventually followed, in which realism and fantasy were combined in the same action. The story told of two innocent lovers long separated by various tribulations, who had to overcome the obstacles strewn in their path by wicked gnomes who stole human hearts and kept them prisoner in a fortress, the "Castle of Hearts" of the title. The fairies would be able to capture the castle if the two lovers, through the purity of their love, recognized one another.

Even before *Le Château des Cœurs* was finished, Flaubert was taking steps to get it put on. He sent the scenario and the first four tableaux to the director of the Vaudeville theater; but he found the style "limp" and finally rejected it. Flaubert, by no means discouraged, worked away at the play all through 1863, and by December regarded it as finished. But the financial backing he had been counting on proved unforthcoming, so he put the piece away for a while and went on to *L'Education sentimentale*. When he began writing it on September 1, 1864, nearly two years had gone by since the publication of *Salammbô*.

A Secret Wound

HAD THOSE YEARS been well or ill employed? *Le Château des Cœurs* is not lacking in ideas or imagination, or even in a sort of mythical truth capable of getting across to the audience. But it does alternate between the realistic and the fantastic, and it is hard to make out whether the tone is intended to be serious, naive, or ironical. In this latest struggle between good and evil in which virtue triumphs, the author seems to take a sarcastic view of a dénouement which can be predicted very early on. The plot hangs fire; the characters are childish in the fantastic parts and caricatures in the realistic scenes. Flaubert, believing one had to write broadly for the theater so as to be immediately understood, lost the feeling for nuance and truth of detail which distinguished him as a novelist. He over-wrote, strove after effect, and found it either in Jarry-like antics or in false ingenuousness. The result was a mass of conflicting elements. On the other hand the play has many novel scenic effects which anticipate the cinema: dissolves, superimpositions, sudden passages from one image to another, metamorphosis of characters before the audience's eyes. On the whole the play can be read with pleasure. Whether it could be produced is another question, which theater managers in Flaubert's lifetime and since have always answered in the negative.

Flaubert himself never doubted his play was a good one and would be put on. He watched for a favorable opportunity. In 1866 he heard that the manager of the Gaîté was in fact looking for a fairy-play that was out of the usual run. He hurried up to Paris, but after much chopping and changing and procrastination his suggestion was rejected. He made another attempt in 1869, after Bouilhet's death. Raphael Félix, manager of the Porte Saint-Martin, was complimentary, but put off by the cost of mounting the show. In 1872, 1873, 1874 and 1877 Flaubert made fresh attempts, and met with fresh failures. He applied for help to an agent, a minister (his friend Agénor Bardoux), Ernest Daudet, Maupassant, and Carvalho, director of the Théâtre des Nations. Every time he thought he was just about to bring it off, but every time he was disappointed.

So he decided to publish it. Charpentier, his publisher, supported a review called *La Vie moderne*, edited by Bergerat. Flaubert agreed to let the play appear in it in instalments. But he was angry at once because of the way it was divided up for serialization, and because the illustrations were misleading and vulgar. He was going to go and tell Charpentier what he thought of him when he was prevented by death. And so to his dying day *Le Château des Cœurs* had been a permanent worry and probably a secret wound.

In the Service of Bouilhet

WHEN BOUILHET DIED he left several plays in his friend's charge. One of them, *Mademoiselle Aïssé*, had been accepted by the Odéon, "subject to revision." Flaubert immediately set about polishing it up, and as soon as the Commune was defeated, saw to it that the play was put on as agreed at the next most important theater in Paris after the Comédie Française. Not without difficulty, it opened in January 1872, but the audiences grew smaller and smaller and it closed after twenty performances. Flaubert had thrown himself without reserve into organizing rehearsals, directing the actors, supervising the staging, and even providing props. But in doing so he was satisfying one of his deepest pleasures, and he considered it well worth the trouble. But two other plays of Bouilhet's were awaiting resurrection: *Le Cœur à droite* and *Le Sexe faible*.

The Letters do not make much mention of *Le Cœur à droite*. It may be that after an unsuccessful attempt to get it put on at the Théâtre de Cluny, Flaubert decided it was not good enough to warrant further efforts.

But *Le Sexe faible* he considered worth any amount of trouble. He thought the theme—the power women acquire over men—had great philosophical and factual truth, and it seemed to him one could easily add to it comic strokes which would make it effective satire. He set to work with a certain amount of enthusiasm, changing Bouilhet's outline, re-writing whole scenes, and drawing the characters more boldly. When the war was over he went to see Carvalho about it. Carvalho professed to be very keen, and sure it would be a success. Once again, Flaubert saw to almost everything, including the casting. By September 1873 all was ready for rehearsals to begin. Then nothing more happened.

Had Flaubert deluded himself again? It seems from the Letters that he took Carvalho literally, whereas in fact the latter had not really made up his mind and did not like to say anything disobliging to the author of *Madame Bovary*. Perhaps Flaubert's worst mistake was to tell Carvalho about his plan to write *Le Candidat*, a political satire. This gave Carvalho an excellent excuse for postponing *Le Sexe faible* in favor of a topical play that was bound to be "more successful still"! *Le Candidat* opened on March 11, 1874. It was a flop. After that there was no question of Carvalho asking for more trouble with *Le Sexe faible*.

But as usual Flaubert dug his heels in, even to the point of sacrificing his own pride. He offered *Le Sexe faible* to the Comédie Française, who rejected it, to the Odéon, who were not keen on it either, and thereafter descended by degrees to the Cluny (a "dive") and the Gymnase. The result was the same everywhere. George Sand, Turgenev, and the Goncourts were astonished to see their friend lowering himself to such humiliating procedures. He reminded them of how much Philippe Leparfait, Bouilhet's illegitimate son, needed money. But these seem only to have been pious pretexts. While

Flaubert may not have hoped to obliterate the failure of *Le Candidat* with *Le Sexe faible*, he did think his revised version of Bouilhet's play was worth any number of other pieces, and that it was his duty to get it performed. But finally he gave up and put it back in its pigeon-hole.

Was it really a good play? What strikes one on reading it is how didactic, and consequently how schematic, it is. We do not know the text Bouilhet bequeathed him, but certainly its subject appealed so much to Flaubert the old bachelor and misogynist that he flogged it for all it was worth. He did so according to his own conception of the theater, broadening every stroke, clarifying with superfluous asides a plot already only too clear, and substituting caricatures for characters. The comedy of manners was changed into satire, which missed its mark because the characters were all of a piece and too far-fetched, or into farce, which despite some happy inventions, would not admit itself as such. One character, Paul Duvernier, is slightly more developed and more moving than the rest, but he gropes about in a world of robots and marionettes. While Flaubert succeeds, through the banality of the situations, the insignificance of the talk, and the artless cynicism of the human relationships, in conveying the sense of an empty and conventional world, the world of the bourgeoisie of the salons, he fails to arouse interest in people reduced to mere social mechanisms. *Le Sexe faible*, instead of being in the line of the great satirists, is more like a mildly entertaining farcical diversion. But did Flaubert think he had written a farce? It is unlikely.

The Candidate

ON THE OTHER HAND, *Le Candidat* was all his—subject, plot, and characters—and owed nothing to Bouilhet. It is also the most interesting of Flaubert's dramatic efforts.

Carvalho's enthusiasm on reading it had acted as a great fillip. Flaubert abandoned his preparatory reading for *Bouvard et Pécuchet* and threw himself with childlike pleasure into his new enterprise. "It amuses me *enormously*," he wrote to his niece, "but I've calmed myself down a bit, because last week my elation went too far." He told George Sand that if the play was performed—he was becoming more prudent—it would shock people greatly: "I'll get myself torn to pieces by the populace, banished by the government, anathematized by the clergy, and so on." What sort of a bombshell was he concocting?

He wanted to write a political play, or, more exactly, a satire on political manners, aiming at all parties—the supporters of the Comte de Chambord, the Orléanists, reactionaries of every kind, as well as staunch republicans. What he intended to go for first and foremost was the election fever which seemed to have seized everyone since the establishment of the Third Republic, the "aberration" which put power in the hands of men whose abilities and character were thought irrelevant so long as they had been placed where they were by universal suffrage. As we know, Flaubert had long been a determined opponent of this method of election, which he saw as a sign of decadence and stupidity. As he had the same distaste for all parties, factions, and ideologies, he thought he would be sufficiently Olympian to hold the balance between all the corrupt judgments, debased ideas, and other follies of the political animal.

His main character is a M. Rousselin, an idle bourgeois suddenly seized with election fever. As he is well-to-do, and slightly more limited in intelligence than his fellow-citizens, he may well think of getting himself made a deputy. Then he would be an important personage in his *département*, and able to go and live in Paris, a prospect which enchants his wife. He would be able to choose for a son-in-law the suitor most able to further his own ambitions. But even these sordid calculations pale beside the obsession of actually winning votes. He has no program whatsoever, not even a single idea; he runs through the whole political spectrum in obedience to each particular situation, aspiring to some vague, indefinite shade that will please every audience. To his one end he sacrifices his daughter, his wife, some of his precious money, and even his honor, of which, by the time he is elected, not a shred remains. The other characters are types, guided by self-interest or other morally reprehensible motives. Politics has corrupted everything around it, and plunged everyone it touches into abjection.

Flaubert worked all out, and at the end of November 1873, after two months which according to him left him "dead-beat," he wired triumphantly to Carvalho that *Le Candidat* was finished. Carvalho came running, and was not sparing in his praise. However, he did suggest corrections and changes. This exasperated Flaubert: he saw it as a device to diminish his play and force him into concessions. He refused, agreed, refused again, then went back to his first version and agreed to make alterations in that. He was in a state of agitation which he camouflaged by an affectation of proud indifference, pretending that all he wanted was to make some money from the play in order to help him in his financial difficulties.

"A Flop"

WHAT FOLLOWED is well known. Despite the presence at the first night of such friends as Daudet, Edmond de Goncourt, Zola, Maupassant, and Bergerat, who tried to induce success by influence and their own applause, the audience remained unmoved and even derisive. Undisguised disappointment and cat-calls from the gods gave way to "pitying gloom." Once again Flaubert was toppled from the heights of his illusions. "It's certainly a flop and no mistake," he wrote next day to George Sand. With characteristic pride he withdrew the play after the fourth performance, though perhaps had he waited the tide would have turned.

It is no surprise that the critics man-handled him as usual. "Not very funny," was their refrain, as it had been with the audience in the intervals. Sarcey wrote that "in M. Flaubert's play everything is false, or at least seems so." Auguste Vitu, in *Le Figaro*, said that M. Flaubert had no talent at all for the theater and "saw the world through dark-colored spectacles which made everything look ugly into the bargain." Vitu too considered these "disagreeable pictures" to be "absolutely false." Flaubert's friends tried to soften the blow. It was not possible to put over "a repugnant subject too real for the stage and treated with too much love for reality," wrote George Sand in a letter. Banville said much the same. What it all amounted to was that in the theater one had to lie in order to seem to tell the truth.

In fact Flaubert had neither lied nor told the truth. What he had done was transpose on to the stage his vision of the world and of things as that vision may be divined from his novels, but in this case without the methods and devices of the novel, and, on the contrary, with the exaggeration he considered necessary in the theater. Instead of adding stroke to stroke, the good mingling with the bad to create life, he limited himself to those traits which built up a character or a situation, or contributed to a development of the plot. In order to make everything light and rapid, he had made everything flash into place like a pattern in a kaleidoscope, hurrying towards a long foreseeable dénouement. The result is that there is no time for the audience to get interested in the characters, or to sort out a complicated plot which suddenly emerges too clearly.

Although the characters in Flaubert's novels are governed by a rigorous determinism, they never give the impression—Frédéric Moreau gives it even less than Emma Bovary—of being manipulated by the author. Life is always confronting them with crossroads, choices, alternatives. But in the theater Flaubert sets his characters on rails and makes them follow the route prescribed without even the possibility of looking right or left. For him, the station-master, the journey is over before it begins; what happens on the train is of little consequence. That which the reader or spectator should be able to see emanating from the play, materializing and rising up with all the circumstantialness and unexpectedness of life, and even with its imponderables, gives the impression, in *Le Candidat*, of having been experienced far away and long ago, and to be worth no more than a mere recapitulation. It is one which is intelligent, sarcastic, bitter, written in telling language full of strokes that go right home, but it is nonetheless no more than a mere account, full of gaps and lacunae. The reporter has forgotten to tell us whether Louise Rousselin may have felt anything for any of her suitors, or to show us the actual jealousy of a husband so spectacularly deceived. We are not told exactly what feeling impels the poet-journalist to seduce a respectable bourgeoise who for all we know may have something of Emma Bovary in her. Flaubert the novelist would have told us all this —would have analyzed it lengthily, subtly, cruelly. A true dramatist would have shown it to us. Flaubert merely flings it in our face.

The Theater as an Outlet

THE RESULT WAS that on March 11, 1874, instead of assisting at a comedy or satire from which they could have gone home satisfied and with an easy conscience, the audience of Flaubert's play felt as if they had been drenched by a jet of spleen. All that concerned politics disgusted him so much, and in the theater he was so unskilful at hiding that disgust, that the spectators wondered with alarm whether his venom were not directed against the whole human race. That was really what people resented, and that was what he expected. His mistake lay in the means he used, and when George Sand accused him of being *trop vrai*, too real, she really meant he had been too rough and clumsy.

Flaubert had in fact used the theater as he had refused to use the novel—as an outlet for his moods and beliefs, a legitimate and even popular way of giving free rein to his fancy, imagination, and personality. His view was that he did not need to be "impersonal" in the theater, since the stage was by definition impersonal, a place where the actors embody the thoughts and feelings and philosophy of the author. He had long meditated on the example of Shakespeare, Aeschylus, Sophocles, Molière and Voltaire—could one see *them* through their plays? While not actually attributing to the medium as such the virtues of the authors themselves, he did think he ran no risk in the theater, and that as he was striving to be a great writer he must necessarily be a good dramatist. After all, it was not a question of magic. He even saw himself as an innovator, enabling the theater to benefit from his work as a novelist and his high standards as an artist. He thought he knew the theatrical point of view, the secrets of the boards, ever since he had revealed his gifts as an actor and his promise as a writer at school and on his father's billiard-table. Although his condescending attitude was not based on vanity, it was a condescending attitude just the same, and his love of Shakespeare and others ought to have preserved him from it. He was learning to his cost that even if contemporary dramatists did write "like cabmen," theater was not just a matter of style.

But Flaubert's mistake was not as tragic as all that, and even though his plays are weak they are amusing and entertaining to read, and clearly the work of an interesting temperament and a writer. Even when he is falling below his own highest standards he is pointing the way for others: *Le Château des Cœurs* heralds Rostand's *Chantecler*, Maeterlinck's plays, and Symbolist productions; and *Le Candidat* foreshadows Antoine's innovating and liberating Théâtre Libre. In addition, Flaubert's plays reveal what his novels give only a glimpse of—his bitter philosophy of life. It is in this part of his work alone that he dares to treat life according to its merits as he sees them; in other words, as a farce which is not funny. It is here he unburdens himself. And that helps us to understand Flaubert the man better, and perhaps Flaubert the novelist too.

14

ART AND INSURRECTION

R EADING THE LETTERS Flaubert wrote during 1871, one
might think he would find it difficult to get over the
blow of the war, the Prussian occupation of Croisset,
the Paris rising, the French defeat—all that he described as "the
end of a world."

Although he had never been taken in by a régime where
everything, from light women to "respectable" literature,
seemed to him "fake," Flaubert saw the death of the Empire
as the collapse of a society in which as a writer he had found a
place. With the sudden breaking of his links with the old
milieu, class, and way of life, he became conscious of his existence
as a social being, and stood up for it against the occupier and
the Communards. The anarchist, anti-patriot, and artist of
the "ivory tower" stood revealed as a Frenchman, a bourgeois,
and a property-owner.

He feared above all for art and literature. What importance
would these modern times accord to such "gratuitous" activity,
such "luxury trades"? It seemed to him that with the rise of
democracy, the new importance of "the people," and the
triumph of utilitarianism, the only thing for artists to do, and
he among them, was to immerse themselves deeper in solitude
and aloofness.

But things were not so disastrous as he had imagined. When
he returned to Croisset in April 1871 he found the house intact
and his study almost as he had left it. There was nothing to
stop him sitting down and addressing himself for the third time
to his *Saint Antoine*. He finished it on July 1, 1872, and then put
it away for a couple of years.

Life went on. After the defeat of the Commune he stayed in
Paris and went to see Princess Mathilde, now back at Saint-

Gratien. In November 1871 he was visited at Croisset by Elisa Schlésinger, widowed six months earlier. The ground had trembled under his feet, but things were settling down again.

The new régime represented the triumph of an avenging bourgeoisie of which Thiers was the personification. Flaubert, having castigated the Communards, proceeded to vilify the Versaillais in almost the same terms: for him they were just alternative faces of the new barbarism. He gave his support to what was to become the Republic, considering the demands of the claimants to the throne outmoded and the agitation of the Bonapartists childish. He continued to stand above all parties and to abominate politics. In 1873 *Le Candidat* was full of the disguised resentment of an outraged bourgeois.

The Bourgeoisie on Trial

HE DEVOTED HIMSELF to the memory of Bouilhet. We have already seen the trouble he went to over *Mademoiselle Aissé* and *Le Sexe faible*. He also wrote a preface to a book of verse which Lévy published in February 1872 under the title of *Dernières Chansons*. He besieged the town council of Rouen to get them to put up a bust in honor of Bouilhet, but they were less sure than Flaubert was of his friend's poetic distinction, and rejected the idea. Flaubert then proceeded to denounce not only them but their whole class: "I no longer address you alone, Messieurs, but all the bourgeois."

He ranks them with the "populace" to which they think themselves superior. They are "conservatives who conserve nothing," and they have the same tastes as the masses, "the same love of money, the same respect for the *fait accompli*, the same need of idols to destroy, the same hatred of everything superior, the same spirit of denigration, the same crass ignorance." They think that to "despise intelligence" establishes them as "practical": they forget that their fathers were "intelligent" enough to acquire the power they wield, and that if they were ignominiously defeated by the Prussians it was because "the dreamer Fichte reorganized the Prussian army after Jena, and the poet Kœrner sent certain Uhlans against us in about 1813." They ought to realize that "intelligence," "dream," and "poetry" are not without their uses. And are they themselves as "practical" as they suppose? "You, practical? Nonsense! You can't handle either a pen or a gun! You let yourself be stripped and imprisoned and butchered by a lot of convicts! You've even lost the brute instinct of self-defence . . . With all your capital and respectability, you can't form an association to come up to the *Internationale*. Your sole intellectual effort consists in shaking in your shoes about the future . . ." What he reproached the bourgeois with was having lost the pride, the ruthless virtues, and even the simple instinct of self-preservation of their class. They were just part of the general decadence. They had taken refuge in the defence of sordid self-interests, and they were doomed to die.

The Artist's Profession of Faith

THE COMPANION-PIECE to this diatribe is the preface to the *Dernières Chansons*: this is the artist's profession of faith, the statement of a splendid isolation directed at once against the bourgeoisie and the people.

Bouilhet is put forward as an exemplary figure. "Though poor, he managed to remain free." While "the meanest bourgeois is in search of a pedestal, print is the meeting-place of all pretentiousness, and competition between the stupid is becoming a public menace," Bouilhet "was proud enough to exhibit nothing but modesty." His virtue was that while still young he responded to beauty; he went on worshipping it despite a laborious and difficult life; he tried to be "an absolute devotee of literature, curious in seeking out metaphors, similes and images, and unconcerned about all else."

That, for Flaubert, was "independence of mind." And nothing is more difficult to maintain when "style, art, by its very nature, always seems insurrectional to governments and immoral to the bourgeoisie." It was because he was a genuine artist that Bouilhet endured suffering, misunderstanding, insults—"all the things that plunge you deeper into despair, all the things that wound you to the heart." It was no wonder that even his death-bed had been "violated" (an allusion to the harassments of Bouilhet's two pious sisters), and that a "Catholic writer" had "slung mud" at his grave.

Did the burghers of Rouen deny that Bouilhet was a genius of the first order, and that he deserved the honors Flaubert was claiming for him? Who were they to say? And were they not confusing genius with success? Bouilhet knew what one had to do to succeed, and hedec lined. "He hated Académie orations, apostrophes to God, harangues to the people; the reek of the sewer and the whiff of vanilla; literature affectedly high and literature affectedly low; both the pontifical and the shirt-sleeve style." He wanted to be an artist and nothing but an artist, and he made his life conform to his vocation. "He was a man whose existence was completely devoted to an ideal, one of the rare servitors of literature for its own sake, one of the last fanatics of a religion on the point of extinction—or already extinct."

In penning Bouilhet's panegyric Flaubert was pleading his own cause, with all his own pride and rebellion and contempt. It is strange to see him, on the one hand, proclaiming the immeasurable gulf between Bouilhet and the bourgeoisie, between the bourgeoisie and himself, and at the same time calling on them for a sympathetic hearing. Did he really expect them to honor the martyr of "a religion on the point of extinction—or already extinct"? But in fact he expected it so little he did not think it worth mincing his words. He seized the opportunity to hurl his rage and beliefs at them, and to declare himself yet again the enemy of all those "who think meanly." He raised his own memorial to Bouilhet in his proud and furious address.

Misfortune did come upon him, but not, as he feared, from the change of régime, the breakdown of public and political morals, and the disappearance of the social setting he needed as a target and a sounding-box. Troubles came, and not singly, from less general and distant causes, and hit him all the harder.

A Mother's Death

HE LOST his mother on April 6, 1872. She had been getting older and weaker, but nonetheless her actual death struck him like a bolt from the blue and "tore out his vitals." It was the end of fifty years together.

Flaubert had never left his mother except on rare occasions, and then always with regret or remorse. She ruled his life. She was the being he loved most in the world; it was partly because of her that he had adopted the strange life he lived at Croisset. For her sake he sacrificed his love-affairs, his mistresses, even harmless pleasures she feared might be bad for him. He had declared his love for her in every possible way, including some which have excited the interest of psychoanalysts, who have produced a body of criticism which thinks to penetrate the secret of an author's work by making bold hypotheses about his life. Had he not promised his mother she would never have a "rival," that she would always be "the first in his heart"? And had he not kept his word? He organized his emotional life in such a way as not to upset her, breaking with Louise Colet when she forced her way into the holy of holies, and seeing to it that his heart was not involved in his later liaisons. This devotion certainly had something unusual, if not abnormal, about it. It makes one think of Baudelaire and Poe, and other gloomy geniuses who sought maternal warmth and were haunted by incurable nostalgia.

Flaubert found it hard to realize that this time the umbilical cord was cut for ever. His love took on an element of fetishism. He would spend hours and even days gazing at an old gown or shawl or hat. It was like a second bereavement to him when he had to look on at the division and dispersal of his mother's things. His niece made him go away to Bagnères-de-Luchon, where he did nothing but sleep, stupefied with fatigue, sadness and disgust. He thought he would "never get over it."

He was also profoundly shaken by other deaths, apparently less close. For months he had been following anxiously the lingering last illness of Théophile Gautier. "*Le bon*" Théo, whom Flaubert had honored as a writer from as far back as his schooldays, had been one of the first to recognize him as an artist, and to welcome him into the charmed circle. The man in the red waistcoat, the "impeccable poet" and "perfect magician" as Baudelaire called him, the maestro, had become a friend. True, he had indulged in journalism and hackwork, but Flaubert, instead of condemning him for deserting his principles, put him forward as an example of the artist as a sacrificial victim, forced to sell himself to society in exchange for his deepest convictions. "For," wrote Flaubert to his niece, "he died of long-drawn-out asphyxiation caused by the stupidity of the modern world." At the loss of this friend and confidant whòm he had come to love "as a brother," Flaubert felt at once "crushed and enraged." He openly envied him for being dead, and wished he could "rot instead of him."

A year later it was the turn of Feydeau, who had been paralyzed for years. "So much the better for him!" said Flaubert. In the general rout, there went yet another whose fate he envied.

But he had not touched bottom yet. Another kind of misfortune hung over him. For years it had been gathering strength, and now it was ready to attack the very existence he had carved out for himself in order to offer as little scope as possible to the world's hostility, in order to devote himself completely to his art.

Money Troubles

ALTHOUGH HIS INHERITED private income diminished in value with the rise of the industrial society, Flaubert had never had to take much thought for the morrow. He was able to write his books in peace, keep a pied-à-terre in Paris, and travel if he had time and inclination. In a way it was easy for him to despise money and social success and other commonplace ambitions, and to prefer incentives which he happened to like better. But from 1871 on his modestly privileged position was less certain than it had been, and in 1875 he was ruined.

Fate is not only malicious, it is also ironical; it strikes where it is least expected, from the quarter where you think you have least to fear. Flaubert, in order not to have to worry about money either on his own account or on that of his family, had agreed to his niece's marrying a "grocer" rather than a "starving artist," and in spite of various reservations accepted Ernest Commanville, a timber merchant, as a suitable husband for her. He was just as much taken in by the "practical" man as the burghers of Rouen. He entrusted Commanville not only with his niece, but also his own fortune and its management. He left it to the new nephew to lay the money out well and manage expenditure.

But the timber-merchant was incompetent and unlucky. He responded more and more dilatorily to his uncle's requests. When war broke out he confessed he was in difficulties. Flaubert was obliged to remind him to pay his taxes and to meet the bills for wine, for the furniture of the pied-à-terre in Paris, forre pairs at Croisset, and even for the most ordinary expenses. He was put in the humiliating position of one who has to beg, and is kept waiting. Even when the war was over the nephew's situation did not improve, and it was Flaubert who had to help him out by borrowing on his behalf.

The death of his mother made Flaubert dependent in another way also. Mme Flaubert had left Croisset to Caroline. It was a condition of the bequest that Flaubert should be allowed to go on living there, but supposing the niece took it into her head to sell? Supposing she was obliged to? Before the settlement of his mother's estate Flaubert was already wondering whether he would have enough to live on now, and whether for economy's sake he would not have to give up the apartment in Paris. A letter he wrote to Turgenev suggests that the division of the spoils hardly went in his favor: "I prefer to be rooked rather than defend myself—not out of disinterestedness, but out of boredom and lassitude. When it comes to money matters I'm seized with a sort of furious disgust bordering on madness."

In November 1872, in a letter which she omitted to include in the Letters, his dutiful niece suggested that he moderate his expenses and keep an eye on his servant. Flaubert sadly acknowledged the hit, then rebelled. "My life is abominably arid—without pleasure, without amusement, without relief. But I am not going to carry asceticism as far as niggling about the cooking. Things are dreary enough as it is. Now let's say no more about it." Caroline had gone too far, and this was a warning not to repeat the offence.

For two years the Commanvilles sought a solution in Sweden and Germany, but by the beginning of 1875 their position was alarming. Flaubert gave up his apartment in the rue Murillo, and decided to put up in rooms next door to his niece when he came to Paris. In July he learned that the Commanvilles had a deficit of a million-and-a-half francs and were threatened with bankruptcy. He was overwhelmed at the news: it meant not only his own ruin but also that Caroline might have to sell Croisset. "I can't breathe for holding back my tears, and so I let them flow. On top of everything else, the thought of not having my own roof over my head, a '*home*' [Flaubert uses the English word], is unbearable. I look at Croisset now like a mother gazing at a consumptive child and saying to herself, How much longer will he last?" But he was less concerned for himself than for his niece, and to stave off the bankruptcy he sold his property at Deauville, and contracted loans which were guaranteed by his friends Raoul-Duval and Edmond Laporte. The trouble and expense Flaubert had gone to were only partly rewarded. Commanville's name was saved, but on October 1 his firm was wound up. "I have the feeling I'm finished," he wrote to Turgenev, "I've been hit so hard on the head my brains are crushed."

The news of Flaubert's ruin soon reached his friends, the people he knew in Paris, and the literary world. George Sand offered to buy Croisset herself so that he could go on living there. Raoul-Duval and Agénor Bardoux, now a minister, tried to find him a sinecure post. Flaubert was touched, sometimes to tears; he was also humiliated. He refused various offers, and thought if he lived "stingily" he might get by till he died, which he hoped would be soon. Although he felt some bitterness at this outcome of a life of labor and "austere study," he bore his nephew no grudge. He tried to console him, showing no regret for his ill-placed confidence or the many acts of generosity he had performed in vain. He had not acted according to either interest or reason, but according to his heart. That was enough for him.

New Projects

IT WAS AT THE END of 1872, after having had *Sainte Antoine* copied, that Flaubert met young Georges Charpentier, son and successor of the founder of the Bibliothèque Charpentier. Charpentier offered to publish Flaubert, but Flaubert, though he had finally broken with Michel Lévy over the promotion of Bouilhet's *Dernières Chansons*, had to wait for the expiry of his contract with him. But in 1873 Charpentier brought out new editions of *Madame Bovary* and *Salammbô*, and in April 1874 he published *La Tentation*. This latest work disconcerted people even more than its predecessors. Barbey d'Aurevilly, always ready for the fray, described it as "Flaubert's ultimate suicide."

Following a now familiar swing of the pendulum, Flaubert next thought of writing a "modern" novel. The setting would be the Second Empire; the title might be *Sous Napoléon III* or *Un Ménage parisien*. Did he see it as a sequel to *L'Education sentimentale*, which he regretted not having continued up to the fall of Napoleon III? Or was it to be, as an outline of 1871 suggests, "the story of the degradation of man by woman"? He intended one of the characters to be a prefect (he named the original as Janvier de la Motte, the father of his friend the Baronne Lepic) who rapes a little girl; the girl later becomes a prostitute and small-time actress. In this new satire on the age he lived in Flaubert would reveal the seamy side of a régime and a society he knew well. He worked out various outlines, sketched characters from various social levels, added a number of observations and suggestions, and then abandoned the whole thing in favour of a project thirty years old—the story of the "two clerks."

Before he had decided exactly what his heroes would be like and what their adventures would be, Flaubert told Mme Roger des Genettes, Léonie Brainne, and Ernest Feydeau that "It will be vast and violent." He wanted to write a book in which he would "breathe forth his anger" and vent the spleen that choked him—"all with the sole object of spitting out on my contemporaries the disgust they arouse in me." It was to be an epic of stupidity which could be taken seriously. He intended to include in it the *Dictionnaire des Idées reçues* he had long been meditating.

Between July 1872 and June 1874 he read "from two to three hundred volumes" on the encyclopedic range of subjects to which his two "stooges" were to address themselves. With his friend Laporte he prospected in Normandy for a suitable place for them to retire to. On August 1, 1874 he wrote the first sentence of the new novel, and copied it out to his niece. To Turgenev he wrote, "I feel as if I am about to embark on a very long journey, a journey to unknown regions from which I shall never return." Alas, he was a good prophet. *Bouvard et Pécuchet* was never finished, and did not appear until after his death.

The Legend of Saint Julian the Hospitaller

FOR A WHILE he set the new project on one side, discouraged by the failure of the Commanvilles' business, his own ruin, and the "frightful difficulties" he encountered in the actual writing. He was afraid that "by its very conception" such a book was "fundamentally impossible" to write. He went and took refuge in Concarneau with a biologist friend, Georges Pouchet. After spending some time musing over his life, his youth, and former ambitions, he fell back, as if to keep his hand in, on a less demanding subject: the legend of Saint Julian the Hospitaller. This was another old project, for which the idea had first come to him in 1845 or 1846, from looking at a stained-glass window in Rouen Cathedral. He had made notes for it quite recently during a visit to Rigi-Kaltbad, in Switzerland, with Laporte. He had mastered all the books on the art of hunting, *La Légende Dorée*, and the technique of painting on glass. He finished writing the story in Paris during the winter of 1875-6.

Beset by sorrows and endless harassments; so doubtful of his own genius that he seemed likely to give up writing for good or even commit suicide; deliberately withdrawn into a spiritual solitude which alienated him more and more from the world around him; he was still driven on in spite of everything by a force within, a furious determination to pursue the task which continued to be his sole reason for living. Though he sometimes compared himself to Binet in *Madame Bovary*, and said writing was of no more importance than making napkin-rings, it was the only activity which counted for him, and he subordinated all others to it. After a few days of forced leisure at Luchon or Rigi-Kaltbad or Concarneau, he would fall into a state of deathly boredom and "stupor," which for him was a kind of disintegration of his being, a kind of death. He would have to start sketching out novels, making notes, writing outlines, all the time counting the days till he could get back to Croisset. He had compared writing to a drug. It was, rather, the medicine that kept him alive.

The Help of Friends

As SOME FRIENDS DIED, Flaubert clung all the more to those who remained, and even made new ones. When he lost Bouilhet he turned to Du Camp, who however had other things to do than provide consolation. After Sainte-Beuve's death, Flaubert drew closer to Théophile Gautier, George Sand, and young writers like Edmond de Goncourt, Zola, and Alphonse Daudet, some of whom became his literary followers. He made a friend of the "Muscovite", Turgenev. He even arranged to see Victor Hugo, now returned from exile, and be invited to dine with him; *"un homme adorable,"* he called him. He took under his wing Guy de Maupassant (son of Laure de Poittevin and so nephew of Alfred, the friend of Flaubert's boyhood who had died young).

Flaubert transferred to the nephew some of the love he had felt long ago for the uncle.

So great was his need of affection that though he had been momentarily irritated by George Sand's "perpetual blarney," he returned to his *"chère maitre"* with tears in his eyes when she offered to buy Croisset. He was sensitive, loyal, tolerant. The care he took of Philippe Leparfait, Bouilhet's natural son, was nothing short of devotion. There is no gossip or scandalmongering in his letters. If he happened to meet anyone he did not like—Dumas the younger, for example—he did his best to avoid him. But he did not throw himself at those he did like: he admired Taine and Renan, but kept his distance.

He also had less illustrious friends: Georges Pouchet, son of Pasteur's unsuccessful rival; Raoul-Duval, who played an important role in politics; Charles Lapierre, editor of the *Nouvelliste de Rouen*, whom he had put in his place about an article hostile to Victor Hugo; above all, Edmond Laporte, his neighbor just across the river at Grand-Couronne, who had been introduced by "little Duplan" and was completely devoted to Flaubert. They saw each other almost every day, went together in search of a suitable retreat for Bouvard and Pécuchet, and spent several weeks together in Switzerland. Flaubert had only to ask and Laporte would rush to do whatever service was required. It was he who guaranteed the loans to stave off Commanville's bankruptcy; yet in 1879 it was Flaubert's niece who made mischief between and finally succeeded in separating the two friends. When one thinks how lonely Flaubert was, it seems one of her least pardonable sins.

Flaubert still had plenty of women friends too. Princess Mathilde was back in France, and he resumed his visits and went on writing to her. Mme Roger des Genettes was now ill and living in retirement at Villenauxe, but though she was no longer the exuberant Edma whom Bouilhet had loved, Flaubert, maintaining with her an intimacy both frank and respectful, sometimes reminded her of the old days of Louise Colet and the rue de Sèvres. He did no more than correspond now with Jeanne de Tourbey, who had become Mme de Loynes, and with

Suzanne Lagier, now rarely cast in any but small parts. But he had resumed contact with Elisa Schlésinger, his one and only love, the love of his youth, and tasted somewhat different pleasures with a new friend, Léonie Brainne.

The Return of Elisa

ELISA became a widow in May 1871. A few months later she came to France from Baden, with her children, to wind up her late husband's interests in the Grand Hotel at Trouville. She stopped a night at Croisset.

What was their interview like, and what did they say to each other? We do not know. But they must have exchanged many memories, and spoken of the past with tenderness and regret. After this glance back at what had been and what might have been, Flaubert no longer addressed his letters formally to "Madame Maurice." "My old affection (*ma vieille tendresse*)," he wrote, "I cannot see your writing without being stirred . . . the old days appear again as if bathed in golden mist. Against this bright background, from which beloved ghosts stretch out their arms to me, the face which stands out most radiantly is yours!—yes, yours." In spite of the years and the distance between them (Mme Schlésinger went on living in Baden, and died there, insane, eight years after Flaubert), Elisa remained "*la toujours aimée*." He even told her so, unwalling just that much the "royal chamber" in which he had enclosed the greatest love of his life. When Elisa's son was married in Paris in June 1872, Flaubert wept "like an idiot" at the wedding.

Léonie Brainne

WITH LEONIE BRAINNE it was Flaubert's senses that were involved rather than his heart. She was Mme Lapierre's sister, and these two, together with the actress Alice Pasca, were the "three angels" who alleviated his solitude in Rouen. The first of the angels granted Flaubert quite terrestrial favors, though this was only suspected until certain letters, abstracted by the modest Caroline, eventually came to light. Flaubert was smitten by the young widow in 1872, and met her in Paris as well as Rouen. Later, though he shared her anxieties about her son's ill-health, he could not help, in the free and playful tone he used with her, making allusions that leave no doubt as to the nature of their relationship. It is not certain that another of the three angels, Alice Pasca, was satisfied with merely "smoking cigarettes and chatting" during the long visits she paid to her "*grand Flau.*"

The thought of these friendships corrects the impression of gloom that might emerge from too brief a summary of the years in which sorrow struck so often. However despairing Flaubert claimed to be, and often was, these friendships helped him to face it out. Sometimes they could drive away depressing thoughts; they wove a protective web around him, within which he could carry on his work, more perfectionist than ever in *Trois Contes*, more ambitious than ever in *Bouvard et Pécuchet*.

15

"THE WORK OF MY WHOLE LIFE"

"IN THE MIDST OF MY SORROWS I am finishing my *Saint Antoine*," Flaubert wrote to Mlle Leroyer de Chantepie on June 5, 1872, "It's the work of my whole life: the idea first came to me at Genoa in 1845, looking at a picture by Breughel, and ever since then I have never stopped thinking about it and reading for it."

"*L'œuvre de toute ma vie.*" The description was also true in the sense that in *Saint Antoine*, under the veil of fiction, Flaubert posed all his great questions, about himself, the world, his vocation, and his destiny as an artist. He took up his position at a watershed of history, Alexandria in the fourth century, and showed the astonishing fragility of religious beliefs and philosophical concepts, and the eternal resurrection of myth. The old beliefs, concepts, and myths had been replaced by others, but in the decadent nineteenth century they seemed no more likely to last than their predecessors.

Whereas Montaigne could still find a firm basis in his own individuality, Flaubert could find no assurance in his own existence. He had to believe in art as Saint Anthony had to believe in God, and his faith, like that of the saint, was assailed from all sides.

The conclusion was already there before the premises, and the resulting shadow-boxing camouflages an anguished confrontation between the author and himself. In 1872, as in 1849 and 1856, Flaubert was still searching after his own identity. Twenty years of life, of experience and work, and the attempt to embody himself in the ideal character of the "artist" had not got him any further forward in this respect. Every time he addressed himself again to *La Tentation*, he tried not so much to plunge into it as to struggle free, to distance himself sufficiently to let the work stand independently. As he stood on the brink of old age, *La Tentation* presented him with the nihilistic creed he had made it the vehicle of in his youth. That creed had now become a bitter statement of fact, one which he could make the basis of a work of art. His difficulties, and his fierce determination to overcome them, all arose from the fact that he and his hermit were indistinguishable. Flaubert, having invested Saint Anthony from all sides, was unable to treat him as a free and autonomous character.

The Various Attempts

WHEN "the idea first came to him" he was twenty-four, and he wanted to become for others what hitherto he had been only for himself: a writer. He still confused creation and expression. He thought that in setting his ideas one against the other he could create a work of art, and that the more important the problems dealt with, the more lofty the work. He was so bound up in the latter that to question its value was to deny his own personality and vocation. His first reaction to Bouilhet and Du Camp's criticisms was a cry of horror and protest; his second was a period of dejection and rumination which lasted two years.

Under the impetus of *Madame Bovary* he felt ready to tackle *Saint Antoine* again, and that this time he would be able to put over the ambitious venture which had come to grief before. It would demonstrate the potentialities which had been in him even then, show him in what he considered his true light as a writer, and incidentally enable him to avenge himself for the verdict on *Madame Bovary*, which deep down he still regarded as iniquitous. He took care not to make Saint Anthony put on Mme Bovary's corset: all he did was prune the 1849 version, lightening the content and tightening up the action. He took the public's temperature by publishing extracts in *L'Artiste*, but the reception was cool almost to the point of indifference. Rather than expose himself to failure, Flaubert put the 1876 *Saint Antoine* away in a drawer.

There was another factor too. He wondered whether pruning

was enough; whether the whole thing did not need re-writing in depth.

The reason he did not set about doing so right away, but turned to *Carthage* instead, was to give himself plenty of time, and to avoid yielding to considerations incompatible with the original impulse of the work. To publish *Saint Antoine* at once would be to "adapt it to the needs of circumstance," to take advantage of a success which he considered a misunderstanding —a certain method, in his view, of going to the dogs. He also thought that if he made *Carthage* "more entertaining, more comprehensible," it would prepare the way and lend him enough authority to be able to "let himself go in *Saint Antoine*." His fears were on the same scale as his ambitions. On the one hand, the public might not be ready, but he also realized his project was going to require a lot of hard work before it was really finished and able to win the reception he hoped for.

When *Salammbô* was completed he was surfeited with antiquity and returned to the "modern" novel with *L'Education sentimentale*. War and defeat drove him back on himself, and he tried to drown his bitterness and rage in *Saint Antoine*, which he took up again in August 1870. But before long he was forced to leave Croisset. When he returned after the occupation he "threw himself" into the work again "like a madman." He had never been so "worked up"; he was full of "terrifying excitement." He finished the fifth part of the new version in November 1871.

He spent the winter in Paris looking after Bouilhet's interests, and returned to Croisset on March 30, 1872, for the death of his mother. *La Tentation* was a sort of refuge, and he completed it on July 1. He had completely overhauled the two previous versions, and the version which resulted was shorter, better constructed, and more dramatic. Further time and trouble would probably not improve it. But still he did not publish it.

Two Years of Hesitation

HE MAINTAINED that even though peace and order were now restored "the times were not propitious." But when would they be? He also said he was "disgusted with everything" and in no hurry to publish. In actual fact he was paralyzed by considerations linked to his youth which he would not admit to.

What they were is suggested by his telling Laure de Poittevin how he had talked about the book to his "dear Alfred" six months before he died; the *Tentation*, he told her, was "still dedicated" to him. Flaubert had re-lived, with all the intensity the past always aroused in him, the evenings he had spent with his friend long ago, their endless discussions, their refusal to compromise, their contempt for all that was not art. *La Tentation*, the repository of all their demands, was still linked to a period of Flaubert's life when his ideal and his vocation found their purest embodiment. He was afraid lest in publishing it he might be profaning a memory and a friendship, of turning the ambitions of his youth to material advantage. For him the book was both a testament and a relic.

This was also why he had to publish it—but he preferred to choose the moment, and to publish it "at the same time as another book entirely different." He had in mind *Bouvard et Pécuchet*: its grotesque though melancholy comedy would counter-balance some of the more solemnly lyrical passages in *Saint Antoine*, and prevent their being taken as too literal a manifesto of militant nihilism. By 1872 this belief had come to seem as hollow as any other. Although he was still a "demoralizer," his method was now more ironical and sharp, as *Bouvard* would show. There was also a further and more prosaic reason for delay: he had broken again with Michel Lévy, this time for good. And he had not yet arranged for a new publisher.

It may be that Flaubert never did consider the "work of his whole life" finished. Even after he said it was completed, he still went on working at it in the intervals of reading for *Bouvard* and writing *Le Candidat*. Nearly a year later we are surprised to find him writing to George Sand about Saint Anthony's final vision: "I'd like to replace the three theological virtues by the face of Christ appearing in the sun. What do you think?" And it was not only the end he thought of modifying. He also talked of "strengthening the massacre at Alexandria," and "clarifying

the symbolism of the fabulous beasts." To different correspondents at different times, months apart, he wrote, as if the
matter still lay in the future, "*Saint Antoine* will be finished once
and for all . . ." and again, "As for *Saint Antoine*, I won't do
another thing to it." In June 1873 he told Mme des Genettes
that he had had "enough" of it and that it was time to leave it
alone. "I'd only spoil the general effect. Perfection is not of
this world. We'd better resign ourselves."

A new publisher presented himself—the young Georges
Charpentier. Flaubert hung back and wanted to wait: again a
new work by Hugo, this time *Quatre-Vingt-Treize*, threatened to
steal the limelight. Finally he gave in. He told George Sand that
parting with this "old companion" cost him "a very sad
quarter of an hour."

A Hostile Reception

THE ONLY *Tentation* published during Flaubert's lifetime appeared in April 1874. Of course the critics were almost
unanimously against it. The more honest among them confessed
they could not understand it, and said they were incapable of
judging it since they were not "theologians." Others professed
to be "horrified." Barbey d'Aurevilly, an old enemy, spoke of
"sad self-execution" and "definitive suicide." The "merciless"
boredom the book inflicted on him was not French: it was "a
German boredom, the boredom of Goethe's second *Faust*, for
example, which *The Temptation of Saint Anthony* resembles." Malice
sometimes lends lucidity. Barbey, trying to annihilate Flaubert,
placed him correctly. He acknowledged the fact that the young
writer who in 1849 had set out under the influence of Goethe to
write his own *Faust* had done what he meant to do.

Le Figaro, La Revue des Deux Mondes, La Gazette de France and
Le Constitutionnel presented a united front against the book. It
was the same situation as with *L'Education sentimentale*, and once
again Flaubert asked himself what he had done to be the object
of such ready and general hatred. Hugo sent benedictions, Taine
and Coppée sent compliments, but this was not enough to heal

the wound. Fearing the book would not sell, Flaubert invoked the help of Renan, who wrote an article, but grudgingly and not very fast. The "work of his whole life" was greeted with incomprehension, sarcasm, and admonitions to give up writing; with just a few it had a *succès d'estime*.

Once more people thought he was trying to disconcert the reader, whereas every time he set out on the "long journey" of writing a new work it was himself he wanted to surprise. In this case he had gone back to his beginnings, retraced a path from which he had early turned aside, and, as if to see where this neglected possibility of his nature might have led, tried to present the best of himself, long buried, with all the resources of a dearly acquired mastery. But in 1874 the metaphysical anguish, the philosophic despair, and the barely-disguised romanticism of a young man of 1850 were out of place.

Flaubert himself was so well aware of this that he re-worked *Saint Antoine* entirely, trying to reconcile the original inspiration and general design with recent developments in science and history. While, as in the previous versions, he still set out to annihilate the religious and philosophical beliefs men had constructed for themselves through the ages, he now did so not from the nihilist point of view of his youth, but by adopting 19th-century relativism. His Devil was still Spinozan, but less sure of himself and less eager to convince. He expounded his position more briefly; what had formerly been blunt assertions now became questions. No conclusion was to be drawn from the appearance of Christ's countenance in the rising sun. It merely corresponded to one fact about the history of religion, and another about the character of St Anthony. The issue lay elsewhere.

Flaubert Divided

IT LAY in Flaubert himself. In 1872, as in 1849, he was still divided, torn between a fundamental skepticism about the things of this world and an instinctive confidence in the creative forces of life.

His "ego" bore the brunt of this conflict, sometimes disappearing into an unfathomable void, sometimes being diffused throughout the whole universe. The only time Flaubert held it in his grasp for a moment was in artistic creation, by dint of time and toil, through a kind of transubstantiation of his being, spiritual and material. That was the price he had to pay to give himself a sense of existing. He placed the ideal artist midway between heaven and earth, and tried to embody that ideal by becoming an "indefatigable describer" of everyday life and a demiurgic creator. Only the artist brings together, unifies, integrates, and tries to possess the world he himself breathes life into; he is both Man and God. It was an all but unattainable ideal, and Flaubert only approached it, by an ascetic discipline, in his moments of "*exaltation*." When he came to afterwards he fell back again into non-existence, the void, nothingness.

Baudelaire had been drawn by *le néant*, Kierkegaard was being attracted by it now, and Mallarmé would be attracted by it later. The tendency began about 1850; it ran right through the second half of the 19th century; in our own it has taken some bizarre forms. It has always been accompanied by anguish and despair.

It is natural enough that the Devil, in *Saint Antoine*, should proclaim, "All is illusion. Form may be an error of your senses, Substance an invention of your mind. Are you even sure that you're alive? It may be that there is nothing." But these questions are really meant. They go beyond mere metaphysics, and express the doubt which undermined Flaubert all the time: if he was not an artist and a creator of beauty, he was not even Gustave Flaubert, he was nothing. When this abyss engulfed him, he would cry out for death, and even simulate it by apathy or prolonged sleep.

But in moments of creation he apprehended a totality apt for an age which had proclaimed "the death of God," and in which divinity had become indistinguishable from its creation. Neither Anthony nor Flaubert suffers too much at having to send the Queen of Sheba back to her kingdom, the ordinary world back to its wallowing, the philosophers to their systems, and the god-makers to their dreams. There is another temptation, the supreme temptation, to which they yield. It rises up from the depths of them, and aims at filling the unbearable void of being by avidly swallowing life in all its manifestations, including the most monstrous. Anthony's aspiration as he kneels before Christ is not at all Christian.

> *J'ai envie de voler, de nager, d'aboyer, de beugler, de hurler. Je voudrais avoir des ailes, une carapace, une écorce, souffler de la fumée, porter une trompe, tordre mon corps, me diviser partout, être en tout, m'émaner avec les odeurs, me développer comme les plantes, couler comme l'eau, vibrer comme le son, briller comme la lumière, me blottir sur toutes les formes, pénétrer chaque atome, descendre jusqu'au fond de la matière— être la matière!* (I want to fly, to swim, to bark, to low, to howl. I'd like to have wings, a shell, a bark, to breathe smoke, to have a trunk, to writhe, to divide myself everywhere, be in everything, waft with odors, grow like plants, flow like water, vibrate like sound, shine like light, cling to every form, penetrate into every atom, descend into the depths of matter— to *be* matter!)

This is Flaubert's ancient yearning: to enter into and exist in the whole of creation, as if all barriers were removed between him and it; as if, by totally merging into it and by a kind of perpetual osmosis, he could draw on all its manifold and various forces. The philosophers, metaphysicians, and theosophists had tried to construct an intelligible universe by means of the intellect alone, and all they had succeeded in doing was heaping ruins on ruins. The opposite method was the right one: concentrating on life, tracing it to its source, seizing it just as it emerges throbbing out of lifelessness, blossoming forth with it in its manifestations. Then consciousness, hitherto empty, becomes consciousness of the world. It is by losing itself at the limits of the universe that it finds itself. But had Flaubert still the strength?

The Definitive "Saint Antoine"

IN THE EARLIER VERSIONS Anthony simply returned to his faith. Having looked on unmoved at all the assaults made on it, he took refuge in God and his cave, in a victory consisting in refusal to engage. In fact, his faith cut him off from life and kept him within easily defined frontiers. He knew both sides of the argument in advance, and the temptations he was exposed to were too feeble for him to yield to.

But the conflict takes place on a higher level, and the dénouement is not at all a mere return to the point of departure. Anthony is wrong if he thinks his faith remains intact. He has assisted at the disintegration of one world and the emergence of another, and a glimpse of this other is enough to send him into ecstasies. His mystical jubilation must have some other source than an overwhelmed creature's appeal to his creator; it bears a very close affinity to the "positivist" aspirations of Flaubert's own century. To want to "descend into the depths of matter" is to seek truth elsewhere than in the sky; it is to replace adoration of materialized spirit by communion with spiritualized matter. Whereas the universe used to find its justification in God, it now remained religious only in the sense that its elements were established in balance and harmony by a vital fiat. The old Spinozism had left the ideal realms of thought to embody itself in a philosophy of nature *à la* Haeckel; absolute belief had been transformed into relativism *à la* Renan. Instead of being swallowed up in the divine, man now formed part of a life which included the divine.

The conclusion of the 1872 *Saint Antoine* was not a negative one. Unlike the two earlier ones it presented a possible way out, in that, as Flaubert wrote to Goncourt, "the scientific cell" rendered faith superfluous, and knowledge gradually reduced the extent of the unknown. Saint Anthony does not think the unknown can ever be reduced to nothing. But his return to God is conditional, a sort of provisional choice of the lesser of two evils.

Flaubert found himself in the same ambiguous position. He shared the aspirations of the age of Darwin, Spencer, Marx, and Renan. He wanted to establish a scientific, impersonal literature which would further knowledge of man and the universe. But the goal seemed always to recede. Beyond the ever-widening frontiers of the known lurked vast continents inaccessible to merely human powers. Without even wishing to go into the final ends of life and the universe, Flaubert observed that they elude our grasp, and that although the problem may be stated more and more precisely, it remains unsolved. All man can do, therefore, is adopt an attitude; and between the religious attitude and the scientific there is nothing to choose. The job of the artist, a combination of saint and scholar, is to reconcile the two. He has to work in the sphere of the relative, while bearing in mind a certain image of the absolute.

Flaubert had moved away from the Faustian conception of the first two versions of *Saint Antoine*. Whereas in 1850 he had hastened towards unknown spiritual countries, made his greatest intellectual voyages, and made no attempt to disguise the insatiable enthusiasm which made him try to assimilate and possess the whole universe, in 1872 he fell back on life as an ultimate and sufficient reason. He knew now that he had at once to know it and invest it, to approach it from both angles, instead of harboring the youthful delusion that the universe created by the artist is the exact equivalent of divine Creation. The most the artist can do is to imitate it, and, while he himself is creating, believe himself back once more in the universe from which birth banished him. It was this "faith" which supported his work, justified his activity, even justified his existence. But this faith was not life. Flaubert was deliberately to produce "art" in the *Trois Contes* and establish a "burlesque critical encyclopedia" in *Bouvard et Pécuchet*. But he had given up hope of discovering, conquering, and rising above himself through a work of which he could speak as he had when he said "*Madame Bovary, c'est moi.*" Returning to his art as Saint Anthony returned to his prayers, he no longer believed that art could equal life, could *be* life. He regarded it now as simply the nearest and most lofty substitute vouchsafed to him.

Saint Antoine is thus a dual testament—that of his youth and its ambitions; that of his lost illusions. Like Lautréamont and Rimbaud, who made the same attempt at the same time as he, he had tried to barter life for existence; having failed, he was left with the alternatives of contradicting himself or being silent.

But he chose a third way, in keeping both with his temperament and with his habit of hard labor. This third way consisted in regarding artistic creation as a grim duty.

16

THREE TALES

*U*N CŒUR SIMPLE, *La Légende de Saint Julien l'Hospitalier,* and *Hérodias* were composed in the intervals of writing *Bouvard et Pécuchet,* the major work to which Flaubert devoted the last ten years of his life, dying before it was finished. Bereavements, ruin, attacks of depression and despair deprived him of strength and energy to work unremittingly at the novel itself. So to give himself a breathing-space and prove to himself that his genius was intact, he undertook shorter works on different subjects and in different styles, requiring a less massive effort. They emerge as products of a professionalism, experience, and aesthetic which have become part and parcel of the author himself, so that he need no longer suffer all the "throes of style."

Whereas in each of his major works up till then Flaubert had gone into the attack with a new vision and a new method, in the *Trois Contes* he trusted himself to his talent, and allowed himself to exploit the riches he had accumulated in the course of years of research. There was no question of just letting his pen run away with him. The sort of second nature he had attained to was made up of rigor and meticulousness and a feeling for beauty which allowed no half-measures. He researched, organized, corrected, and relied on his skill. But at least he did not despair of doing something worth while, or doubt of his success. He was like a virtuoso who after long practice and having overcome countless difficulties is completely master of his art, and can play the most difficult scores from memory.

And like a virtuoso, Flaubert entered into possession of worlds he had already explored and long inhabited, performed new variations on his own well-known themes, and thus allowed himself a pleasure he had almost always denied himself before. Different as they are from one another, the *Trois Contes* give the impression of an act of creation in which inspiration, theme, and writing all combine to form a single object, marked unmistakably with the stamp of Flaubert's genius.

The Legend of Saint Julian the Hospitaller

FIRST, CHRONOLOGICALLY, comes *La Légende de Saint Julien l'Hospitalier*. Flaubert had already thought of writing it several times, ever since he had studied the naive images illustrating the life of the saint in a stained-glass window in Rouen Cathedral. That was in 1846. Ten years later, in 1856, he returned to the project, then abandoned it. In 1875, after the Commanvilles' and his own ruin, when he had taken refuge at Concarneau with his friend Georges Pouchet, Flaubert, worn out and looking back over his life and the memories of his youth, thought he might kill time and distract his mind from his woes by at last putting this old project into effect.

In 1874, on the visit to Rigi-Kaltbad with his friend Laporte, he had made notes on the subject and done a good deal of reading, ranging from *La Légende Dorée*, written by Jacques de Voragine in the 13th century, through various treatises on hunting, falconry and painting on glass* to contemporary works by Lavallée and Blase.†

The story was to be broadly drawn, its general tone that of medieval legend such as it might be handed down by popular and religious folklore. Flaubert wanted to show a simple man a prey to human instinct, and subject, like Oedipus or Orestes, to a terrible fatality, from which he is ultimately saved by Grace. He had to steer a middle course between fairy-tale and hagiography, between plausibility of character and social and historical background and a certain atmosphere of magic. This magical element would give a deeper meaning to Julian's murderous sadism, and allow the whole of Creation to become

Essai historique et descriptif de la Peinture sur verre, by E. H. Langlois (1832), tells the story of Julian as depicted in the stained-glass window in Rouen Cathedral.

†*La Chasse de Gaston Phoebus, Conte de Foix*, by Lavallée (1834); *Le Livre du Roi Modus et de la Reine Ratio*, by E. Blase (1839).

active and vocal. Flaubert aimed at creating an effect of wonder, not through unbridled imagination or inordinate use of symbol, but by placing everything within a single consistent universe which lent its own values to men, events, and the world. Divine intervention itself would seem quite natural against a long tradition of the lives of saints and martyrs.

Flaubert had not taken on any difficulties which he could not overcome in a few months, and in February 1876 the story was finished.

The meaning he had wished to impart to "the story of Saint Julian such, more or less, as it is to be found in a church window in my country" is transmitted so clearly through the richest, most dense and beautiful prose Flaubert ever wrote that it placed Taine among the foremost of Flaubert's contemporary admirers. He wrote to the author: "It is not the Middle Ages itself, but the world as imagined by the Middle Ages. What you were aiming at when you tried to produce the effect of a stained-glass window is achieved: the pursuit of Julian by the animals, the leper—all this is the authentic mentality of the year 1200."

Men of letters as well as philosophers and historians gave their approval. From the time the story first appeared in serial form in *Le Bien Public* in April 1877 right up to the present day, everyone used the word *"chef-d'œuvre."* In 1893 Marcel Schwob exclaimed how hard it was "to imagine the miraculous transformation which decked in purple and gold" the simple figures of the legend as transmitted by tradition; he pointed out the skill with which the author had made Julian's soul human and the setting of the story vivid. Gustave Flaubert had succeeded in fusing into "one miraculous literary enamel all the trappings of chivalry, together with the simplest of popular religious tales."

In 1922, Albert Thibaudet was also struck by the "dazzling fusion," which, as Schwob said, enabled us to know "a soul very close to our own." Thibaudet went on: "Julian is caught up in the vortex of fate, a vortex which will not release him because it is his very nature, because it is our very nature." Flaubert seemed to have written this masterpiece of French prose "in a state of grace in which human affairs took on an absolute symbolic value, and in which everything, including style, unfolded with a kind of fluid necessity." Thus, by a paradox which has few parallels, the story Flaubert wrote by way of a "rest" from pressing anxiety turned out to be one of the greatest achievements of literary art.

Un Cœur simple

FLAUBERT WAS STILL in his "state of grace" when, with *Saint Julien* only just finished, he began to write *Un Cœur simple*. This story, too, was quickly written: he finished it in August 1876.

This time Flaubert plunged into his own legend, into the memories of his childhood and youth, among the people he had known in a world now vanished.

George Sand had criticized his earlier works for lack of feeling, harshness towards his characters, too critical an attitude towards life and the world, deliberate and systematic cantankerousness, and inhuman objectivity. *Un Cœur simple* was intended to show her that a novelist did not have to appear in his work and bedew it with tears in order to show the qualities prized by the *"chère maître,"* and that the milk of human kindness could flow from the author to his characters through the simplest, most naive, and most "realist" of stories. After George Sand's death Flaubert wrote to her son: "I began *Un Cœur simple* just for her, with the sole object of pleasing her. She died while I was in the middle of it. Thus is it with all our dreams."

While he was still "in the middle of it," in June 1876, he wrote to Mme Roger des Genettes: "I want to move, to bring tears to the eyes of the tender-hearted; I am tender-hearted myself." He summarized the work itself as follows: "The story of *Un Cœur simple* is just an account of an obscure life, the life of a poor country girl who is pious but mystical, faithful without fuss, and tender as new bread. She loves in turn a man, her mistress's children, her nephew, an old man she looks after, and then her parrot. When the parrot dies she has it stuffed, and when she too dies she confuses the parrot with the Holy Ghost." Then, anticipating Edma's smile, he added: "This is not at all ironical, as you suppose. On the contrary, it is very serious and very sad."

Life continued to rain blows on him, snatching away family and friends: Louise Colet's death in 1876 meant the loss of another part of his youth. He was haunted by the thought that by withdrawing from life in order to represent it better he might have made a fool's bargain. "I was a coward when I was young," he wrote to George Sand, "I was afraid of life. But everything has to be paid for." So he plunged more and more, as he grew older, into the nostalgic world of childhood, of his uncles and aunts, of his connections and acquaintances in Honfleur and Pont-l'Evêque. He saw again the lush water-meadows by the Touques, and the sunny landscapes of Trouville. And then, as Thibaudet says, he "cast a net over his former life," in order to dredge up the treasures hidden there. In the guise of the harsh and touching story of a loyal servant-girl—partly the Léonie of his friends the Barbeys at Trouville, partly his own old Julie—he brought to life again, sometimes under their real names, people he had known in the old days, and, in their real colors, places he had recently revisited, his heart full of sensations from the past.

Mme Aubain in the story is great-aunt Allais. Paul and Virginie, himself and his sister Caroline when they were young. Félicité's nephew, Victor, who dies of yellow fever in Havana, was really the nephew of Captain Barbey, who had already figured in the same way in the first *Education*. The Marquis of Gremanville was great-great-uncle Charles-François Fouet, better known to all his relations as "Councillor" de Crémanville from his post under the *ancien régime* as councillor-auditor to the Cour des comptes at Rouen. Even the parrot Loulou had a model in a stuffed bird Flaubert obtained from the Rouen Natural History Museum and kept in his work-room. The places in which the story was set were still unchanged when Gérard-Gailly visited them half-a-century later. "I went to Gefosses," he writes. "I walked up the sloping courtyard and saw the house in the middle, and the pond where Paul skimmed stones; and, from the highest point in the meadow, I made out, beyond a beautiful landscape, the 'grey patch' of the sea."

The sources have a special importance here. Flaubert, by making a dramatic transposition of his memories and composing the story of Félicité, intended to revive in himself, as accurately as possible, real episodes of his childhood, and to see the people and places concerned in their light. This was a substitute for the memoirs he had wanted to write but had abandoned; and he did not mean to have the story of his old servant found ridiculous. Into his account of this existence buffeted by all life's cruelties, he put all his heart, his regrets, and his nostalgia; he did so without departing from his aesthetic, thus accomplishing a *tour de force* from which all tension and effort seem absent. In this masterpiece of naturalness, noble sentiments do make excellent literature, in spite of Gide, and no one but Flaubert has the right to joke about this unexpected aspect of his talent. *"Cette fois-ci, on ne dira plus que je suis inhumain. Loin de là, je passerai pour un homme sensible, et l'on aura une plus belle idée de mon caractère,"* he wrote, when he had brought his story to a successful conclusion. ("This time they won't say I'm inhuman. On the contrary, I shall be considered a man of feeling, and people will take a nobler view of my character.")

This is not to say his philosophy had become gentle and optimistic. Though in the case of Félicité he was operating at the level of very elementary feelings, once again he was depicting the injustice of fate and the emptiness of all hopes. Whether one asked little or much of life, it always gave the same tragic and disillusioning answer.

"Hérodias"

FLAUBERT STARTED *Un Cœur simple* in March 1876. Already, in April, while he was still writing it, he was thinking of a tale in a completely different vein which in color, atmosphere, and characters would form a contrast with the "humble reality" he was now in the midst of. On August 17, immediately after finishing the story of Félicité, he wrote to his niece: "Herodias presents herself, and I *see* (clearly, as I *see* the Seine) the surface of the Dead Sea shimmering in the sun. Herod and his wife are on a balcony from which you can see the gilded tiles of the temple."

He had been caught up again in his dream of the East, this time linked to another image from Rouen Cathedral, where in a tympanum over one of the side doors Salome was sculpted dancing on her hands before Herod, with the executioner brandishing his sword nearby, preparatory to decapitating John the Baptist. The story was in the line of *Salammbô* rather than of the Scriptures, a tale full of ferocity and lust, in which Flaubert meant to wrest a morsel of living flesh from a confused history of Jews, Romans, Arabs, pagans, and sectaries of a faith in the process of being born. He also wanted it to be a significant episode, in the course of which, in a medley of races and religions, amidst the rebellions of subject peoples against Rome and their wars among themselves, Judaea, still awaiting a Messiah, became the true Promised Land. Flaubert isolated the moment of Salome's dance and the beheading of John the Baptist, the moment when history ceased to be the history of Mediterranean antiquity and became the history of the modern world.

He made use of the legend of Herodias. But what the Gospels of Saint Matthew and Saint Mark could not give him were the characters of the historical figures he wanted to portray, the psychological explanations of Herodias's victory over her husband, what lay behind the bold stratagem by which she extorted the monstrous promise from the Tetrarch. If *Salammbô* is like a fresco, *Hérodias* resembles one of those antique jewels engraved with some legendary or symbolic story, in which the infinite diversity of human feeling is expressed in myth.

Herod Antipas, a weak ruler whose power may be snatched away at any moment either by those above him or by those below, represents the craven cruelty of man governed by his appetites and in a chronic state of fear. Herodias, a mixture of "Cleopatra and de Maintenon," embodies the restless hatred of an ambitious woman who has backed the wrong horse and shrinks at nothing to rectify matters. Salome, so charming and innocently shameless, is a girl who is not unaware of the strange effect she has on men, and lets herself be used to pull other people's chestnuts out of the fire. Flaubert's other characters, while not drawn in depth, are vividly depicted: they are either borrowed from history or legend, or defined by their part in the action. Around them is a vast cacophonous choir of different races, bands, crowds and armies. And over and above all this, East and West meet in uncertain battle.

Flaubert condenses this prodigious panorama of political and religious history into a few pages, and shapes it with a few strokes. He did not achieve his object with the same facility as in the other two stories. He undertook harassing bibliographical and archaeological research for it; he got friends and acquaintances to help him with the vast documentation necessary; the worst worry of all was the fear that he might repeat the effects of *Salammbô*, when what he needed was an entirely different human and material climate. He exploited his own recollections of the Holy Land, and made Salome dance with the same wanton movement of the hips as Kuschiuk Hanem. It was only by a series of adjustments and readjustments that he finally managed to hold the balance between history and psychological truth. He was walking a tightrope and performing balancing acts at the same time. And yet sometimes he himself was astonished at the speed with which his pen raced across the paper; he said he was prey to "*une effrayante exaltation.*" He finished *Hérodias* in three months, at the end of January 1877.

A Cordial Reception

IN MARCH he sold *Hérodias* and *Un Cœur simple* to *Le Moniteur* and *La Légende de Saint Julien l'Hospitalier* to *Le Bien public*. At the end of the month Charpentier sent him the proofs of the book, which came out at the end of April. For these various publications Flaubert received what he considered enough to live on for a year, and his state of euphoria was the more pronounced because, for once, the critical reception was almost unanimously cordial.

Edouard Drumont talked of "marvels"; Saint-Valry, in *La Patrie*, of "an excellent combination of accuracy and poetry"; Charles Bigot, in *Le XIXe siècle*, spoke of "perfection"; even old enemies like Sarcey at last paid homage. Naturally, Flaubert's friends and admirers from the beginning were not to be outdone. Once again Théodore de Banville used his theater column to salute "three absolute and perfect masterpieces, created with the power of a poet sure of his art, who should only be spoken of with the respectful admiration due to genius." Karl Steen (Mme Alphonse Daudet) and Guy de Valmont (Maupassant) gladly joined in the raptures. Only Brunetière, espousing the old quarrels of *La Revue des Deux Mondes*, considered the *Trois Contes* "certainly the weakest thing Flaubert has done"; he alone saw in them "the sign of an imagination that is drying up." But this sour small voice was drowned by the acclamations of the "young men"—Paul Alexis, Henry Céard, Léon Hennique, J.-K. Huysmans, Octave Mirbeau, and Maupassant—who on April 16 gave a dinner in Flaubert's honor. Goncourt and Zola were also invited, and this caused the papers to announce the birth of the "*l'école naturaliste*."

The public reception was more reserved; or rather, the public's curiosity was soon satisfied. Their attention was distracted by a political crisis which led to the government of May 16, and this affected sales. At the beginning of the month Charpentier was selling three hundred copies a day, but this dwindled to a half-dozen or so. Flaubert changed his tune. "As for my poor book, it's completely flattened. All I can do is rub my belly." He returned to Croisset, "sick to death of Paris" and disillusioned once more. "To the dreariness of my private affairs is added the disintegration of public ones. My whole horizon is black." So he bravely set to again on *Bouvard et Pécuchet*.

"A Rather Strange Book"

WHILE *Trois Contes* served as a distraction for Flaubert during the more ambitious work he had in progress, and while it has not the weight of *Madame Bovary* or *L'Education sentimentale*, it does not deserve to be put in the shade by the books he took longer to write. These three short narratives are more like shoots off the main plant which take only a few weeks to flower. They bear witness to the vigor and potential of the tree itself. The *Trois Contes* also showed that Flaubert was not the mere plodder ill-informed criticism had made him out to be, but that he could mobilize his resources without undue time or trouble.

But the comparison must not be pushed too far. The usual view is that *Un Cœur simple* belongs to the same world of everyday reality as *Madame Bovary*, the description of which caused Flaubert to be dubbed a "realist." Still according to this view, *Saint Julien* derives straight from the religious and legendary world of *La Tentation*, while *Hérodias* comes from the highly-colored and barbaric world of *Salammbô*. All this would make the book a sort of synthetic summary of the author's talents, containing the three complementary aspects of his inspiration. But this is a very rough and ready account of the matter. In each case the story is not so much the issue of the novel concerned as a distant relation. But if Flaubert included them all in a single volume, he did so for good reasons.

Although he was hard up, he was too scrupulous to indulge in just putting a book together. And his usual indifference to publication absolves him of the suspicion of wanting to give his audience something to keep it going. It was after *Saint Julien*, while he was writing *Un Cœur simple* and thinking of *Hérodias*, that he spoke of publishing *"un livre assez drôle"*, that is, a book that would probably surprise people because of the obvious contrasts of subject and style, but which would in fact be an original and independent work, not intended to be too closely associated with his previous books. He did not see Félicité as Emma Bovary, and he does not make us enter into her consciousness. Saint Julian, unlike Saint Anthony, is not a man always asking himself questions, usually insoluble ones. And the Judaea of A.D. 30 bears no resemblance to Carthage. Nor are the mechanics of creation the same in *Trois Contes*. Flaubert had turned aside from the novel and from the "fundamentally impossible" book he was working at, the exact nature of which he was not sure

about. He wanted to try a new register he had felt he had a gift
for when he was young—as if he wished to prove to himself he
had not been wrong.

The Colors of the Past

IN HIS PREVIOUS WORKS Flaubert had tried to fill a void in
himself, though he never entirely succeeded in doing so, and
each book, once finished, left him still unsatisfied. In *Trois
Contes*, though he did not make this attempt, he did make use
of the same live substance, made up of different combinations
of reality and dream, observation and vision, myth and symbol,
intuition and deduction. This substance took form in accordance
with an internal logic which resolved each problem on a
different level of the past. For convenience, these levels may be
labelled historical, legendary, and personal; but Flaubert's
material in fact constituted a single imaginary world, subject to
Fate and sometimes to Grace, a world in which human resolves
are undone by life, and which is full of signs, premonitions, and
myths. The past invoked by Flaubert had in fact been remade
by men, as if to give it a meaning and prevent it falling into
oblivion.

Flaubert did the same with his own past. The story of
Félicité, like that of Hérodias and Julian, resembles a stained-
glass window or rough-cut image in stone.

Flaubert made this past actual by preserving its colors.
Whereas in *Madame Bovary* and *L'Education sentimentale* he wrote
from a present which unfolds before the reader's eyes, producing
in him the illusion of finding out what happens at the same time
as the author, in *Trois Contes* he retraces in each case a history
already over. For a greater or less time it has already been
consigned to the annals of history or memory, and Flaubert sets
his characters in motion against a framework given in advance
by public or private events. Instead of evolving freely, as in the
novel, and conducting the author towards new discoveries about
themselves, life, and himself, the characters obey a destiny
already sealed for ever.

The story-teller describes lives which are ended for good and all, and he has no power to intervene. He simply describes them, with art, accuracy, and verisimilitude.

This is perhaps why *Trois Contes* is not the first book of Flaubert's one turns to for excitement, surprise, and a lesson on life. But it does give us the opportunity of studying an example of perfect art, an art which consists in the extraordinary economy of the narrative and the vivid evocation of the characters and the very special worlds they live in, all expressed in a style which the author can modulate at will between dazzling and tense, dramatic and dreamy, sober and subtle. His only object is to enjoy, and to make us enjoy, his talents and his mastery of them. If it were anyone else but Flaubert one might think the creator had been given a holiday to leave scope for the artist. What *Candide* is to the 18th century, *Trois Contes* is to the 19th—one of the great triumphs of French prose.

17

BOUVARD AND PECUCHET

LAUBERT had not finished *Bouvard et Pécuchet* when he died
suddenly on May 8, 1880 in his study at Croisset, just as he
was getting ready to go to Paris.

Like *La Tentation de Saint Antoine*, the "story of the two clerks"
was "the work of his whole life." He had had the idea for it in
his youth, and he had devoted his last ten years to it. They were
the most difficult and exhausting years. What would the book
have been like if it had been finished? We can only conjecture,
and sift the various possibilities.

Caroline Commanville published it in April 1881, having
copied out Flaubert's notes for a "last chapter." This "last
chapter" makes a convincing enough epilogue to his two heroes'
adventures: discouraged by the failure of their experiments,
they decide to go back to "copying as before"* and find
happiness in returning to their former occupation. In so doing
they say goodbye to the world which has disappointed them
and trampled down their naive ambitions. They have not been
able to live in accordance with morality and justice, using reason
as their guide and applying the treasures of the accumulated
knowledge of mankind. Like both *Madame Bovary* and *L'Education sentimentale*, *Bouvard et Pécuchet* is on its own plane a novel of
irremediable failure. In it Flaubert attacks even more fiercely
than before humanity, the world, and life; what emerges most
specifically is man's weakness.

The novel appeared first serialized in reviews, then in book
form, but provoked little comment. In the year since his death,
much had been said about Flaubert and his work, and people

---

*The words "as before" (*comme autrefois*) were added by Flaubert's niece.
See Alberto Cento's critical edition of *Bouvard et Pécuchet* (Naples and Paris,
1964).

thought they knew what to think about both. For Barbey d'Aurevilly, *Bouvard et Pécuchet* confirmed the image of an "impotent" writer who had wallowed in "vulgarity" and "baseness" and who in his last work sometimes attained the "odious" and "disgusting." Barbey was not sure that if Flaubert were alive he would have wanted to publish the book, the appearance of which was due to the greed of the "jackals of posthumous literature." Some of Flaubert's friends were embarrassed. They could not make out why he had devoted the last ten years of his life to a work whose significance escaped them, and which seemed to be outside the bounds of the novel, perhaps even of literature itself. As for the established critics of the time, they remained prudently silent.

"An Affirmation of the Universal Stupidity"

BEFORE *Bouvard* was published, Zola (to whom Flaubert had spoken about it) said: "According to the author, *Bouvard et Pécuchet* is meant to be to the modern world what *La Tentation de Saint Antoine* is to the world of antiquity: a negation of everything, or rather an affirmation of the universal stupidity."

Maupassant expounded more fully. "It is a review of all the sciences as they appear to two minds which are fairly lucid, but undistinguished and simple. It is . . . above all a prodigious critique of all scientific systems, set one against the other, destroying one another through contradictions of fact or through contradictions in laws which are accepted without examination. It is the story of the weakness of the human intelligence . . . the eternal and universal stupidity." Maupassant, too, compares it with *Saint Antoine*: "What Flaubert had done for the old religions and philosophies . . . he did again for all modern learning." The book showed "the uselessness of effort, the futility of assertion, and always the eternal poverty of everything."

Maupassant based his views on a fact that was known to Flaubert's niece but which she did not mention. This was the existence, in addition to the novel proper, of a "shattering" collection of stupid remarks and observations, a "mountain of notes left too scattered and unorganized ever to be published in their entirety." According to Maupassant this "dossier of human folly" was to have formed the "crown . . . conclusion . . . and dazzling justification" of the novel. He reproduced the main chapter headings and some samples: slips, blunders, absurd periphrases, and other howlers perpetrated by philosophers and writers, some of them very illustrious. He says this was the material which the two "copyists" were to copy out. "Flaubert intended . . . to make a whole volume out of this material. To make the collection of absurdities lighter and less tedious, he would have interspersed it with two or three stories in a vein of poetic idealism, these also copied out by Bouvard and Pécuchet."

Maupassant knew what he was talking about, and exegetists and commentators might have saved themselves a lot of trouble in the last eighty years if they had paid attention to what he said. Maupassant is categorical: the book as published lacks not only one chapter—the chapter copied out by Caroline Commanville—but also a second volume, a second part probably equivalent in length to the first, which would have "crowned" the whole structure and been its "dazzling justification." Maxime Du Camp repeats and confirms this in his *Souvenirs littéraires*: "The book which death did not leave him time to finish and which has been published under the title of *Bouvard et Pécuchet* has only one volume. But Flaubert intended it to have two." And Du Camp, like Maupassant, says this second volume was to have been "a collection of supporting documents justifying the first." Du Camp was pleased this second volume had not in fact appeared: it would have contained a dozen or so of his own expressions which Flaubert had described as "beautifully silly," together with some bloomers by Flaubert himself. This "mountain of notes" is now in the Library in Rouen.

An Old Project: The Dictionary of Clichés

THE EXISTENCE of what, following Maupassant, has been called *Le Sottisier* (Jestbook), extracts of which have been published, throws a strange light on what the real scope of Flaubert's last work must have been. We recall a letter he wrote to Bouilhet from Damascus in 1850: "You do well to think about the *Dictionnaire des Idées recues*. This book, properly got up and preceded by a preface in due form, explaining that the object was to recommend tradition, order, and universal convention, and set out in such a way that the reader doesn't know whether his leg is being pulled or not, might make an unusual piece of work—maybe a successful one too, for it would be completely topical." It appears from this that it was a project the two friends had in common; they had probably begun to carry it out.

Two years later, while he was working at *Madame Bovary*, Flaubert came back to his "old idea" and told Louise Colet about it.

> I sometimes have frightful itchings to slate the human race, and I'll do it some day ten years hence, in some long, wide-ranging novel. Meanwhile, an old idea has come back to me, my *Dictionnaire des Idées reçues* (do you know what that is?). The preface especially excites me, and the way I see it (it would be a whole book) no law could touch me although I'd attack everything. It would be a historical glorification of everything that is approved of. I'd show that majorities have always been right, and minorities always wrong. I'd sacrifice the great men to all the imbeciles, the martyrs to all the executioners, and all this in a far-fetched and pyrotechnical style . . . This apology for all aspects of human scurviness, ironical and vehement throughout, full of quotations, proofs (which prove the opposite), and hair-raising extracts (that'll be easy), would profess as its object the finishing off once for all of every kind of eccentricity. I should thereby join up with the modern democratic idea of equality, and Fourier's dictum that great men will become superfluous. And this, I shall say, is the object with which the book was written. It would therefore contain, in alphabetical order and on every possible subject, all you need to say in public to pass for a decent agreeable fellow . . .

After giving a few examples, he concludes: "The whole book must not contain a single word of my own invention, so that once anyone has read it he'll be afraid to utter, for fear of letting out one of the phrases in it."

Flaubert did write the *Dictionnaire*, or at least part of it. He made use of it for both *Madame Bovary* and *L'Education senti-mentale*, and one can form an almost complete idea of it from the published extracts of *Le Sottisier*. But a question remains: is *Bouvard et Pécuchet* to be taken as the "preface" of which Flaubert spoke to Bouilhet, or as the "long, wide-ranging novel" he mentioned to Louise Colet?

Another Project: the Story of Two Clerks

FLAUBERT GOT THE IDEA of writing the story of "two clerks" after *Salammbô*, while he was hesitating between various projects, one of which became *L'Education sentimentale*. In a notebook which Mme Marie-Jeanne Durry published in 1950, he sketched portraits of Dumolard (or Dubolard)—"fat," "fair curly hair," based on "old Couillère," a mayor of Trouville he had imitated in his youth—and Pécuchet, described as having a "pointed nose." They meet on a bench in the Boulevard Bourdon, dream about the country, then go and live there and begin their "fruitless experiments." Flaubert notes briefly: "Gardening, agriculture, politics, literature, history, socialism, metaphysics, religion, science, they try to adopt a child, education, two children, hoping to marry them off later." He knows how it will all end: "In the copies, antithetical pictures—crimes of kings and peoples and their good deeds are sometimes difficult to distinguish.—Moral problem." In 1863 he had already sketched the plan for *Bouvard et Pécuchet* and the *Sottisier*, which, though it would grow more complex, was not to be seriously modified.

No doubt he recalled *L'Histoire naturelle*, *Genre commis*, which he had published when he was fifteen in *Le Colibri*; he may well also have remembered a short story by Barthélemy Maurice called *Les Deux Greffiers*, published twice in 1841 (in *La Gazette des Tribunaux* and in *Le Journal des Journaux*) and reprinted in 1858 in *L'Audience*. It was the story of two clerks who retire with their wives to Touraine to live as they please. They undertake various unsatisfactory experiments in hunting, fishing, and gardening, have "words," return on the sly to their "copying," and confess that "their sole pleasure is to resume, in make-believe, the arid task which for thirty-eight years had been the occupation and, perhaps without their knowing it, the happiness of their lives."

Flaubert never mentioned Maurice's story either in his letters or in conversation. When Daudet, after his death, discovered what he took to be the "source" of *Bouvard et Pécuchet* he told Edmond de Goncourt about it in confidence. Goncourt, in his *Journal*, did not beat about the bush. He expressed astonishment "that Flaubert had not been restrained by the knowledge that some day or other this sort of plagiarism would be discovered". Another disciple of little faith went one better: Goncourt notes that Henry Céard says "*Le Candidat* is taken outright from *Une Journée d'Elections* by Lezay-Marnésia, and that everything is there, even the romantic journalist." Since then, fortunately, people have read *Les Deux Greffiers* first-hand, and Descharmes and Dumesnil have made a detailed analysis of *Une Journée d'Elections*. And Flaubert's shade can rest in peace. He certainly read Maurice's story, but at the most it only served to remind him of his old project, confided long ago to Du Camp, of writing the "story of two clerks," or perhaps even provided him with a background. He was in so little haste to "plagiarize" that after having made a few notes in 1863 he decided the idea was not yet ripe enough and turned to *L'Education sentimentale*. He returned to the project in 1870, before the desire to rewrite *La Tentation* prevailed once more over anything new.

Perhaps the *Tentation* was a necessary preliminary, perhaps he had to deal with ancient follies before depicting modern ones. At all events the old project began to be translated into fact after the third version of the *Tentation*, and in 1872 he told George Sand he would like both books to appear at the same time. That was one of his reasons for holding back publication of *Saint Antoine*: "I'm working on one now which could be a companion-piece to it . . . a modern novel, forming a counterpart to *Saint Antoine*, which will lay claim to being comic." While for him the two books are to be "quite different," he still considers them as part of the same purpose. Both are to be against "stupidity."

Preparatory Labor

WHEN *La Tentation* was finished in July 1872, Flaubert embarked on a "colossal" program of reading in order to bone up on all the subjects in which his heroes were to plunge, and also so that he himself should know the "last word" on the various sciences, from the philosophy of medicine to ethics and metaphysics, taking in on the way all the diverse branches of knowledge suggested by circumstance, chance, and the two students' desire to be encyclopedic. Flaubert devoted two years to this reading, interrupting it only to attend to Bouilhet's affairs and to write *Le Candidat*. He "ruined" himself buying books, spent days in the Bibliothèque Impériale and the library at Rouen, and borrowed books from them to use at home. In June 1874 he told Mme Roger des Genettes he had read 294 volumes; six years later the figure was "over 1,500." And according to the most recent commentators this figure is probably an under-estimate.

The object of all this reading was to compile, as he had announced long ago, *"une encyclopédie critique en farce"* (a burlesque critical encyclopedia), or in other words to assemble, listed under authors and subjects, as many howlers, contradictions, and absurdities as possible, committed by people of serious reputation. The reader was thus to be convinced of the nothingness of the human intelligence, of *"l'eternelle misère de tout* (the eternal poverty of everything)." While the failure of two minds which are avowedly "simple" and even "undistinguished" and yet "fairly lucid" is due in part to their own "lack of method," it constitutes even more the failure of science, unable to give clear, intelligible, and sound explanations of the world, history, and human actions. Just like the old religions and philosophies, science, for all its pretensions, is foiled by the unknowable. It has replaced fables, myths, and visions by explanations scarcely less fantastic, and often just as dependent on self-interest, opinion, and convention. It has substituted for the old fanaticisms new obligations to believe, and, as it claims to be based on reason, its laws and decrees are heavy with threats. It leads straight to the barracks of industrialism, to a "*pignouflisme universel*," universal oafishness.

The Breath of Wrath

FLAUBERT WAS NOT in any frame of mind to carry out this inquiry coolly and objectively. On the contrary, his principles of impassivity seem to have been undermined by the defeat of 1870, inflicted by "educated men" and "scientists" in uniform, sacking and slaying; by the insurrection of the Communards, whom Flaubert dismissed as "mad dogs"; by his numerous bereavements, especially the death of his mother; and by his disgust for his contemporaries and congenital hatred of the "*bourgeois*." Gone was the time of the impersonal artist, reigning throughout his work like God in Creation. Now, from the top of his ivory tower, he meant to "spit on his contemporaries."

A few days in a single month in 1872 show him sharpening up his weapons. "I'm pondering something in which I'll breathe forth my wrath," he writes to Mme Roger des Genettes. "Yes, at last I'll get rid of what's choking me. I'll spew out on my contemporaries the contempt they inspire in me even if I break my ribs in the attempt. It will be vast and violent . . ." The same day he writes to his friend Mme Brainne:

> *Tout cela dans l'unique but de cracher sur mes contemporains le dégoût qu'ils m'inspirent. Je vais enfin dire ma manière de penser, exhaler mon ressentiment, vomir ma haine, expectorer mon fiel, éjaculer ma colère, déterger mon indignation—et je dédierai mon bouquin aux mânes de saint Polycarpe . . .* (And all this with the sole object of spitting out on to my contemporaries the disgust they inspire in me. At last I'm going to say what I think, exhale my resentment, spew forth my hatred, expectorate my spleen, ejaculate my anger, deterge my indignation—and I shall dedicate my book to the shade of Saint Polycarp . . .)

And he continues:

> *Mais avant de crever, ou plutôt en attendant une crevaison, je désire "vuider" le fiel dont je suis plein. Donc je prépare mon vomissement.*

Il sera copieux et amer, je t'en réponds . . . (But before I croak, or
rather in the meantime, I want to void the spleen that fills me.
So I'm preparing my vomit. It will be copious and bitter,
I can tell you . . .)

People have been surprised that this "wrath," this "hatred,"
this "spleen," were channelled into a story evoking laughter,
even though the comedy is sometimes sinister; they have been
surprised that the "vomit" turned out to be a jest-book arousing
amusement rather than indignation. Is it that we have become
more tolerant, or blasé? Do we not now regard as a cliché the
fact that the human mind is fallible, and that truth is sometimes
revealed through the accumulation of error? Might it not be
that Flaubert, who often makes his heroes his spokesmen, is
almost as naive as they?

And yet *Bouvard et Pécuchet* really is *"le livre des vengeances"* that
was promised. Its revenge is subtle: by insidious inlets it seeps
into the reader's mind and saps the foundations of both the
commonest and the most grandiose ideas. The artist has played
a part, adding to what might have been just a lampoon several
extra dimensions which transcend the author's original intentions and the time and place of the writing, stretching across
eighty years to link up with our present preoccupations. If, like
many a masterpiece, *Bouvard et Pécuchet* remains an enigma, this
is not for the reasons alleged by its contemporaries, but because
its author depicted in it a mystery which is part of the human
condition.

A Long Journey

OUR BEST PROOF that the artist prevailed over the man of
resentment and wrath comes two years later in the letter Flaubert
wrote to Turgenev on July 25, 1874, when he was confronting
the actual writing of his "infernal" book: "I feel I'm about to
embark on a very long journey, a journey to unknown regions
from which I shall never return." He had felt the same about the
previous "long journeys," those of *Madame Bovary, Salammbô,*
and *L'Education sentimentale.* Once again, although his plan was

perfectly clear, he was setting out for the unknown; he even had a presentiment of the fact that he would not come back. This "anchors aweigh!" is absolutely typical of the Flaubert we admire as man and as artist; for him it had always been something more than just a departure for literature. If he died in harness, it was because his task was also an exacting and ambitious quest, which literally wore him out.

About the book which he intended to be comic he wrote to Turgenev: "One could make it into something serious and even appalling." To his niece he wrote: "The difficulties of this book are frightful. I'm capable of passing out in harness." Can he really be talking of the fairly simple story of his two clerks? "This book is diabolical!" he wrote to Caroline on another occasion. And to George Sand: "You'd have to be absolutely crazy to take on a book like this. I'm afraid it may be, in its very conception, fundamentally impossible . . . Ah, if I brought it off! . . . what a dream!" Months, years went by, and it was always the same: the "cursed," "infernal," "horrible" book sometimes "dazzles him by its immense scope," sometimes makes him tremble and seems to yawn beneath him like a "gulf that grows wider at every step." In 1878 he told Mme Brainne: "It's something so audacious I could completely break my back at it."

What was all this really about? It was about an attempt which no artist before him had dared to make with the same rigor and the same method: it attacked what had been the private preserve of philosophers, reformers, and moralists, and did indeed seem an "impossible" venture. Where others had made people laugh at individuals and their follies, vices, and absurdities, Flaubert wanted to make comedy out of the thoughts and ideas which constituted the common stock of contemporary life. It was no longer a matter of making the reader laugh at the expense of his neighbor, but of taking the gentle reader himself as the target, and forcing him, if he wants to avoid branding himself a coward, into a profound self-examination. By placing the reader on various roads to knowledge which all end in an impasse, Flaubert aims at forcing him back on his own lazy or frivolous retreats, driving him back on question marks, and making him admit that what he took to be true is neither certain nor sound nor even very reasonable. He wanted to sow so much doubt in his mind that he would even doubt his own existence. He told Mme Brainne that his "secret aim" was "to disconcert the reader so much that he goes crazy (*ahurir tellement le lecteur qu'il en devienne fou*)." But he had not reckoned with men's power to delude themselves and their capacity for indifference. And indeed these qualities had to exist for his book to be regarded as comic, for his critical encyclopedia to be taken as a "burlesque." And Flaubert's hatred of humanity was not so great that he could not offer it two scapegoats, and let it have a comfortable laugh at Bouvard and Pécuchet.

Out of His Depth

IN MAY 1875 Flaubert was swept out of his depth: when he heard of the Commanvilles' débâcle and his own ruin he let his bitterness overflow. Then, at Concarneau, he wrote *Saint Julien l'Hospitalier*, and, back in control again, spent 1876 and the beginning of 1877 writing *Un Cœur simple* and *Hérodias*. The *Trois Contes* were well received, and it was in quite good spirits that he returned to his "*deux bonshommes*." As early as March he was writing to Mme Roger des Genettes: "This evening, at last, I've put back on my desk the files on my big interrupted novel, and I'm going to try to resume my task." He was not to leave it again until his death.

His problems were of all kinds. Of documentation in the first place. Also of the distribution of material, for his two heroes had to make a more or less comprehensive tour of human knowledge in a sequence which would both seem natural and be of mounting difficulty. There was also the problem of literary organization: for Flaubert intended to write a real novel, with interesting characters and situations, and with its theme not weakened but reinforced by chance, surprise, and accident.

The preparatory labor was enormous. The papers he left have only recently been seriously interpreted. They contain no fewer than seven complete and detailed synopses, and there are a large number of break-downs for different chapters to be devoted to some particular science or branch of learning. When they were published in 1964 these papers ran to nearly three hundred large printed pages. They show Flaubert mastering the knowledge his two heroes were to attempt, forming an opinion about the way the various "authorities" distinguished themselves, and drawing his own conclusions before handing over the reins to the two clerks. Flaubert had to possess the critical approach which Bouvard and Pécuchet lacked in order that they might happen at the right moment on the howler or inconsistency or evasion which evokes their indignation or surprise. It is then that they turn, disappointed and disgusted, to another subject. At the risk of some implausibility, Flaubert had to save time by prompting them with his own conclusions. It has often been asked whether they expressed Flaubert's opinions. The answer seems practically certain when we read in one of the synopses: "They may . . . after making a study, formulate their opinion(=mine) by desiderata in the form of axioms."

And yet they are absurd, and there is no doubt that Flaubert intended them to be so. But "they are not just a couple of imbeciles," he wrote in the original plan of the novel. And it is true that in addition to their touching zeal and thirst for knowledge they have preoccupations which are not at all ignoble. Flaubert saw them as "having many feelings and embryonic ideas which they find it hard to express." He adds that "by the very fact of their contact with one another they develop." They are not the same at the end of the novel as at the beginning. Their new attitude towards the people of Chavignolles arises from the fact that they have developed, and come to understand a certain number of things.

The Discovery of Stupidity

WHAT MAKES US LAUGH just as much as their "lack of method" is their ever-renewed and always ill-rewarded enthusiasm, their indefatigable patience, in short their belief that the vast realm of knowledge is open to them, without any previous apprenticeship, by mere virtue of the fact that they want to explore it. They suffer from the drawback of all autodidacts, or rather from the even more widespread ill of average humanity, which, unable to go back to the originals, has to fall back on popularizers, the general opinion, clichés, *idées reçues*. It is in fact the authors of textbooks, catechisms, summaries and treatises that Flaubert is fustigating—the dogmatism, intolerance, and conformism of all these popularizers and pseudo-savants. If Bouvard and Pécuchet are ridiculous for growing melons according to the precepts of a book on gardening, when in such a case experience and practice are at least as important as knowledge, they are excusable when they follow the "distinguished" intellects who undertake to reveal to them the mysteries of the various religious, philosophical, and metaphysical systems. Copyists by profession, they are disposed to believe what they are told, and the printed word has for them religious force. They are outraged by the way people ill-use the truth, which for them becomes more and more elusive, until they finally doubt, despite the assertions of the authors they have consulted, whether it exists at all. In short, they discover that life is not at all like what the books say.

They arrive at this discovery through their reading itself, and through the comparison they are obliged to make, say, between the teachings of Christianity and the behavior of the Abbé Jeufroy, or between the ethical precepts of Foureau and what he does. They see those who possess knowledge and power, the local worthies, acting in contradiction to their convictions and the ideas they profess, and obeying instead self-interest, fear, and received opinion. Once they have perceived this complacent and aggressive form of stupidity, it is not long before they are unable to "bear" it. And at the thought of there being "other Coulons, others Marescots, and other Foureaus from here to the antipodes," they feel as if "the weight of the whole earth" is bearing down on them. They had made such progress, according to their author, that "their evident superiority was offensive." They then ceased to be harmless and became subversive, and the gendarmes were sent after them.

Whatever had been their methods of acquiring knowledge, and though each time they started from scratch without having learned anything from sad experience, they did end up by penetrating the mystery of a world based on quite other realities than ideas, ethics, and knowledge. By dint of trapping in their humble snares a truth which always evaporates, leaving in its stead a doubt so agonizing that they think of killing themselves, they end by emerging into a certainty with which they arm themselves to bring about the rule of justice. At this antepenultimate stage of the novel they are touching rather than ridiculous. Their good-will and naivety, which might almost be called a love of the absolute, have saved them. They return to their copying because the world which oppresses them is too heavy to be lifted. They do as Flaubert has done: they shut themselves up in their ivory tower, and avenge themselves by cataloguing, with a sort of morose delectation, all the stupidities they have ever read or heard of.

An Osmosis

DESPITE HIS DETAILED SCENARIOS telling the story from A to Z before it was actually written, Flaubert was unable to withhold from his two heroes the same sympathy which had led him to side with Emma and Frédéric. This time the characters he created were very distant from himself; he meant to make people laugh at them; their way of life was one of those he abominated most, yet he could not help raising them to the level of his own concerns, and launching them as executors of justice, latter-day Don Quixotes against the windmills of Chavignolles. Dressed up as archaeologists, mesmerists, or utopian socialists, armed with textbooks and pamphlets, they recall the Knight of the Woeful Countenance spurring his steed into action, lance in hand and lettuce on head. Don Quixote believed in the romances of chivalry: Bouvard and Pécuchet believe in science. The absurdity and illusion are the same, except that Flaubert's contemporaries scarcely realized it, worshipping as they did the same idol of a positivist age, and thinking to find the answer to all their questions in the unlimited progress of science.

The distance Flaubert set between himself and his characters dwindled as the work advanced. "I'm afraid of having exhausted my brain," he wrote in 1874. "It may be that I'm too full of my subject, and the stupidity of my two heroes is invading me." Again in 1875 he says he is "invaded" by them, "to such a degree that I've become them. Their stupidity is mine and it's killing me." He was, in fact, beginning to resemble them. In naivety: he said that if he brought off his novel the earth "would not be worthy" to bear it. In harking after the absolute: "If I succeed it will, seriously, be the highest peak of Art." He had become them because they had become him, like Emma and Frédéric. Though they were absurd characters, laughably credulous, they gradually became his spokesmen; when the novel was almost finished, they even became his executors! In 1880 he told Auguste Sabatier that *Bouvard et Pécuchet* was his "testament"—"a résumé of my experience and my judgment on man and the works of man." He conveyed his last wishes to posterity through the two clerks. How much black humor there was in their story is suggested by his remark to Du Camp: he said he wanted "to produce such an impression of lassitude and *ennui* that in reading the book one might think it had been written by a cretin."

A Nameless Work

"A PURELY philosophical work. Nothing could be less like a novel," wrote Henry Céard when *Bouvard et Pécuchet* was published. He was right, if one thinks in terms of *Madame Bovary* or *L'Education sentimentale*. Flaubert seems to have given up wanting to "represent life" in a certain way or according to a certain aesthetic,* and although he still pays a modicum of

*Though he said he wanted to "return to the novel" when he had finished *Bouvard et Pecuchet*, and indeed had two or three projects for novels in mind.

attention to realism and verisimilitude, he is less concerned with the psychological evolution of each of his heroes than with their shared intellectual adventures. That was his theme and he stuck to it. Bouvard and Pécuchet are only "typical" in so far as they represent average humanity. Their actual case is exceptional. And in order to lend it scope, the author has to abstract them from the world, life, and their own individuality, leaving the traditional raw material of the novel in the background and making it serve as a touchstone or foil. When Bouvard and Pécuchet return to the world their adventures—and the novel— are almost over. The same is true of Robinson Crusoe and Don Quixote. Bouvard and Pécuchet have even lived outside time: according to the dates given in the novel, they are about to embark on a new life at the age of eighty-five. Historical events such as the 1848 revolution and the *coup d'état* of December 2 punctuate a lapse of time of much longer duration. In a way, everything has taken place in their heads. Is it not because they are dreamers that life has confounded them so calamitously? "There is probably no name for my book in any language," Flaubert said. It might perhaps be called a philosophical novel, or a *conte*, but the question is of no importance. Once again, Flaubert was attempting something different from before. And *Bouvard et Pécuchet*, because of the encyclopedic sweep of its subject and the urgent and fundamental questions it poses, takes its place naturally by the side of the *Odyssey*, *Pantagruel*, *Don Quixote*, and *Robinson Crusoe*, all of them unclassifiable works which succeeding generations interrogate each in their own way, and which remain permanent sources of warmth and life, patiently abiding all question and all commentary.

Views

ACCORDING to Paul Bourget, Bouvard and Pécuchet suffer from a disease which gets worse as their century wears on: excess of thought, intellectualism. They symbolize the human race "playing with thought like a child playing with poison." Instead of staying within their class, sticking to their last, and being content to live according to their instincts, they take it into their heads to meddle with the dangerous substance which, as Mme Flaubert told her son, "dries up the heart." In Bourget's view, this was the disease which afflicted Flaubert himself. He wanted to be an "intellectual," he had never known "love, happy and fulfilled effusion, the soft abandonment of hope." He was ignorant of "happiness of the strict observance, the serenity of moral and religious obedience." The sin for which Flaubert was punished was that of wanting to think for himself. Happiness in life, like the happiness of the soul, resided in obedience to the beliefs and opinions of the community, and it was vanity and folly to want to do otherwise.

Jules de Gaultier, who had invented and worked out the idea of "*Bovaryisme*," also thought the two copyists were wrong to harbor thoughts which were above them. Like Emma, they aimed at what was beyond them and ended up living in illusion. They "symbolize humanity," and exhibit "the enormous disproportion between the goals the human mind sets itself and the results of its researches." Flaubert had written not so much an epic of stupidity as an epic of intelligence, always fallible and never still.

Emile Faguet contented himself with considering the book from the point of view of literature. For him it was a "*roman manqué*," and, worse still, "boring." Flaubert was justly punished for his "pride," and it was a good thing he had died before the book was finished, for it would have been very painful to him to see it fall so far short of his hopes.

So opinions differed. Strangely enough, comment on the book tended to take the form of glosses, as if the disease Bouvard and Pécuchet suffered from was contagious. Critics took refuge in general or pseudo-philosophical ideas, or converted these into considerations dictated by circumstance or the opinion of the moment. *Bouvard et Pécuchet* is a mirror both for readers and for critics, and the latter, though they have often enough looked in it, have rarely shown the cautiousness of Albert Thibaudet, who suspected that any judgment passed on Flaubert's last work was itself a likely candidate for the *Sottisier*. He saw in this a proof of the book's "plasticity" and "validity." In fact the novel is a snare for critics; they infallibly get caught up in its toils, as in those of *Ulysses* (Joyce owed much to Flaubert and to *Bouvard et Pécuchet* in particular) and of the novels of Kafka, another of Flaubert's admirers. Perhaps it is wisest just to say, with Remy de Gourmont, that "*Bouvard et Pécuchet* is amusing in the profoundest sense of the word," but that not everyone can appreciate it. It is "pre-eminently a book for the strong, for it has much bitterness in it, and its whiff of the void strikes right home."

Not even all Flaubert enthusiasts have liked the book. Some have said that since it was unfinished it should not have been published. Others have praised it lavishly, while secretly regretting that Flaubert did not go as far as Jarry, for example, in his satire. In any case, how was one to see, in this combination of diagram and caricature, the highly subtle author of *Madame Bovary*, or the painter of the *Education*'s intermittences of the heart? Not until the "literary reign of terror" about a quarter of a century ago did it become fashionable to admire only *Bouvard et Pécuchet* among all Flaubert's works. But although traces of this attitude still persist, the two clerks are not colorful enough to be the figureheads of a new movement. And who could love them for themselves, or draw lessons in conduct from their behavior? Although they are heroic, they are anti-heroes *par excellence*.

A Course of Modesty

AMONG OUR CONTEMPORARIES only a Bouvard-et-Pécuchetist of long standing, whose admiration dates from before the "terror," has dared to say straight out that *Bouvard et Pécuchet* is "one of the master works of Western literature," comparable, in its relation to the modern world and its concerns, to what the *Odyssey* was to Ancient Greece. According to Raymond Queneau, author of *Les Enfants du Limon* and *Exercices de Style*, just as *Ulysses* does something more than catalogue the countries of the Mediterranean basin, so Bouvard and Pécuchet do something more than catalogue human knowledge. They believe in "the absolute validity of the human mind confronted with phenomena," in a strict correlation between the capacity to know and the material to be explored; and to perceive that the two only encounter each other by chance fills them with rage and disgust. Through their experiments they learn not so much their own limits as the limits of the human condition.

Queneau does not see Flaubert as a declared enemy of science, and this corresponds with what we ourselves have learned of him. He is on the same side as science in so far as it is "skeptical, reserved, methodical, prudent, and humane," in so far as it does not show the arrogance of things exclusively of the mind. What he attacks—with less chance than in the *Tentation* of making allies and friends—are the dogmatists who claim, as he wrote a few months before he died, to have "*le bon Dieu (ou le non Dieu)*" in their pocket, and who take their stand on a single explanation of things. For him they are "ignoramuses . . . charlatans . . . idiots" who see only one side of things and never the whole, and because they have committed the "ineptitude of drawing conclusions" they seek to impose their solutions on their contemporaries and dominate over them. To ensnare them in their own blunders and absurdities is more than a healthy amusement; it is a necessary measure of hygiene.

It may be that Flaubert, an admirer of the East writing under the eye of his big porcelain Buddha, intended *Bouvard et Pécuchet* to give to mankind a course of modesty *à la* Zen.

18

THE LAST YEARS

LAUBERT'S LAST YEARS were years of sadness, solitude, and seclusion. More than once he invoked death, hoping for "a good attack" which would deliver him both from his "impossible task" and from life. Completely occupied as he was with *Bouvard et Pécuchet* and his *"misère* (poverty)," which was known and publicly lamented, he scarcely heard the murmur which rose around him of admiration for his work and his example, and of friendship for himself. He thought he had sacrificed his honor and his independence as a writer by making various advances which were repugnant to him, not realizing that by the dignity of his life he had won the respect even of the indifferent.

He managed his budget from day to day, only going up to town when necessary. "If I don't go to Paris," he wrote to Maupassant, "it's because I haven't a penny to bless myself with. That's the explanation of the whole mystery, in addition to the fact that I have no place to stay—I leave the one I had to my niece . . ." What distressed him even more than "privations" and "the complete absence of freedom I'm forced into" was the business activity the Commanvilles had reduced him to taking part in: he had to sign bills, authorize powers of attorney, cope with process-servers, let himself be encroached on by all the maddening "base preoccupations" with which he had always refused to have anything to do. *"Je me sens souillé dans mon esprit,"* he wrote to Léonie Brainne, "I feel as if my mind is *soiled.*"

"Chère Caro," instead of trying to preserve her uncle's peace, was more concerned with making use of his credit and connections. Without even the excuse of necessity she brought about a rupture between him and Edmond Laporte, one of his best friends.

Caroline and the "Vieux Chéri"

LAPORTE was a small-time businessman and local worthy at Grand-Couronne until he was ruined in 1877. Nearly every day he crossed the river to visit his neighbor, see if he needed anything, and help him in his labors. It was he who had come and joined him in Rigi-Kaltbad in 1874, and he accompanied him on his journeys in Normandy in search of a suitable retreat for Bouvard and Pécuchet. When Flaubert slipped on the ice in the garden at Croisset on January 25, 1879, fracturing a fibula, Laporte was the "*sœur de charité*" who for three months came and sat with the invalid and acted as his unpaid secretary.

Flaubert did not let his "*vieux chéri*" outdo him in kindnesses. He sent him the morocco-bound manuscript of *Trois Contes*. After Laporte's ruin, Flaubert interceded with Agénor Bardoux, Minister of Education, to find him a post, and in June 1879 Laporte left to become divisional inspector of labor in Nevers. In spite of the distance they remained close friends. Flaubert still needed his "Bab" to copy out new material for the *Sottisier*, and to chase after information and books. In September he wrote: "I've amassed some notes for the second volume, and we'll have to get down to it this winter, *mon bon*, when you've done with all your public duties."

Caroline, who knew Laporte's devotion to her uncle, had at various times got him to act as her husband's guarantor, and in 1879 when the Commanvilles' situation grew desperate yet again, she asked Laporte to renew his guarantees. Laporte, who saw the situation more clearly than Flaubert and knew Commanville was heading for disaster, refused; in any case, he had lost his own fortune and was not in a position to take the risk. Caroline got her uncle to write to him, but Laporte still declined; and Caroline, furious, forced Flaubert to break with him. Several months later Flaubert wrote to his niece that he still thought often of Laporte, adding cryptically, "That's something I haven't found it easy to swallow." But Caroline did not give up a grudge in a hurry: in 1929, fifty years later, she still took pleasure in remembering that when Laporte came to pay his last respects immediately on Flaubert's death, Maupassant turned the "traitor" out of the house.

The Search for a Sinecure

THE ONLY PLOT Laporte had had anything to do with had been the friendly conspiracy of Turgenev, Zola, Daudet, Goncourt and others to try to get Flaubert the post of Librarian of the Mazarine. The difficulties were not so much on the side of officialdom as on that of the hermit himself. He kept hesitating and changing his mind, and when he finally did agree his candidacy failed because of a change of government, and "the excellent Monsieur Baudry", Librarian of the Arsenal, was appointed. But Flaubert was apparently to be spared nothing. *Le Figaro* published an article on his "poverty" which made him weep with humiliation and rage. New advances were made, particularly by Turgenev, to get him some sort of supplementary income. He finally accepted a pension disguised as the post of Supernumerary Librarian of the Mazarine. It seemed to him he had surrendered what he valued most, his honor as a writer. *"C'est fait! J'ai cédé! Mon intraitable orgueil avait resisté jusqu'ici. Mais hélas! je suis à la veille de crever de faim, ou à peu pres"* ("It's all over! I've given in! My obstinate pride resisted up till now. But alas, I'm on the verge of starvation, or almost . . ."), he wrote to one correspondent. The reprinting of *L'Education sentimentale* had brought him in 700 francs, and that of *Salammbô* 1,000; but because of the Commanvilles unknown creditors were claiming 50,000, and even seized the gardener's wages. He asked his niece for an explanation, but she was not to be moved. She had found in religion enough serenity to bear the misfortunes of others, and preferred to talk to Père Didon about her salvation.

Disciples and Friends

ANY PLEASURE Flaubert enjoyed during this period came from those, like Turgenev, who were also preoccupied with art and creation, or from people like Zola, Daudet, Goncourt, and Huysmans who regarded him as a *"maître"* in every sense of the word. But he loathed doctrines and theories, and took good care not to fall a prey to his "disciples." He poked fun at the peremptory dicta of Zola, and was "indignant" at his "materialism." He considered *La Fille Elisa* "sketchy and anaemic," *Le Nabab* "a jumble," the style of *Les Sœurs Vatard* "abominable." Nevertheless he did recognize his own influence sometimes, and before other people he defended or even praised books like *L'Assommoir* or *Nana*, which seemed to breathe a genuine greatness. For Maupassant, nephew of his dear friend Alfred Le Poittevin, he showed an almost paternal affection, and nearly quarrelled with Léonie Brainne because she was shocked by *Boule-de-Suif*. Was she stupid? he asked himself. With all these younger novelists, some of whom were to unite under the banner of "naturalism," he kept up a sustained and friendly correspondence. Any criticisms he made of their work were always affectionate, and offered with the sole object of helping them master and perfect their art. One of the greatest pleasures of the last months of his life was the party he held at Croisset for Goncourt, Zola, Daudet, Maupassant, and Georges Charpentier, who was publisher to them all. When, a few days later, he received the first copy of the *Soirées de Médan* with an affectionate collective dedication, he could reflect that he would not die without posterity.

His friends in Rouen—Lapierre and his wife, Léonie Brainne and Alice Pasca—all did their best to cheer things up for him. Every year they organized a dinner on the feast of Saint Polycarp, of whom Flaubert claimed to be a reincarnation (the saint was always shutting up his ears and lamenting the state of the world), and on April 27, 1880 they excelled themselves. There was fancy dress, complimentary verses, presents, letters and telegrams from various parts of the world, and mock delegations. The *"bon géant"* was touched. Let people like Du Camp seek official honors and a seat in the Académie. To *"père"* Hugo," who offered to introduce him into that "illustrious company," and to Daudet and Goncourt, who urged him to enter it, he answered, "Not if I know it!" He relied on his work rather than on a green coat for "immortality."

On Saturday May 8, 1880, as he was getting ready to leave for Paris, to see his friends, to scold Charpentier again, and to finish *Bouvard et Pécuchet* in the flat in the Faubourg Saint-Honoré vacated for him by his niece, he was struck down by cerebral arteritis and died a few hours later. The burial, which took place in the Monumental Cemetery in Rouen on 11 May, was like the other funeral ceremonies he had often described, and which had seemed to him to present a perfect image of the wretchedness of the human condition. Goncourt noted that Commanville was chiefly concerned about the money he might get out of Flaubert's works; Caroline, meanwhile, was trying to make a good impression on Hérédia. Du Camp did not come, because of his rheumatism—or perhaps he was adding a last touch to his *Souvenirs littéraires*, weeping over the genius of his departed friend, "stunted" (as he said) by epilepsy. Before the end of the end of 1881, Croisset would have been sold and demolition begun.

Flaubert's posthumous life began with *Bouvard et Pécuchet*, which first appeared between December 1880 and March 1881, and with the publication, before the end of the century, of the *Correspondence*. The latter, although expurgated and incomplete, made those who had remained resistant to the writing, which they considered too tightly controlled, revise their judgment. They saw from the letters the struggle that lay behind it, and on what molten lava it had been built. For all the writers of the next century, even for those such as André Gide and Paul Valéry who did not really like him, Flaubert became an example.

Uncompleted Projects

THE PAPERS which Flaubert's niece Caroline retained until her death in 1931, and which were then dispersed in libraries or auctioned, not only reflect a prodigious amount of work in connection with the published works. They also contain many notes of all kinds, synopses and plans, and projects for novels which Flaubert would probably have gone on to if he had not died at the age of fifty-eight. There are traces here of all the things he talked of in his letters, to Jules Duplan, Turgenev, George Sand, Zola, Mme des Genettes, and even Princess Mathilde.

As early as 1852–1853, Flaubert (thinking of Alfred Le Poittevin and having read Balzac's *Louis Lambert*) spoke to Louise Colet of a "metaphysical novel with visions" which he would have liked to write if the subject had not scared him "from the healthy point of view." He said it was "the story of a man who goes mad through thinking of intangible things," and who "manages to have hallucinations in which he finally sees the ghost of his friend." He would deal with a subject to which *Louis Lambert* was only a "preface," and because of his experience of them would be able to paint certain states of mind better than they had ever been painted before. His own nervous illness had revealed to him the existence of "curious psychological phenomena which no one has any idea of, or rather which no one has ever felt." While his brain was beset by a tumult of images, and he could feel his soul ebbing away "as one feels the blood flowing out of an open wound," he at the same time tried to observe what was taking place in him. Each time it happened he had the sensation of dying, and tried to register in his mind every moment of the transition. Then he realized madness was not far away, and took fright. After noting down an outline for *La Spirale*, he put the project aside, turned towards an aesthetic of masterly control and objectivity, and set to work again on *Madame Bovary*.

"La Spirale"

THROUGH THE STORY of a painter who had travelled in the East and acquired the habit of taking hashish, *La Spirale* would have attempted to fuse into one continuous sequence the events of ordinary life and the events of dream. The hero cultivates hallucinations in order to spend his whole life on the plane of the imagination, to make real and imaginary life inter-react and interpenetrate and form a single whole. By this means he would attain superior knowledge. The image of the spiral indicates that he was to pass through "successive trials," stages in his initiation, and the moral of the story would be that:

> *Le bonheur consiste à être fou . . . c'est-à-dire a voir le Vrai, l'ensemble du temps, l'absolu. Il considère comme présent le passé et l'avenir. Il converse avec les Dieux et voit les types.* (Happiness consists in being mad . . . that is, in seeing the Truth, the whole of time, the absolute. He regards both past and future as present. He talks with the Gods, and sees the original types.)

Flaubert conceived of it as a fantastic novel with a metaphysical bearing. One regrets all the more that Flaubert never wrote it because (though the plan we have of it dates from 1861, after Baudelaire's *Les Paradis artificiels*) it foreshadows comparable modern attempts such as those of André Breton in *Nadja* and *Les Vases communicants* and those of Henri Michaux. Moreover, if *La Spirale* had been written it might have prevented the stupid label of "realist" from ever being attached to Flaubert.

The Fairy-Plays

WE SEE THE SAME DESIRE or temptation to cross the frontiers of reality, or at least to see beyond ordinary life and its artistic "representation," in the numerous projects for fairy-plays which Flaubert noted down in the summer of 1862, after the publication of *Salammbô*, though this employed to the full his visionary powers. *Le Château des Cœurs* did not fulfil his aim of renewing the genre and making it into "a splendid and vast dramatic form." These projects show him, nevertheless, amusingly translating colloquial expressions into series of visual puns; another modern idea is a "Locution Island," the inhabitant of which "has the power of seeing all his thoughts realized." In *Une Résurrection* he raises all the dead in a cemetery—"dressed according to their calling and full of joy, they set out to begin life again." The sequel can easily be imagined. Flaubert also intended to present "the follies of Love," love being regarded as "a force independent of the individual." The action was to take place "in an imaginary Asia—by means of much moral quaintness." There is a magician with the power of reading the hearts of married couples and lovers, whose real thoughts and dreams become visible to the audience. In yet another outline Flaubert proposes to convey three grocers imperceptibly "into their dream," and then, he adds, "Illusion begins." For him, the fairy-play should be something far removed from panto-mimes for children. He saw it not as an escape from reality, but as a means of integrating into what, even though it includes feeling and passion, may be called the rational part of life, the unknowable element which man approaches in dream and the free flight of imagination.

But what he wrote after *Le Château des Cœurs* was *L'Education sentimentale*, the chronicle of his youth and unsuccessful loves, in which he brings to life again his memories, imaginings, and desires. But though still obeying in it the principles of his own aesthetic, Flaubert did not decide to devote himself to this disguised confession without hesitation and much prospecting of more devious routes. Various synopses show he intended at first to write a novel closer to *Madame Bovary* and even more objective.

A Novel about the Second Empire

HE THOUGHT UP many plots in which love, adultery, and money so predominated that he was afraid of repeating the same effects as in *Madame Bovary*. In *Un Ménage moderne*, which was to be set in "*le milieu Chaussée-d'Antin*," a husband, wife, and lover are seen in an extremely unappetizing relationship: the wife extorts money from the lover to give to the husband, who is only too happy about the whole business. One has the feeling that the author himself was disgusted by this picture of typical bourgeois sordidness. On the other hand, he was enthusiastic for a while over the princely though scarcely more edifying adventures of Kœnigsmark. He noted down a plot on this subject which makes an already confused history somewhat more confounded. But apparently he soon abandoned it, attempting to write a "History of Official Art," thinking of telling the story of the two clerks, and being more and more often visited by the face of Madame Moreau—Elisa Schlésinger. The vision eventually prevailed, and one project predominated over all the rest. Flaubert decided to write *L'Education sentimentale.*

After it was finished and published, and there had followed the German occupation of part of France and the Paris Commune, Flaubert was sorry he had not taken the story up to the fall of Napoleon III. He thought this would have made the picture more complete and significant. While rewriting *Saint Antoine,* reading for *Bouvard et Pécuchet,* and telling the fantastic adventures of St Julien and the ingenuous ones of Félicité, he was thinking all the time of the great novel on the Second Empire which he alone could write. It was to be a fresco of society and a study of manners. He would aim not so much at psychological analysis as at bringing to life a whole age and society which he knew at every level, from the peasants of his native Normandy to the Court at Compiègne, and at showing the spirit of decadence which in his view that society embodied. Everything about it was "fake," he wrote in 1870, "from the *cocottes* to literature."

It may be wrong to relate all the plans and outlines from 1871 to 1877 to the great novel on the Empire, especially as the title keeps changing—*Sous Napoléon III, Un Ménage parisien, Monsieur le Préfet*—and as Flaubert also had other projects in mind, such as the *Battle of Thermopylae* which he mentioned to Turgenev and Goncourt, and the modern novel on the East of which he spoke to Jules Duplan and Mme des Genettes. It would probably be more accurate to think that, just as he did before deciding to write *L'Education sentimentale,* Flaubert pursued several lines at once, developing one or another of them in turn to see its possibilities, and then returning to the work in progress—one of the *Trois Contes,* or the "infernal" *Bouvard et Pécuchet,* which soon left him no time to think of anything else.

At all events it seems that for Flaubert, the misogynist, the main theme of the Second Empire novel would have been to show "the degradation of man by woman." He wrote those very words in an outline belonging to 1871, and the choice of characters, settings, and plots always reinforced this theme. He would show a republican lawyer who sells himself to the powers-that-be to win a "Catholic *grande dame*" and ends in disgrace; or a poet who, for the same reasons, prostitutes his talent first in journalism and then in government service; or an unsuccessful playwright who launches into pot-boiling and then into politics and business. In this way Flaubert would have been able to show every social circle with its sordid intrigues, and the fundamental immorality of all that claimed to be "official" and respectable. He gave himself the vigorous advice: "In *the modern Parisian novel*, mix in as much ass, as much money, and as much piety (Saint Vincent de Paul, etc.) as possible." He wanted to tear away appearances and reveal the seamy side of things. At one time, using the title *Monsieur le Préfet*, he thought of using a real Prefect of the Empire, Janvier de la Motte, a strong man famous for his peculations. As for the "whores" who became devout and bourgeois while keeping their husbands on a tight rein, Flaubert noted down some colorful examples.

None of these projects came to anything. They were too large and sometimes too fragmentary, and above all Flaubert was unable to find a "tight plot" which would link together the various social circles he wanted to depict "otherwise than through the development of the hero." The poor reception of *L'Education sentimentale* was still present in his mind, and this time he wanted to write a novel which would be a colossal success. He was too involved in his subject, too eager for revenge, too didactic and satirical, to bring to these projects the necessary creative detachment. He made up for it in *Bouvard et Pécuchet*, and since the years left him were so few, there is no cause for regret.

19

THE LIVING FLAUBERT

THE *Correspondence*, the uncompleted projects for plays, fairy pieces and novels, and the notebooks, with their observations and reflections, all correct the traditional picture of Flaubert as a "realist" who overcame his own romanticism, as a fanatic for form, a slave of outworn theories, a craftsman who became an artist through hard work rather than through his talents. People think of genius as something so free, spontaneous, vast and strong that it is almost easy, a force of nature which creates under dictation from the gods. Although this over-simplified picture does apply to a certain degree to Flaubert, he is usually thought of more as a diligent worker, with *Madame Bovary* grudgingly admitted as a masterpiece. At any rate, this attitude provided a good excuse for relegating Flaubert himself to a safe distance among the saints of literature, and for treating *Madame Bovary* as a kind of relic.

Or so it was until François Mauriac and Henri Guillemin perceived he was a "mystic without knowing it," a "seeker of God" in spite of himself, and until Jean-Paul Sartre set him among the Pantheon of bourgeois gods. And now he has become the patron of the "*nouveau roman*," a guinea-pig for psycho-analysis, and (because of a few phrases in a letter to Louise Colet) an advocate of euphuism. All these ways of exploiting him show either that he is still very much alive, or else that he has risen miraculously from the dead. People, especially young writers, have a feeling that he still has something, and something of importance, to say.

To find out what this something is, there is no need to call on all the formidable methods of investigation available to modern criticism. All that is necessary is to read his books as he wanted them to be read, letting them give one food for dream; or to

allow oneself to be moved by what he wrote in the ordinary
course of his existence, unpreoccupied by art; or to sympathize
with the human being who outside his work concealed nothing
of his thoughts and feelings and moods, and who looks us, as he
looked his contemporaries, straight in the face. One need never
mistrust Flaubert: there is never any guile or subterfuge or
swagger. He was called *"le bon géant,"* the good giant, and it is
this simplicity, frank and direct sometimes to the point of naivety,
which makes one feel towards Flaubert as towards a friend.

The Family

It all began, of course, in his childhood, among the family
of Rouen *notables* whose head, by his profession, education, and
character, was much more than a local dignitary and won the
respectful admiration of his young son. Gustave was also very
attached to his mother and sister. He could not imagine a
better family, a warmer or more propitious background, or
greater intellectual freedom. Perhaps that was the cause of the
trouble, of his trouble. If he wanted to live on his own account
and assert himself as a person, he would have to reject all that,
in principle if not in fact—good families, noble professions, the
respectable class to which he belonged.

His first reaction was to reject a future too assured, to rebel
against a present which, after the heady follies of Napoleon,
witnessed the triumph of the bourgeoisie, the business men and
the dignitaries, with their commercial good sense. Flaubert, a
bitter and frustrated "child of the age," came too far after the
great Romantics to be able to participate properly in their
revenge through the imagination. To their disillusions he added
his own, and realized he must go farther than they in rejecting
the existence prepared for him. He would not found a family.
He would not be domesticated by any profession, position, or
office. Until he died he would go on proclaiming his hatred and
disgust for the enemy the bourgeois, who had reduced the
world to the dimensions of a piece of "private property." By
becoming an artist he escaped from the prison of society, and

could ward off a certain number of evil spells. But this was on condition that he stood alone, apart, and against everyone. On condition that he expressed thoughts and feelings and produced works which all pronounced the same vengeful negative on the cramped life and universe fashioned by the respectable for their own purposes. On condition that he told the truth.

The "Demoralizer"

FLAUBERT DID NOT do badly at keeping his promise—through his life, led resolutely outside all civic and social structures and outside literary circles; and through his work, based on a deepseated irony which destroys the high-sounding values on which man in society rests. Emma the suicide joins hands with Frédéric the failure; both are stifled by the same mud, Parisian or Norman. The man of Carthage or Alexandria who disembowels and slays in the name of the gods is no more to be envied than the man of the nineteenth century, whom science threatens to imprison in an industrial and military barracks. Flaubert tears away all the veils which conceal the sinister reality: conformisms, religions, philosophical beliefs and all forms of idealism, "*blague*" and illusion, for ever fascinating and for ever born again. Instead, here are men as they are, stripped, naked, the playthings of a nature beyond their control and a universe which has insinuated itself into them and maneuvers them as it pleases. They are victims; the time for heroes is past. Life, deprived of its disguises, and among them the most specious of all, the search for happiness, keeps none of the promises the credulous believe in. Life is failure, perpetual failure.

A Dream with the Dimensions of Reality

FLAUBERT DEFENDED HIMSELF against George Sand's accusation that his work aimed only at being "satirical" and "critical." He did not see writing as a cleansing of wounds: if he threw himself into it without reserve it was so that it might evoke for himself and others a life which had nothing in common with the life

which had been thrust upon him, and one rich in the surprises
that provide the heart and mind with nourishment. For him, to
write a book was to embark on a "long voyage," with unknown
adventures and no certainty of reaching the goal. What mattered was not so much the route and the halts on the way,
carefully though these were established in advance, but the
setting out, the going. The aim of the work of art was *"faire
rêver,"* to draw the reader, spectator or listener into a spiral
movement which goes beyond ordinary life and reaches the
limits of feeling, thought, and imagination. The author is only
occasion, support, and sometimes guide. As soon as a dialogue
is set up between him and the reader, both have transcended
their normal condition and found a common language of which
the book itself only babbles the grammar.

For Flaubert, truth and beauty were not absolutes, but
inducements to enter a world whose doors would otherwise
remain closed. "Is it with fictions that one can discover truth?"
If he had only been concerned with truth he would never have
gone beyond the "realism" of some of his successors. If he had
only been concerned with beauty, he would have been content
with the historical visions of Carthage and the mythological
visions of *La Tentation*. Out of these two ways, sometimes
parallel but more often divergent, he tried to make a single path
which he thought, eighty years before the moderns, "ought
to lead somewhere."

If Emma and Frédéric belong to the substance both of our
life and of our dreams, it is because they are not merely two
human beings knocked about by life. Flaubert the *"descripteur
infatigable"* could have gone on piling up stroke on stroke and
telling their life in detail, but that would never have given them
the mythical dimension which makes them escape the book and
inhabit us. Painted from life? So what? Typical? What does it
matter? They no more make us think of Delphine Delamare in
the one case than of the over-timid lover of Elisa in the other.
Flaubert has dreamed them and given them life, with all the
resources of an observation which saw "into the very pores" of
things, a memory which could revive the atmosphere and colors

of the past, and an imagination which aimed at being sufficiently inductive to suggest the secret causes of the blinking of an eye. Flaubert dreamed them to life as Baudelaire did his *"géante,"* as Rimbaud did his infernal loves. If the dream has the dimensions of reality, it is because the poet has been able to deepen reality, to push back its limits until it becomes capable of displaying the unknown potentialities of which it is full. There is even that vibrating fringe whose presence, merely suggested, is the very hallmark of life. As long as men can read, Emma will always be entering the hotel where she is to meet Léon and making the laces of her corset hiss as she undoes them in their room. Frédéric will always be going up the Seine aboard the *"Ville-de-Montereau"*. Where the realist merely sees, observes, and describes, the visionary of the real builds, even for a tiny detail, a spectacle in which all his senses, his whole being participates. He causes the world in all its modes and tenses to enter into it. The "thing seen," banal and fleeting, becomes a fragment of eternity.

Flaubert's labor in pursuit of form is only an exercise, a method designed to bring forth, sharpen, and realize the vision. The obstinate phrase or elusive cadence he pursues for days are signs for him that the vision is as yet vague and cluttered, or partial, or commonplace, or incongruous. He has not yet sufficiently "made himself feel" what is to be said, what should gush forth in a unique correlative of images, sounds and colors, like an artesian well from soil hitherto prospected in vain. Flaubert is not trying to express better but to express, as one for whom the word is an event, the manifestation of a reality which language has buried beneath its strata. If he works like a cart-horse, it is because there are heaps of words to be cleared out of the way, dead, empty, ossified words which sometimes form almost insurmountable obstacles. He must sweat and grunt his way through to give his vision its proper amplitude and scope.

Ecstasies, Visions and Hallucinations

FLAUBERT HAD ONLY to sit in the sun in the bay of Sagone, or to look at the sea from the cliffs of Normandy, to feel his being quit its mortal envelope and become at once sun, sea, sky and the whole of nature, together with the wind that was blowing and the tree or fisherman's cottage in the distance. The being which abandoned him on the shore gradually dispersed further and further until he was filled with cosmic exaltation.

Conversely, he had only to gaze fixedly at "a stone, an animal, a picture," and he felt himself enter into them, take on and live their existence. He escaped into the objective, and the objective entered into him, to such a degree that "it made him cry out." He was traversed by a two-fold current which sometimes arose within him, sometimes arose and took possession of him from without. He was at once the point of intersection and central source of what Orientals call the respiration of the world. With the sensibility of a "great hysterical girl,"* he had faculties so hyper-acute he could hear a whisper behind closed doors and follow the secret life of his own internal organs. And his nervous illness drew him down into abysses from which he sometimes feared he might never return. He realized with horror that he might drift into continuous hallucination.

We should not be misled by his technical mastery, his attempt to penetrate the pores of matter as if to anchor himself there more firmly, or his desire to learn from the great classics. These were so many defences, sometimes the last defence, against what when the charge of imagination becomes too strong is called mental derangement. All the self-imposed discipline, all the strict commands of his aesthetic could not prevent him from vomiting when Emma took the fatal dose of arsenic, or from finally adopting the naive and simple views of Bouvard and Pécuchet. If he had been less on his guard he would have become like the hero of *La Spirale*—victim of the imaginary world he himself had created.

Excuse and Alibi

IF HE WAS A RIGORIST LOVER of form, a strict student of phrases,

---

*It is strange that his doctors, Dr. Fortin and Dr. Hardy, both used almost the same description.

it was with good reason: there lay his alibi and his excuse. It is less certain that Valéry was right when he accused him of being the slave of documentation. Although he had a need to see, to observe, to note, and although he was not only influenced by an age which was "historicist" and obsessed with natural history but also undertook to translate its ambitions into literature, reality was not so much a starting-point for him as a means of confirming his vision. This can be seen by the search he went on with Laporte to find a retreat for Bouvard and Pécuchet. When in his notes he puts the names of living people well-known to him under the names of the characters whose story he is going to tell, commentators have tended to jump to the conclusion that observed models were his point of departure. But were they not rather references and tests? To convey the sensation of "certain mildews of the soul" he used not only the unhappy love affairs of Delphine Delamare but also the story of an unmarried girl full of mystical imaginings; in *Salammbô* the documentation he had amassed on Carthaginian civilization was not so essential as his desire to capture a "purple" mirage. Ordinary reality only entered into his inspiration as a guest, to serve as reference and touchstone. He gives back more than he takes from it, thereby escaping the transitory, the ephemeral, the period photograph, and capturing the constants of the heart and mind, of which the most detailed observation can only ever proffer the appearances.

"To represent life" is something quite different from remaining at the level of phenomena as a whole, of which we never see more than a part, and the significance of which escapes us. It is "to place oneself above everything, and one's mind above oneself." As Flaubert wrote to Maupassant in 1878, "Reality, in my view, should only be a *springboard*," thus refuting those of his disciples for whom reality was "the whole of Art." "Nothing is true," he added, "except relationships; that is, the way we perceive objects." The "superior view-point" he aimed at is impartial as between subjective and objective. Beneath it they freely interchange their elements, fuse together, and reappear, transfigured, in a new totality which allows Flaubert to say without inconsistency both "*Madame Bovary, c'est moi,*" and "She is suffering and weeping at this moment in twenty villages of France." *Le "vrai"*, the truth, which Flaubert attained has a thousand faces, though that does not make it an essence or an absolute. It can co-exist with the observation, either bitter or ironic, that there is nothing true, that all is illusion.

In Quest of Being

AN EXPERIMENT, even though it was successful, never made any contribution to the next. Nothing was established. Each time it was necessary to start from scratch. Flaubert was no more— and no less—master of his trade at the end of his career than he was at the time of his earliest compositions. There is no progress from *Madame Bovary* to *L'Education sentimentale* or from *Salammbô* to *Bouvard et Pécuchet*. Some subjects for novels he had in mind all his life; others were noted down fifteen or twenty years before he actually wrote them. There is not even any development: his was not the kind of talent that deteriorates or improves. What did evolve were his ideas, and, to a lesser degree, his aesthetic and his sense of existence. What remains constant throughout, right up to *Bouvard et Pécuchet*, is the desire to attain an evident, permanent, and indestructible reality in which his self, present but invisible, would partake of the same qualities. Though some have called him a craftsman, and he saw himself as a "workman in the luxury trade," what he was fashioning was in fact Gustave Flaubert, the being who chose not to live outside his own creation, and whose creation continually gives him life again. He is close to the great Romantics of the nineteenth century. But, in his preoccupations and his poetic method, he is closer still to writers his own age largely ignored— to Baudelaire, Rimbaud, and Mallarmé.

A "Mysterious Chemistry"

FLAUBERT'S TOIL would have been less exhausting than it was if all it had been aiming at was "just expression." But in fact he was performing a difficult, even heroic ascesis, designed to bring him to the state where the self, having cut adrift from all its moorings, re-enters its mortal vesture in possession of all that has been won in the interval. Flaubert confronted chaos and moved through disorder until, through expression, a lasting precipitate was formed. It was with this "*chimie mystérieuse*" in view that he was constantly preparing himself, assembling his materials, emptying himself, putting himself in a state of preparedness. There were certain moments when the smallest external impression upset him, the slightest disturbance was overwhelming. Time and space no longer existed for him, he did not know what he was doing, his nearest and dearest were like ghosts, and he entered into a state of catatonia.

Was he really just a writer in the "throes of style"? Was his state not rather that of a mystic awaiting his god, a scientist on the brink of a discovery? If the god remains deaf or the experiment fails, the only thing to do is try again, with more faith, more scrupulousness, more care. What the profane regard as wasted time, barrenness, or sterility is really the time of ripening, of travelling towards light and revelation and harmony.

Flaubert told George Sand in a letter that in the initial phase he was "*un bonhomme en cire*", a wax dummy: "Everything prints itself on me, ingrains itself in me, enters into me. I have to make great efforts to collect myself, for every moment I'm boiling over." He was crammed with sensations, impressions, and feelings; invaded, and yet mute. Before the word could be born, the way had to be prepared for it, the humble, natural way. He had to create silence around it, and a void in himself, and wait in what seemed a wilderness. It was not a matter either of conquest or of setting his mark on whatever material offered. The author was absent, far from such vain preoccupations. And then when the word was eventually born, he ceased to be a "wax dummy" and became alive and self-determined, active, sensitive, released from his own weight, omniscient, omnipotent, the chaotic and anonymous reality which hitherto encompassed him now emerging as animate, with ordered causes and effects, and with a meaning which was not inconsistent with mystery. "I am an '*homme-plume*,' " wrote Flaubert. "I feel through my pen, I feel in relation to it, and I feel much more with it in my hand." He created through literature; literature created him.

CHRONICLE

Main Events in the Life of Gustave Flaubert

1821 December 12. Born at the Hôtel-Dieu at Rouen, where his father is chief surgeon. His mother, Justine-Caroline Fleuriot, belongs to a family of doctors and shipbuilders in Pont-l'Evêque.

1832 February. Enters the "eighth" class of the Collège Royal, Rouen.

1834 At school, edits the handwritten journal *Art et Progrès*.

1836 Writes his first tales. At Trouville, during the school holidays, he makes friends with the Schlésingers, and falls in love with Elisa Schlésinger, *née* Foucault. Begins to write *Mémoires d'un Fou*.

1837 Publishes *Une leçon d'histoire naturelle, Genre commis* in *Le Colibri* (Rouen).

1838 Writes *Agonies* and *La Danse des Morts*. Finishes *Mémoires d'un Fou*.

1839 *Smarh; Les Funérailles du Docteur Mathurin; Rabelais*. At the end of the year, leaves the Collège and prepares his *baccalauréat* on his own.

1840 August 23, passes his baccalauréat.
End of August-October, journey to the Pyrenees and Corsica with Dr. Cloquet. At the Hôtel Richelieu, rue de la Darse, Marseilles, he has a love affair with Eulalie Foucaud de Langlade. On returning home, writes travel notes.

1841 Enrols to read law in Paris.

1842 Exempted by lottery from military service.
July-August: in Paris, first at 5 rue Le-Peletier, then at 35 rue de l'Odéon.
September: at Trouville, where he meets the Colliers.

November: settles in unfurnished rooms at 19 rue de l'Est.

December 28: passes first-year exam.

In Paris he frequents the Colliers, Pradiers, and Schlésingers.

Finishes *Novembre* on October 25.

1843 February: begins *L'Education sentimentale* (first version).

May: inauguration of railway between Paris and Rouen.

August 21: fails second-year exam.

End of December: visits Vernon, the village where Elisa Schlésinger was born. Makes friends with Maxime Du Camp and Louis de Cormenin.

1844 January: Returning from Deauville, on the road from Pont-l'Evêque, suffers the first attack of his nervous illness. Gives up law.

April-May: Dr. Flaubert sells his property at Déville and buys Croisset.

1845 January 7: Flaubert finishes the first *Education sentimentale*. March 3: his sister Caroline marries Emile Hamard. The family accompanies the couple to Italy.

May: in the Balbi gallery in Genoa, Flaubert is struck by the Breughel painting called *St. Anthony*.

Return journey via Milan, Geneva, and Besançon.

Flaubert makes scene-by-scene analysis of Voltaire's plays.

1846 January 15: death of Dr. Flaubert.

February 21: Caroline Hamard gives birth to a daughter also named Caroline.

March 23: Flaubert's sister dies.

April: he retires to Croisset with his mother, his niece, and the servant Julie.

July 6: his friend Alfred Le Poittevin marries Louise de Maupassant.

July 29: Flaubert meets Louise Colet at Pradier's, and she becomes his mistress.

1847 May-July: trip to Britanny with Du Camp.

1848   February: Flaubert and Bouilhet go to Paris to see what is happening.

March: Flaubert writes to Louise Colet from Croisset, breaking off the affair.

April 3: death of Alfred Le Poittevin.

May 24: Flaubert begins *La Tentation de Saint Antoine*.

1849   April: Du Camp invites Flaubert to go with him to the East.

September 12: Flaubert reads *La Tentation* to Du Camp and Bouilhet and they tell him it is no good.

November 4: Flaubert and Du Camp embark at Marseilles for Egypt.

1850   March 6: spends the night with Kuschiuk Hanem.

July-August: Beirut, Jerusalem. It is probably in Beirut that Flaubert contracts syphilis.

August 5: birth of Guy de Maupassant.

August 18: death of Balzac.

November: Constantinople.

December: Athens.

1851   January: Delphi, Thermopylae, the Peloponnese.

February 10: embarks for Brindisi, Naples, Rome (until May 6).

Visits Florence and Venice with his mother, while Du Camp returns to Paris.

July: takes up again with Louise Colet.

September 19: begins *Madame Bovary*.

December: is present at the *coup d'état*.

1853   Three-monthly meetings with "la Muse" in Paris and Mantes.

The Schlésingers, ruined, go to live in Baden. Bouilhet settles in Paris.

1854   In Paris, Flaubert begins liaison with the actress Beatrix Person.

October: final break with Louise Colet.

1856   Finishes *Madame Bovary*. Du Camp publishes it, with cuts, in *La Revue de Paris*, from October 1.

December 21-28: extracts from *La Tentation de Saint*

Antoine published by Théophile Gautier in *L'Artiste*.
La Revue de Paris prosecuted.

1857   January 29: trial of Flaubert and *La Revue de Paris*.
February 7: Flaubert acquitted.
April: *Madame Bovary* published by Michel Lévy and is a
dazzling success.
June 25: Baudelaire publishes *Les Fleurs du Mal*.
August: Baudelaire fined 300 francs.

1858   In Paris, Flaubert frequents Sainte-Beuve, Gautier,
Renan, Baudelaire, Feydeau, and the Goncourts.
April 16: embarks from Philippeville to visit the ruins of
Carthage.
June 12: returns to Croisset and works on *Salammbô*.

1859   September: Hugo publishes *La Légende des Siècles;* Louise
Colet publishes *Lui,* in which she attacks her former
lover.

1862   Elisa Schlésinger in a mental home in Germany.
February 15: Flaubert finishes *Salammbô*, which appears
on November 24.

1863   Flaubert a visitor at the Princess Mathilde's, and
attends the *dîners Magny*, where he meets Turgenev.

1864   His niece Caroline marries the timber merchant Ernest
Commanville.
September 1: Flaubert begins *L'Education sentimentale*.

1866   August 15: Flaubert made *Chevalier* of the Legion of
Honor.
George Sand visits Croisset.

1867   The Commanvilles' financial difficulties force Flaubert
to contract loans and sell a farm.
March: he meets Mme Schlésinger again (in Paris or
Mantes).
June 10: invited to a ball in the Tuileries.
August 31: death of Baudelaire.

1869   Finishes *L'Education sentimentale*.
July 18: death of Bouilhet.
October 13: death of Sainte-Beuve.
L'Education badly received by both public and press.

1870   June 20: death of Jules de Goncourt.

Flaubert is uneasy about future events, works first at Bouilhet's *Le Sexe faible* and then at *Saint Antoine*. His relatives from Nogent take refuge at Croisset; Caroline takes refuge in England.

November: Prussians at Croisset.

1871   January 28: Armistice.

March: Flaubert, with Dumas the younger, goes to see Princess Mathilde in Brussels, then goes on to London and Dieppe. He returns to Croisset.

May: learns of the death of Maurice Schlésinger.

November 8: Elisa visits him at Croisset.

November 22: goes to Paris, where he often meets Léonie Brainne.

1872   Bouilhet's *Mademoiselle Aïssé* is produced at the Odéon, and Flaubert publishes and writes a preface to Bouilhet's *Dernières Chansons*. Quarrels with Michel Lévy over the latter.

April 6: death of Mme Flaubert.

July 1: *La Tentation* finished.

October 25: death of Théophile Gautier.

1874   *Le Candidat* produced at the Vaudeville. Flaubert withdraws it after four performances.

April: Charpentier publishes *La Tentation*.

Trip to Switzerland with Laporte.

August 1: takes up *Bouvard et Pécuchet*.

1875   Sells the farm at Deauville in attempt to save the Commanvilles.

September: stays with his friend Pouchet at Concarneau.

Begins *La Légende de Saint Julien l'Hospitalier*.

October 1: Commanville's business is wound up. Flaubert is ruined.

1876   March 8: death of Louise Colet.

Flaubert starts *Un Cœur simple*.

June 8: death of George Sand. Flaubert attends the funeral.

Zola publishes *L'Assommoir*, Daudet *Le Nabab*, and

Renan *Dialogues philosophiques* and *Prière sur l'Acropole*.

1877 Flaubert finishes *Hérodias*. Charpentier publishes *Trois Contes*.

1879 Turgenev tries to get Flaubert a post as Librarian at the Mazarine, but Frédéric Baudry is appointed instead. Jules Ferry, minister for education, grants Flaubert a disguised pension of 3000 francs which he never received.

1880 Flaubert enthusiastic about *Boule-de-Suif*, and uses his influence to prevent Maupassant being prosecuted. February 11: Jules Lemaître, a young teacher from Le Havre, visits him.

At Easter, Zola, Goncourt, Daudet, Maupassant and Charpentier stay with him at Croisset.

April: receives *Les Soirées de Médan* with flattering collective dedication.

May 8: dies of cerebral arteritis when getting ready to go to Paris.

May 11: buried in Rouen cemetery.

December 15: *La Nouvelle Revue* begins publishing the unfinished *Bouvard et Pécuchet*.

A SHORT BIBLIOGRAPHY

FLAUBERT'S WORKS

Madame Bovary: Mœurs de province, 1857.
Salammbô, 1863.
L'Education Sentimentale: Histoire d'un Jeune Homme, 1870.
La Tentation de Saint Antoine, 1874.
Le Candidat: Comédie en Quatre Actes, 1874.
Trois Contes, 1877.
Bouvard et Pécuchet (published posthumously), 1881.
Correspondence, 1884 and subsequent editions.
Œuvres Complètes de Gustave Flaubert (28 vols., Conard, 1910-36).
Gustave Flaubert: Œuvres Complètes, ed. Nadeau (18 vols., Rencontre, 1964).

TRANSLATIONS

Madame Bovary: Eleanor Marx-Aveling (1866); H. Blanchamp (1905); J. L. May (1928); G. Hopkins (1948); Joan Charles (1949); Allan Russell (1950).
Salammbô: J. S. Chartres (1886); M. French Sheldon (1886); J. W. Matthews (1901); B. R. Redman (1928); E. P. Mathers (1931); P. Goodyear and P. J. Wright (1962).
Sentimental Education: D. F. Hannigan (1898); D. K. Ranous (1923); A. Goldsmith (1941).
The Temptation of Saint Anthony of 1856: Rene Francis (1910).
The Temptation of Saint Anthony of 1874: L. Hearn (1911).
Three Tales: A. McDowall (1923); Mervyn Saville (1950); W. F. Cobb (1965).
Saint Julian the Hospitaller: M. D. Honey (1925).
Bouvard and Pécuchet: D. F. Hannigan (1896); T. W. Earp and G. W. Stonier (1936).
George Sand-Gustave Flaubert Letters: Aimée L. McKenzie (1922); also a selection by J. M. Cohen (1949).
Selected Letters: Francis Steegmuller (1957).

BIOGRAPHICAL AND CRITICAL WORKS

Barbey d'Aurevilly, J., "Gustave Flaubert," in *Le Roman Contemporain* (1902).

Bart, Benjamin, *Flaubert's Landscape Descriptions* (1956).

Brombert, Victor, *The Novels of Flaubert* (1966).

Bruneau, Jean, *Les Débuts littéraires de Gustave Flaubert, 1831-1845* (1962).

Coleman, A., *Flaubert's Literary Development* (1914).

Dumesnil, René, *Gustave Flaubert, l'Homme et l'Œuvre* (1947).

Fay, F. B. and Coleman, A., *Sources and Structure of Flaubert's "Salammbô"* (1914).

Gaultier, Jules de, *Le Bovarysme: La Psychologie dans l'Œuvre de Flaubert* (1892).

Giraud, Raymond, *Flaubert: A Collection of Critical Essays* (1964).

James, Henry, "Gustave Flaubert," in *Notes on Novelists* (1914).

Levin, Harry, *The Gates of Horn: A Study of Five French Realists* (1963).

Maupassant, Guy de, "Flaubert," in *Œuvres Posthumes II* (1908).

Mauriac, François, *Trois Grands Hommes devant Dieu* (1947).

Proust, Marcel, "A Propos du style de Flaubert" in *Chroniques* (1927).

Riddell, A. R., *Flaubert and Maupassant: A Literary Relationship* (1920).

Spencer, Philip, *Flaubert: A Biography* (1966).

Starkie, Enid, *Flaubert: The Making of the Master* (1967) and *Flaubert: the Master* (1971).

Steegmuller, Francis, *Flaubert and Madame Bovary* (1939).

Thibaudet, Albert, *Gustave Flaubert* (1935).

Thorlby, Anthony, *Gustave Flaubert and the Art of Realism* (1957).

Valéry, Paul, "La Tentation de (saint) Flaubert," in *Variété* V (1944).

Wilson, Edmund, "Flaubert's Politics," in *The Triple Thinkers* (1938).

Zola, Emile, "Gustave Flaubert," in *Les Romanciers Naturalistes* (1890).

ABOUT THE AUTHOR

MAURICE NADEAU was born in Paris in 1911. In the immediate post-war period he was the literary editor of Albert Camus' newspaper, *Combat*. Subsequently he was the leading literary critic of the liberal-left weeklies, *L'Observateur* (1953-60), and *L'Express* (1960-65). He has edited one of the most important French literary monthlies, *Les Lettres Nouvelles* since 1953, and he is at present the co-editor of *La Quinzaine litteraire*. Among his books are a history of the Post-War French Novel (1970) and a history of Surrealism which was translated and published both in England and the U.S.A.